❧ ❧ ❧ *Gender and Genre in Novels Without End*

76
77

Gender and Genre in Novels Without End

The British *Roman-Fleuve*

Lynette Felber

University Press of Florida
*Gainesville / Tallahassee / Tampa / Boca Raton
Pensacola / Orlando / Miami / Jacksonville*

00 99 98 97 96   6   5   4   3   2   1

Library of Congress Cataloging-in-Publication Data

Felber, Lynette, 1951–
    Gender and genre in novels without end: the British roman-fleuve
    / Lynette Felber.
        p. cm.
    Includes bibliographical references and index.
    ISBN 0-8130-1402-6 (cloth)
        1. English fiction—20th century—History and criticism.
2. Cycles (Literature)   3. Trollope, Anthony, 1815–1882. Palliser
novels.   4. Richardson, Dorothy Miller, 1873–1957. Pilgrimage.
5. Powell, Anthony, 1905–   Dance to the music of time.
6. Authorship—Sex differences.   7. Narration (Rhetoric)
8. Fiction—Technique.   9. Literary form.   I. Title.
PR888.C92F45   1996   95-13834
823.009—dc20   CIP

The University Press of Florida is the scholarly publishing agency for the State
University System of Florida, comprised of Florida A & M University, Florida Atlantic
University, Florida International University, Florida State University, University of
Central Florida, University of Florida, University of North Florida, University of South
Florida, and University of West Florida.

University Press of Florida
15 Northwest 15th Street
Gainesville, FL 32611

❧ ❧ ❧   *Contents*

❧ ❧ ❧ *Abbreviations and Editions*

Trollope, the Palliser Novels

Unless otherwise stated, all references are to the World's Classics Centenary Edition (1982–83), each published by Oxford University Press in two volumes, each with separate pagination.

Can You Forgive Her? (1864–65)	CYFH?
Phineas Finn (1869)	PF
The Eustace Diamonds (1873)	ED
Phineas Redux (1874)	PR
The Prime Minister (1876)	PM
The Duke's Children (1880) (one volume only)	DC

Richardson, *Pilgrimage*

All quotations refer to the 1967 edition of *Pilgrimage*, the first complete edition of the *roman-fleuve*, published in London by J. M. Dent and in New York by Alfred A. Knopf. Dates in parentheses refer to the first publication of each individual novel.

Volume One:

Pointed Roofs (1915)	PR
Backwater (1916)	B
Honeycomb (1917)	H

Volume Two:

The Tunnel (1919)	Tun
Interim (1919)	Interim

Volume Three:

Deadlock (1921)	Deadlock
Revolving Lights (1923)	RL
The Trap (1925)	Trap

Volume Four:

Oberland (1927)	O
Dawn's Left Hand (1931)	DLH
Clear Horizon (1935)	CH
Dimple Hill (1938)	DH
March Moonlight (1967)	MM

Powell, *A Dance to the Music of Time*

All references are to the four-volume edition published by Little, Brown and Company in the United States (1951-75).

First Movement:

A Question of Upbringing (1951)	QU
A Buyer's Market (1952)	BM
The Acceptance World (1955)	AW

Second Movement:

At Lady Molly's (1957)	ALM
Casanova's Chinese Restaurant (1960)	CCR
The Kindly Ones (1962)	KO

Third Movement:

The Valley of Bones (1964)	VB
The Soldier's Art (1966)	SA
The Military Philosophers (1968)	MP

Fourth Movement:

Books Do Furnish a Room (1971)	BDFR
Temporary Kings (1973)	TK
Hearing Secret Harmonies (1975)	HSH

✤ ✤ ✤ *Preface*

In the *Poetics*, Aristotle advises writers to consider proportion and aim for "a magnitude which may be easily embraced in one view." Giving fair warning to the novelists who would arrive some 2,000 years later and produce a genre exceeding either the epic or the tragedy in magnitude, he explains: "Nor, again, can one of vast size be beautiful; for as the eye cannot take it all in at once, the unity and sense of the whole is lost for the spectator; as for instance if there were one a thousand miles long" (vii). In formulating his poetics, however, Aristotle failed to account for those faithful, persevering spectators who linger to prolong the pleasurable experience and return for the next play in the trilogy to become better acquainted with the characters. That desire for a continuing relationship is a major motivation for viewers, writers, and readers of serial genres, including the *roman-fleuve*. I confess to being one of those readers. My discovery of Anthony Trollope while reading for my comprehensive exams in graduate school led me from the Barset to the Palliser novels, a dangerous labyrinthine journey into imbricating texts. Trollope is not really to blame: my fascination began much earlier in a childhood addiction to novels that prolong the reading experience—L.M. Montgomery's *Anne of Green Gables*, Laura Ingalls Wilder's *Little House in the Big Woods*, and even Mazo De La Roche's Jalna series. This preference led me to specialize in the lengthy, multiplotted Victorian novel and, ultimately, to this project—a genre study of the *roman-fleuve*.

This study draws upon narratology, reader response, and feminist approaches to construct a poetics of the *roman-fleuve* and support my thesis that it is a genre perceived as feminine and one that shares numerous features with the *écriture féminine* identified by French feminist theorists. The defining features of the *roman-fleuve*—its extraordinary length, the spatial and temporal gaps between volumes, and its problematic closure—

produce a unique reading experience illuminated by contemporary theory that accounts for the dynamics of narratives. The relevance of narrative theory to a genre that embodies—and exceeds—the definition of the novel as "extended prose fiction" is evident. The gaps or blanks in texts emphasized by reception theorists are also germane to my theorizing about readers' response to the *roman-fleuve*, in which the blanks of indeterminacy are transformed into larger and far more literal kinds of intervolume gaps. Less obviously, I am self-consciously working within a tradition of criticism that metaphorically describes (and expresses value) by attributing sexual features to narrative. In my employment of French feminists, Hélène Cixous and Luce Irigaray most notably, I acknowledge that their theorizing about feminine narrative falls, somewhat unexpectedly, within a convention of gendering narrative that dates back to the beginnings of literary criticism, including Aristotle.

The introductory chapter provides a brief history and a theoretical definition of the *roman-fleuve*. In the application chapters that follow, I analyze three significant contributions to the genre that have been inadequately studied and appreciated in the twentieth century: Anthony Trollope's Palliser novels (1864–80), Dorothy Richardson's *Pilgrimage* (1915–38), and Anthony Powell's *A Dance to the Music of Time* (1951–75). My purpose in selecting exemplars from the mid-nineteenth century through the current period is to explore the history, reception, and narrative of the *roman-fleuve* from its earliest to its more recent prototypes. Although Trollope, Richardson, and Powell may seem an unusual trio, my choice is motivated, in part, by a desire to account for the frequently ambivalent reception of the *roman-fleuve* and of these writers, each of whom has had ardent followers and equally vehement detractors, none of whom is indisputably canonized. There have been examples of the *roman-fleuve* produced by women writers whose affinity with a feminine writing is evident: Doris Lessing's *Children of Violence* and Anaïs Nin's *Cities of the Interior*, for example. But to select examples of the *roman-fleuve* that exemplify an *écriture féminine* by women writers is to leave unexplored the distinction between gendered writing and the sex of the writer. By selecting texts by Trollope and Powell, I show that male writers may choose (albeit unconsciously) to work in a genre perceived as feminine and that there is an affinity between the features of the *roman-fleuve*—even at its most conventional—and an *écriture féminine*. Furthermore, diverse as the three are in terms of historical period and conception of the form, their adaptations of the *roman-fleuve* reveal intriguing similarities.

Trollope developed one of the first identifiable examples of the nineteenth-century British *roman-fleuve* in his Palliser novels, often mistakenly regarded as merely a serial. Much criticism still tends to deprecate Trollope for any variance from the nineteenth-century novel tradition, ignoring his innovations in the genre. Traditionally, Trollope has been criticized for weak, suspenseless plots, without a recognition that his novels privilege a narrative dynamics quite different from the climactic model derived from Aristotle's *Poetics* and that they might more productively be viewed from a less traditional critical perspective. In chapter 2, I show how Trollope, dissatisfied with the limitations of the already lengthy Victorian novel, experimented with a form that intensifies the narrative conventions of the "baggy monster." Trollope's Palliser novels comprise a proto–*roman-fleuve*, establishing conventions that prefigure those developed by his successors in the fully evolved *roman-fleuve*. Because the Pallisers establish the prototype for the genre, my discussion of Trollope is the most structuralist of my three application chapters. I use his Palliser novels to define the dynamics of the *roman-fleuve* in its beginnings, middle, and end and to place Trollope's experiments with the genre in the context of nineteenth-century novelistic conventions. Furthermore, I find that many of the narrative characteristics for which Trollope is criticized anticipate those of the *écriture féminine* proposed by contemporary feminists.

Chapter 3 demonstrates that in the thirteen volumes of *Pilgrimage*, Richardson most fully exploits the inherent propensities of the genre. As exemplified in both theory and practice—her aesthetic objectives as a novelist are elucidated in her letters, sketches, and through her protagonist-writer in *Pilgrimage* itself—Richardson, the long-neglected and critically abused first practitioner of stream of consciousness narrative, is also the unrecognized matriarch of a feminine aesthetic. It is no coincidence that the *roman-fleuve* and *écriture féminine* are often associated with the modern period; they both exemplify a modernist aesthetic deemphasizing linear plot, eschewing closure, and privileging synchronic development. Moreover, this chapter demonstrates the relationship between Richardson's aesthetic intent, to create what she terms a "feminine equivalent of the current masculine realism," and her distinctive feminism.

Powell's *A Dance to the Music of Time* represents an adroitly developed contemporary exemplar of the *roman-fleuve*. In the fourth chapter, I argue that there is, nevertheless, a tension in Powell's *roman-fleuve* that results from the simultaneous deployment of conventional and modernist (or, at times, postmodern) narrative techniques. In its use of a multiplot narrative and an intrusive and editorializing narrator, in its shifting emphasis on various groups of characters, and in its detailed, primarily chronological narrative, *The Music of Time* is in many ways a throwback to Trollope's Victorian conception of the genre. (And as a specialist in the Victorian novel, I do not mean this to have derogatory connotations.) However, while Powell attempts to control the superfluity of the *roman-fleuve* and of *écriture féminine* by employing features of the traditional novel (closure, for example), his narrative frequently undermines these features. The resultant narrative-in-tension may itself be viewed as a subtle gesture toward a postmodern aesthetic. *A Dance to the Music of Time* suggests a nostalgic phase in British literature after World War II exemplified by a contemporary *roman-fleuve*.

My book is best read by the same method as the *roman-fleuve* that is its subject, whose ideal reader carefully peruses each of the parts as they contribute to a cumulative understanding. The chapters on Trollope, Richardson, and Powell are parallel and linked rather than interdependent; each may be read in conjunction with the introductory first chapter and, as the three exemplars of the *roman-fleuve* represent different phases in the genre's development and evolution, each chapter explores the *roman-fleuve* and *écriture féminine* from a unique perspective. Because an implicit aim of my project is to popularize a neglected—and often denigrated—genre, I have avoided, as much as possible, technical jargon and the extremes of the critical approaches so that I may reach a wider audience. Finally, in keeping with the primary characteristic of the novel without end, my last chapter is an epilogue rather than a conclusion; I suggest therein further implications of the genre's exclusion from the canon and its place—past, present, and future—in the evolution of the novel.

A project that evolves over a ten-year period, as this one has, accumulates an enormous debt of gratitude. My primary acknowledgment is to Robert S. Baker, who suggested that my interest in Anthony Trollope might take the form of a genre study, since "genre is always inherently interesting and timely." I would like to thank those who read the complete manuscript at an early stage, especially Robert Baker, Joseph Wiesenfarth, and James G. Nelson. At a later stage of the project, Harriet Kramer Linkin offered a thoughtful critique and creative suggestions for the first and last chapters, for which I am deeply grateful. The anonymous readers for the University Press of Florida as well as those colleagues who gave me advice about the manuscript, Jim Payne and Diane Price Herndl, also deserve hearty thanks.

Over the years I imposed on the expertise of staff at several libraries, including the University of Wisconsin and the Beinecke Rare Book and Manuscript Library at Yale University. The University of Wisconsin supported this project through a Knapp dissertation fellowship. My travel to study Dorothy Richardson's correspondence at Yale was funded by a New Mexico State University Minigrant. At NMSU, where most of this manuscript was written, Helen Barber, Donald A. Barclay, and Donnelyn Curtis were invaluable in their research expertise, and when what I sought was not in our library, they worked electronic magic. The interlibrary loan office at NMSU, Jivonna Stewart in particular, patiently and efficiently processed hundreds of requests for materials.

Material from chapter 2 was originally published in *Genre*, vol. 20, no. 1 (1987), 25–43, as "Genre in Search of a Historical Context: Trollope's Proto–*Roman-Fleuve*." Portions of chapter 4 were published as "A Text of Arrested Desire: The Anticlimax of Extended Narrative in Anthony Powell's *A Dance to the Music of Time*" in *Style*, vol. 22 (1988), 576–94. I am grateful for permission to reproduce them here. Permission to quote from Dorothy Richardson's unpublished letters has kindly been granted by the Beinecke Rare Book and Manuscript Library at Yale University.

I owe a special debt to Walda Metcalf at the University Press of Florida, who encouraged me over the long period of review and revision, and Siobhán White, who answered numerous inquiries. My greatest debt, however, is to my husband, Steven Newmark, and my son, Garrett, for keeping the ship afloat during the years I was lost in the morasses of *romans-fleuves*, novels without end.

Chapter One

The *Roman-Fleuve*

Flooding the Boundaries of the Novel

What do such large loose baggy monsters,
with their queer elements of the accidental and
the arbitrary, artistically *mean?*
Henry James, "Preface to 'The Tragic Muse'"

James's disparaging epithet for multiplotted nineteenth-century novels implicitly privileges highly plotted narratives over those with other, non-Aristotelian, dynamics. This bias, however, has not dissuaded novelists from creating the baggiest monster of all—the prolix sequence novel or *roman-fleuve* (literally "river novel"), which pushes the expansiveness of the Victorian triple-decker to an extreme. In origin a nineteenth-century French genre, it has been refined during the twentieth century by both experimental and more traditional writers from Proust to Powell.[1] Despite its significance as the successor to the nineteenth-century serial, the multivolume *roman-fleuve*, or sequence novel, has never gained the popularity of more diminutive serial publications such as the miniseries, the soap opera, or the *roman feuilleton* (an installment novel published in a daily newspaper). Nor has it received a just share of critical attention. In this first theoretical study of the *roman-fleuve* as a genre, I seek to rectify that neglect.

The definition of a subgenre—a slippery both/and kind of endeavor—becomes even more problematic when the species is one as loosely delimited as the novel. Some of the features of the *roman-fleuve* are those of the novel intensified; ironically, the subtype is a hyperbolic form. In this case, however, a quantitative difference produces a qualitative difference. The abundance of characters, often numbering in the hundreds and requiring a "Who's Who" to refresh readers' memories, and the prolonged temporal gaps between the publication of the novels create a reading experience significantly different from that of the serial or long novel. The exaggerated characteristics of the subgenre illuminate, by magnifying, features of the novel itself. Other characteristics of the *roman-fleuve* are unique to the subgenre: it differs from the long novel in its prevalent use of extraneous narrative substructures, extractable narratives within the comprehensive framework of the entire novel. Whereas in the long novel various plot lines and characters eventually converge, in the *roman-fleuve* many are, or seem to be, dispensable. Powell describes his technique as "leav[ing] open a great many cards of reentry, which may or may not have to be used."[2] Not every detail is carried through to the finish; some subplots dead-end. While the *roman-fleuve* in many ways differs from the novel in degree more than in kind, it is nevertheless a distinct subgenre in its own right, distinguished from related genres such as the Victorian serial or the long novel.

It may be that the *roman-fleuve* has been neglected by critics simply because of its extreme length.[3] Though this may seem a superficial issue, it may actually be an issue of superfluity: length is a factor that may relegate a genre to the margins of the canon. Several dictionaries of literary terms include in their definition of the *roman-fleuve* a derogatory qualification (for example, "sometimes also [applied] to a tediously meandering novel")[4] suggesting that length and flow are essentially negative in and of themselves. Thus, the denigration of the genre seems to inhere within the term. While some genres suffer canonical exclusion because of their brevity—as if the epistle and the haiku are too small to merit consideration—it does not follow that more is better where genre is concerned. Ever since James dubbed them "baggy monsters," lengthy, complex nineteenth-century narratives have been regarded disparagingly, and of course James is only the most notable spokesman for this view.

The massiveness of the multivolume *roman-fleuve* poses both practical and aesthetic problems that have contributed to its marginal acceptance within the canon. How much does it cost a publisher to print a 2,000- to 3,000-page novel? Can a novelist sustain excellence—or even sustain a narrative—through 2,000 or more pages of text? The greatest challenge is to the readers themselves. The *roman-fleuve* demands a commitment far exceeding that of any other fictional narrative. Not only must the reader sign on for an extended reading time, but that reading period is often protracted for years or even decades if the work is published incrementally. The publication history of Richardson's thirteen-volume novel *Pilgrimage*, discussed in detail in chapter 3, reveals the impact that length may have on canonical acceptance. The bulk of *Pilgrimage*, the first twelve volumes, appeared in installments from 1915 through 1938, a drawn-out publication that exasperated her publishers. They announced the appearance of the "final" volume of the novel twice: in 1938, when volume twelve was published, and again in 1967, when the final installment and thirteenth "volume," *March Moonlight*, appeared ten years posthumously.

Some of the distinguishing features of the *roman-fleuve* might be considered defects in a conventional novel, and readers at times seem alienated by the ways in which the subgenre differs from its species. The traditional novel, for example, privileges closure. Frank Kermode expresses this value when he argues that we look to the end of a narrative "to bestow upon the whole duration and meaning."[5] However, because of the proliferation of endings between the first and last volumes—each novel having its own ending, which is subsequently undermined by the next volume—the *roman-fleuve* inherently deprivileges closure. This teasing narrative, always threatening to end but always evading closure, both entices and irritates readers. Paraphrasing Kermode, Joseph Frank has commented, "We say *tick-tock* because to repeat *tick-tick* endlessly is a burden that humans cannot bear; where there is a beginning we want an end . . . not simply the hum and buzz of repetition *ad infinitum*."[6] In the case of the *roman-fleuve*, each volume supplies both a new beginning and a provisional ending within the whole. Although the temporal and spatial gaps of the serially published *roman-fleuve* contract when the work later appears in a collected edition (as was the case with Richardson and Powell, and eventually with Trollope), the gaps between individual novels provide an intermission for the later readers as well.

The expectation of the ending, an anticipation often long-protracted in the *roman-fleuve*, leads readers to be hypercritical of that ending when it finally is published. Powell's *A Dance to the Music of Time*, a twelve-volume *roman-fleuve* published from 1951 through 1975, is a case in point. After the last volume was published, a special MLA session was organized, the implication being that the work could then be evaluated in some conclusive way. When essays and books were published that took the final volume into account, it became evident that several critics were disappointed in the neat, circular, anticlimactic ending, which revealed that the entire narrative was a flashback in the mind of the narrator. The very ambitiousness of the genre creates expectations that authors have difficulty meeting.

Practical and aesthetic concerns are just part of the reason the British *roman-fleuve* has gained only marginal acceptance within the canon. Its similarity to "debased" genres and readerships is also a contributing factor. Paradoxically, many of the characteristics of the *roman-fleuve* that make it resemble popular genres—and that may account for whatever popularity it has achieved—are those denigrated by "serious" readers and critics. As with the serial and the soap opera, much of its popularity is based upon its creation of an extended relationship between readers and characters; our familiarity with these seemingly real friends compels us to "tune in" week after week or year after year to see what becomes of them. In addition, the genre may be denigrated because its resemblance to the serial links it to both a female readership and a feminine narrative. Its length would seem to require the time associated with readers or viewers (traditionally supposed to be the unemployed, particularly middle-class women) who have the leisure to cultivate extended relationships with serial characters and events. Its narrative progresses through a nonlinear movement; it is developed through reiterations, parallels, and repetitions, moving synchronically rather than diachronically, emphasizing extended development of characters and subplots rather than forward movement of a major plot. Such narratives are often associated with women's writing or an *écriture féminine*. Damned by its refusal to meet conventional expectations, by its ambitiousness, and by association, the *roman-fleuve* has achieved neither the contemporary critical acceptance of the nineteenth-century serial novel nor the popularity of the twentieth-century television series. There is a paradox at the heart of the marginal acceptance of the *roman-fleuve*: on one hand, it seems too difficult and esoteric to appeal to the average reader; on the other hand, it resembles popular genres disparaged by serious critics.

The genre's often denigrated length and its feminine features are examined—and ultimately, I hope, revalorized—by my thesis: I argue that the *roman-fleuve* is a form that exemplifies narrative characteristics often defined as those of an *écriture féminine* and that is gendered feminine by a cultural construct that describes narratives in sexual terms. Critics who disparage the genre for its feminine features—a practice I examine later in this chapter—reflect a convention of privileging climactic and forward-moving plots that can be traced back to Aristotle, the first literary critic. Continued through his heirs, including Gustav Freytag and Henry James, this convention has recently been reconsidered by French feminists such as Hélène Cixous and Luce Irigaray, who privilege alternative patterns. As both a participant and a critic within the tradition of gendering narratives, I suggest not that narratives reflect essential qualities of women and men, rather that we have *gendered* them feminine or masculine as a descriptive tool, one that reflects—and often resists, in the case of the French feminists as I read them—certain cultural biases under patriarchy.

The hypothesis about an *écriture féminine* is directed not at the sex of the writer but toward the writing itself. Cixous, often considered the primary advocate of an *écriture féminine*, suggests that it is rare in writers of either gender: "To be signed with a woman's name doesn't necessarily make a piece of writing feminine. It could quite as well be masculine writing, and conversely, the fact that a piece of writing is signed with a man's name does not in itself exclude femininity. It's rare, but you can sometimes find femininity in writings signed by men: it does happen."[7] Thus, writers as diverse as Joyce, Artaud, Genet, and Céline have been considered feminine writers, and certain characteristics of narrative or style (such as linear plot or fragmented syntax) may be considered "masculine" or "feminine," whatever the sex of the writer. Some contemporary feminist literary critics have also argued that there are connections between gender and genre, and some theorists postulate that certain genres (the romance, epistolary novel, or even the novel itself) may be feminine, or woman's, genres.[8]

It is not my intent here to rehash the essentialism-constructionist debate, which would take me a considerable distance from my central subject, but I do want to articulate some of its implications for the gender-genre issue.[9] Warnings about the "trap" of essentialism have been articulated mainly by Anglo-American feminists because of a quite legitimate fear of derogatory definitions of the feminine that are used to oppress women. The warnings also reflect an intercultural gap, which provokes skepticism about the psychoanalytic orientation of French feminists and discomfort with the gendering of nouns and their modifiers (characteristic of many languages other than English), a process described grammatically as a *sexe fictive*, or fictitious sex.[10] Generally this fictitious sex is arbitrarily assigned, but at times it clearly does reflect a cultural gender bias: in French, for example, the addition of one man turns a group of 999 *elles* into *ils*.

When narratives are gendered, the process is also fictitious or meta-phoric, not literal. One of the reasons the French theorists have been dismissed by some Anglo-American feminists is that they have been sub-ject to "over-literalist" readings.[11] Jane Gallop, however, argues that "the Irigarayan *poétique du corps* is not an expression of the body but a *poiésis*, a creating of the body," not anatomical but constructed.[12] Thus, French feminist theorization of a multiple-sited female sexuality does not reinscribe the patriarchally conceived woman-as-passive-object-of-desire (though admittedly, it brings its own set of risks). Critics of the "essentialist ploy" need to hear and acknowledge the subversive, playful—sometimes taunting—tone of Cixous and Irigaray. It signals a refusal of assimilation or co-optation, a rejection of patriarchal values as the en-trance fee for equality. To deny women's difference is to risk losing the common bond that is the basis for identity. Defending the existence of a feminine aesthetic, Silvia Bovenschen asserts that "feminine artistic production takes place by means of a complicated process involving conquering and reclaiming, appropriating and formulating, as well as forgetting and subverting."[13]

It is not clear *why* sex and gender have been so prevalently used as met-aphors to describe narrative throughout literary history; Robert Scholes describes the "sexual act" as the "archetype of all fiction" (but imme-diately proceeds to equate it with the climactic Aristotelian model of plot).[14] The notion of textual *jouissance* compellingly suggests that we do not—or cannot—separate our greatest pleasures. Our propensity for assigning gender to everything from boats to animals (who are often dubbed "he" or "she" because of their species, in direct contradiction of their visible sex) would make an interesting study in intellectual history. Narratives are elusive and abstract entities for analysis, in spite of efforts to reduce them to Proppian functions or computer-tallyable features. The designation of masculine and feminine narratives constitutes what Diana Fuss calls a "nominal" device used for "linguistic convenience."[15] To assign them gender is one way to classify them.

In evaluating arguments about gender-genre connections, motivation must also be examined. As Fuss suggests, it is important to examine the ends for which such arguments are deployed: "To insist that essentialism is always and everywhere reactionary is, for the constructionist, to buy into essentialism in the very act of making the charge."[16] In the case of Cixous and Irigaray, it is clear that they wish to reconstruct women's sexuality into a positive, celebratory model. For each, this project is intrinsically related to women breaking silence to write their difference, articulating something other than the status quo, as Irigaray's "two lips" and Cixous's "your body must be heard" make clear. In the context of such a revalorization, the designation of the *roman-fleuve* as a feminine form should simultaneously increase estimation of its so-called feminine narrative features. Richardson in particular valorizes the narrative and social values she associates with women. Her celebration of a feminine writing and consciousness is intended to promote an entire ethos repressed by patriarchy. Although Richardson describes herself as apolitical, her project has a clear affinity with what Rosi Braidotti defines as a "priority issue" for contemporary feminists: "the achievement of equality in the assertion of difference."[17]

It is also important to look at the gendering of narratives in a historical context; this book traces the evolution of a subgenre that emerged shortly after the period when women first entered the marketplace as novelists. When they were allowed for the first time in history to participate in the profession of writing, their success came because they were doing something different in their novels. Although it may not have a direct and immediate bearing on women's position in society, there *is* something inherently subversive about women in a patriarchal society appropriating the right to write their own bodies. Critics who trace patterns of subversive narrative strategies or identify domestic ideologies in texts are arguing that women inscribe their difference on the writing itself—and that male writers may be influenced by and emulate those techniques. It is at this point that the historical converges with gender studies.

Thus, my discussion of the *roman-fleuve* as a feminine genre juxtaposes a number of controversial associations. Readers may wish to place the adjectives "feminine" and "masculine" in mental quotation marks throughout this book in order to acknowledge the problematic nature of these designations. We have found no way to remove ourselves from either biology or culture for the purpose of locating or defining difference objectively; biologists and linguists have yet to resolve the issue of sexual difference as it is reflected in language. In the following pages, I use the term "feminine" to refer to the constellation of features attributed to women (and narratives), with a preference for the French feminists' revisionary construction (see the third section of this chapter). This usage implies that women and men are different, but it does not assume any monolithic, unchanging feminine nature nor deny differences among women. I use the term "feminist" to refer to an ideology that acknowledges society's unequal treatment of men and women and that desires to change society to rectify that injustice. Although I do not believe that a feminine narrative is necessarily a socially transformative device, the convergence of feminine narrative and feminist rhetoric in works like *Pilgrimage* is mutually reinforcing. If reconstructing the feminine gives women a subjectivity they were previously denied, "encouraging women to think, say, and write the feminine is a gesture of self-legitimation that breaks away from centuries of phallo-logocentric thought which had silenced women."[18] At this moment in history, the feminine is a highly contested, unstable, and volatile site.

In the four introductory subsections that follow, I offer a brief history and a theoretical definition of the *roman-fleuve*—a narrative poetics—followed by analyses of the special dynamics of reading the *roman-fleuve*, of its readers, and of the peculiar gendered rationale for its canonical exclusion.

❧ A Narrative History of the *Roman-Fleuve*: The French Connections

Although it would seem appropriate to use an English term when discussing British literature, *roman-fleuve* has a historical and descriptive suggestiveness that makes it a more useful term than any of the alternatives such as the "sequence," the "series," or the "sequel." These terms have never been clearly distinguished, and when a distinction is made, it is often merely a thinly disguised value judgment based on an aesthetic appraisal, or a ranking of genres. The term *roman-fleuve* is usually attributed to Romain Rolland, who used the river metaphor in his preface to *Jean-Christophe* (1906-12) to describe his own work in the genre. According to his account, his novel "m'est apparu comme un fleuve; . . . il est, dans le cours des fleuves, des zones où ils s'étendent, semblent dormir, . . . ils n'en continuent pas moins de couler et changer." [(It) seemed to me like a river; . . . there are, in the course of rivers, zones where they stretch out, seem to sleep, . . . they continue no less to flow and change.][19] In English, the *Oxford English Dictionary* lists the first use of the term in 1936, under a series of compound terms that begin with *roman* (*roman policier*, *roman à these*, and so forth). The usage sentence provided again reveals the seemingly predetermined negative connotations: "Those great *romans-fleuves* whose unnumbered volumes have no other purpose than to show us to ourselves as we appear."[20]

I have chosen the French term in preference to the English alternatives to designate the French origins of the genre, among other reasons. According to Elizabeth Kerr, *La Comédie humaine* is "the first real sequence novel and Balzac was the first novelist to conceive of such a unified series."[21] Trollope himself acknowledged this legacy when he proposed a toast to Balzac at a Royal Literary Fund anniversary dinner: "I am told that he was the man who invented that style of fiction in which I have attempted to work."[22] Richardson also defines her project in relation to Balzac, whose realism she rejects in her 1938 foreword to *Pilgrimage* as one that represents "a relatively concrete and coherent social system." Balzac's *La Comédie humaine* may be viewed both as an international prototype for the genre and as a French predecessor of Rolland's and Proust's more refined twentieth-century versions of the *roman-fleuve*, functioning in French literary history as Trollope does later for the English. Balzac's *roman-fleuve* is much larger and more sprawling than any subsequent exemplars, but it creates an effect similar to that Trollope might have achieved if his Barset and Palliser series— which have some overlap of characters and plots—were combined into one gigantic *roman-fleuve*. The first collected edition of *La Comédie humaine* (1842–48) contained seventeen volumes; Balzac published ninety-one novels and had contemplated 137 before his sudden death at age fifty-one cut short his life's work. The reappearing characters, the reiterated plots, and the encyclopedic desire to create a world through a multivolume novel are carried over from the nineteenth- to the more unified and streamlined twentieth-century conception of the genre.

Significantly, Balzac's statement of intent in his 1842 introduction to *La Comédie humaine* prefigures statements made by subsequent writers in the genre. He describes "the vastness of a plan which includes both a history and a criticism of society, an analysis of its evils, and a discussion of its principles."[23] Balzac's historic intent is appropriated by Powell, while the self-professed social criticism and analysis prefigure the careful moral distinctions made by Trollope. The discursiveness, using fiction, sometimes digressively, as a platform for critical inquiry—often about aesthetics—is adopted by Trollope through his editorializing narrator and by Proust and Richardson in less obtrusive twentieth-century fashion.

Most important, Balzac's encyclopedic conception establishes an emphasis on minute analysis of social class characteristic of all subsequent exemplars. In his introduction, he expresses a desire to create an anatomy, to delineate "differences between a soldier, an artisan, a man of business, a lawyer, an idler, a student, a statesman, a merchant, a sailor, a poet, a beggar, a priest."[24] Powell not only makes abundant references to Burton's *Anatomy of Melancholy* throughout *A Dance to the Music of Time*, but he also completes his own minute anatomy of social class distinctions in the Balzacian tradition. Similarly, Richardson anatomizes the differences between men and woman in *Pilgrimage*. Balzac also establishes connections between his plan and natural history, suggesting to the modern reader biological and social Darwinism: "I, for my part, convinced of this scheme of nature long before the discussion to which it has given rise, perceived that in this respect society resemble[s] nature. For does not society modify Man, according to the conditions in which he lives and acts, into men as manifold as the species in Zoology?"[25] Trollope echoes this sociological statement in his autobiography when he defines as his major objective a tracing of changes in characters over a lifetime (see chapter 2).

Another nineteenth-century predecessor is Émile Zola's *Rougon-Macquart* (1871–93), a twenty-volume sequence of novels that shares Balzac's sociological emphasis. In his naturalistic concern with heredity, Zola also participates in the Darwinistic strain of the genre. Zola's novels shift their emphasis from individual to individual, creating a social panorama. In differentiating between legitimate and illegitimate branches of the family, he shares in the nineteenth-century concern with class evident in Balzac and Trollope. Although it is not as unified as twentieth-century exemplars, the *Rougon-Macquart* introduces the family saga approach of such early modern exemplars as John Galsworthy's Forsyte novels, begun in 1906 and published collectively in 1921 as *The Forsyte Saga*.

Romain Rolland's ten-volume *Jean-Christophe* (1905–12) is a more immediate twentieth-century French predecessor of Proust and Richardson in focusing on a single protagonist in bildungsroman fashion. Two other notable connections among these early modern examples of the genre are their use of digressive discursive material and of musical motifs. Building on Balzac's precedent of discursive statements within a novel, *Jean-Christophe* contains music criticism just as *Pilgrimage* later contains elaborate digressions commenting on writing, translation, and sex roles. Since Rolland's major character is a composer, music naturally forms a major subject within his *roman-fleuve*. Proust's use of the Vinteuil sonata and Richardson's extensive repetition of a Chopin nocturne as major structuring motifs also reflect a precedent established by Rolland.

The most celebrated example of the genre, Proust's seven-novel *A la recherche du temps perdu* (1913–27), was at first intended by its author to be published in one volume under the title eventually bestowed on the collected whole. As a *roman-fleuve*, it fully participates in the repertoire of the genre's features. In his exploration of the themes of memory recaptured and involuntary memory, Proust is aware of the potential of the genre to represent scope and to experiment with stream of consciousness narrative and nonchronological presentation of time, as Gérard Genette has shown in *Narrative Discourse*, his detailed structuralist study of *A la recherche*. Both Richardson and Powell were enthusiastic readers of Proust, although it is important to note that Richardson could not have been influenced by the French writer in conceiving of *Pilgrimage* as a *roman-fleuve*. Extracts of the first volume of *A la recherche* began appearing in *Le Figaro* in 1912, and *Swann's Way* was published in 1913, as Richardson began to write the first volume of *Pilgrimage*. However, she did not read Proust until December of 1922, when *A la recherche* began to appear in England in the Scott Moncrieff translation (1922–31). Her letters to Bryher from 1925 to 1928 and to Peggy Kirkaldy in 1928 are peppered with references to Proust. Powell read Proust at Oxford, and his novel self-consciously echoes *A la recherche*, even to the creation of a mock-Proustian extract in *The Military Philosophers*. Critics disagree somewhat on the amount and kind of influence Proust wielded over Powell: Robert Selig believes that they share many of the same time-deforming narrative techniques defined by Genette while Philip Thody finds a good deal of deliberate contrast and parody.[26]

❧ The *Roman-Fleuve* Defined: A Narrative Oxymoron

Genre criticism must consider all features that may contribute to the definition of a particular genre. Therefore, the most serviceable definition of the *roman-fleuve* is one broad enough to cover a large "repertoire" of features culled from the representative or most inclusive members, while establishing no inflexible criteria for inclusion within the genre.[27] The *roman-fleuve* is distinguished from the ordinary novel primarily (though not exclusively) by its length, scope, and subject matter. Content—as well as the ideology, themes, and motifs that cohere to a specific content—is significant to the narrative characteristic of the *roman-fleuve*. A series of more than three volumes (distinguishing it from the trilogy, which lacks the requisite scope), the *roman-fleuve* achieves unity primarily through consistent narrative presence and/or thematic focus. While the volumes generally can be read separately, as a series they have a cumulative effect. The fluidity of its subject matter, establishing a protracted though often digressive or anachronous narrative, gives the work a seemingly unfinished form. Characterized by scope created more by the reading time than the narrated time dramatized within the work, the *roman-fleuve* chooses vast subjects—such as *bildung*, social change, history, and time.

In its magnification of interchapter gaps and motific repetition, the *roman-fleuve* exploits traits inherent in the novel form. The contrast Wolfgang Iser draws between the serial and the book form of a novel is significantly parallel to the difference between the novel and the *roman-fleuve*: "The reader is forced by the pauses imposed on him to imagine more than he could have done if his reading were continuous, and so, if the text of a serialized novel makes a different impression from the text in book form, this is principally because it introduces additional gaps, or alternatively accentuates existing gaps by means of a break until the next installment."[28] Analogously, the longer the novel, the more significant the imaginative activity. Furthermore, as the novel is unified by repetition, especially the use of motifs or recurring characters linked together by their roles as members of a family or community, so the *roman-fleuve* emphasizes the imbrication of lives and social spheres. The repeated characters, situations, and motifs provide the structural continuity that connects volume to volume, while the accumulation of slightly modified paradigms elicits the variety and universality of human experience. Using a sexual analogy, Peter Brooks defines this function of repetition: it "bind[s] the energy of the text so as to make its final discharge more effective."[29] It is the binding power of the *roman*, harnessing the *fleuve*, that creates tension in this genre, although I will take issue with his generalization about "discharge" presently.

I have chosen the term *roman-fleuve* not only to designate the national origins but also for its descriptive evocativeness. While *roman* denotes a lengthy prose narrative, *fleuve* connotes narrative flow, as in the metaphor of the river of life, evoking the genre's affinity with novels (such as the Victorian novels of Eliot, Dickens, and Trollope) that depict change within the larger social unit, the community, or within the individual. The organic plexus of the form, the profuse effluence of change, the often indirect trajectory of the course of time, as well as the prolixity of the form, resulting from the swelling of the middle, the refusal of the *roman-fleuve* to end at one or even multiple volumes, are all suggested by *fleuve*. As a self-conscious metaphor, its relevance transcends this particular genre; it also suggests the stream of consciousness technique often associated with the *roman-fleuve* because of the work of Proust and Richardson (although the latter despised this term, which she referred to as "shroud of consciousness").

Furthermore, there is a tension between the noun and its modifier: *fleuve* designates the matter, dynamic and unrestricted, whereas *roman* provides the frame that contains and restricts the driving force. The *roman* functions as the structure of narrative, which, according to one definition, "demarcates, encloses, establishes, limits, orders."[30] The juxtaposition of the terms *fleuve* and *roman* suggests the formalist dichotomy of *fabula*, the objective "order of events referred to by the narrative," and *sjužet*, the more subjective "order of events presented in the narrative discourse."[31] Another distinction between these two latter terms, that of Meir Sternberg, based on that first defined by the Russian formalists, is relevant to characteristics of the *roman-fleuve*. He defines *fabula* as "the chronological or chronological-causal sequence into which the reader, progressively and retrospectively, reassembles these motifs; it may thus be viewed as the second-degree 'raw material' (postselected and straightforwardly combined narrative) that the artist compositionally 'deforms' and thus re-contextualizes in constructing his work."[32] In describing the progressive and retrospective movement of chronological sequence, Sternberg describes *fabula* in terms that evoke the wavelike progression of the *roman-fleuve*. Moreover, his differentiation between *sjužet* and *fabula* hints at the rich subjective potential of the genre: "The *sujet* . . . is the actual disposition and articulation of these narrative motifs in the particular finished product, as their order and interrelation, shaping and coloring, was finally decided on by the author. To put it as simply as possible, the *fabula* involves what happens in the work as (re)arranged in the 'objective' order of occurrence, while the *sujet* involves what happens in the order, angle, and patterns of presentation actually encountered by the reader."[33]

In the *roman-fleuve* it is the *fabula* that reflects the continuous, though sometimes indirect, flow of the genre. The Trollopian *roman-fleuve* maintains a high degree of apparent correspondence between *fabula* and *sjužet*, whereas the modernist *roman-fleuve*, such as Proust's *A la recherche du temps perdu* and, to a lesser extent, Richardson's *Pilgrimage*, creates a greater disparity between the two. Of the three British writers considered in this study, Richardson most fully utilizes the subjective and time-deforming characteristic of this genre in recapturing the past through memory.

As a subgenre of the novel, the *roman-fleuve* exacerbates its narrative problems, those of length in particular. Seymour Chatman notes that "narrative is basically a kind of organization,"[34] and in the *roman-fleuve* the organization and recall of a mammoth and potentially wayward series of plot events require an encyclopedic capacity on the part of both the writer and the reader. In the ordinary reading process, as Iser describes it, "all images cohere in the reader's mind by a constant accumulation of references, which we have termed the snowball effect,"[35] but in the *roman-fleuve* the snowball becomes an avalanche. To facilitate comprehension of the whole, some critics have proposed that unity is the salient characteristic of the genre. Kerr, for example, argues that the "most successful sequence novels reveal in the separate parts some inkling of the whole plan."[36] However, this stipulation implies that the writer preconceives the structure of the *roman-fleuve* from the first volume. A thorough preconception of the details and structure of the entire work is unlikely, and furthermore, this requirement fails to consider the dynamics of plot in narrative. Brooks's definition of plot, derived from Freud's *Beyond the Pleasure Principle*, provides a model that is dynamic because it accounts for the force of human desire in motivating narrative, the relations of beginnings and endings, and the extrapolation of meaning from "temporal flux"; his description of plot as "arabesque" privileges continuity rather than unity, especially divergent continuity, and suggests the continuousness of the *roman-fleuve*, the characteristic suggested by the modifier.[37]

One of the exigencies of the *roman-fleuve* is to reconcile the demands of unity—that the collection of individual volumes maintain one major subject—against the free-flowing drive of the genre, the continuity that not only connects the volumes but that, more significantly, also provides the momentum that moves the plot forward. Richardson, like Trollope, believed her work was best read in its entirety. When John Cowper Powys agreed to write a booklet to promote *Pilgrimage*, for which Richardson's publishers wanted her to write a short paragraph on each volume, giving a plot outline and the circumstance of composition, she "told them, since they admitted they had read only one volume of mine, that each volume is a single chapter of one book & cannot therefore be treated in the manner they suggest."[38] This tension between the impulses of continuity and unity reiterates the conflict between the dynamic and static qualities of the genre, a relation elucidated by Paul Ricoeur's definition of the essential relationship of plot and time: "Every narrative combines two dimensions in various proportions, one chronological and the other nonchronological. The first may be called the episodic dimension, which characterizes the story as made out of events. The second is the configurational dimension according to which the plot construes significant wholes out of scattered events."[39] Ricoeur's articulation of this dichotomy of narrative clarifies the tension within the *roman-fleuve*: the *fleuve*, the force of continuity, may be characterized as chronological, kinetic, and forward-moving (though potentially digressive), while the *roman* the embodiment of unity, is in itself essentially nonchronological, restrictive, and backward-looking, generally static in effect.

In part, the *roman* is characterized by restriction because of its selectivity, a device that limits the amplitude of the *fleuve* (and of the *fabula*). Although the *fleuve* impels the work to abandon itself to the flux of time, in reality the genre must somehow curtail the flow if it is to represent the flow, a paradox inherent in narrative itself: "Every narrative, however seemingly 'full,' is constructed on the basis of a set of events which *might have been included but were left out*; and this is as true of imaginary as it is of realistic narratives."[40] Because of its scope and subject matter, the *roman-fleuve* grapples with many of the same problems as historical narrative; in this respect it resembles the "chronicle" that Trollope's narrator repeatedly claims to write. However, the *roman-fleuve*, unlike the historical annals or chronicle forms it resembles, explores the significance of process and isolates segments of it through beginnings and endings, that is, through plot. Plot reconciles, albeit in an uneasy alliance, an inevitable selectivity with the impulse of continuity since, according to Scholes and Kellogg's definition, "plot requires (as Aristotle, who was not afraid to utter a necessary banality, observed) a beginning, a middle, and an end. In historical narrative, this means that a subject must be discerned in the past and cut off from the irrelevant matters with which it has only a temporal connection."[41]

In the *roman-fleuve*, as my discussion of specific exemplars in the following chapters will demonstrate, the beginnings and endings are as problematic as in any historical or quasihistorical form: the emphasis on process conflicts with the selection of cutting-off points; therefore, the genre finds its points of initiation and termination with difficulty. Its inherent propensity for rendering process is best realized in the middle, the realm of the *fleuve*, where selectivity is less restrictive because of the possibility of variation, expansion, and repetition. The problem of reiteration is especially complex when the writer feels the competing needs to make the individual volumes self-sufficient and the *roman-fleuve* a unified whole. Richardson reveals her awareness of this necessity in a letter to the novelist E. B. C. Jones, when she rues the damage done to the opening of a volume by this necessity: "I agree, with groans, as to the opening of 'The Tunnel.' I attempted a compressed retrospect & achieved almost nothing at all. This business of compression, so essential, if the unity & continuity of consciousness is to be conveyed, gets of course more troublesome as the material accumulates, though at the same time it is made a little easier by Miriam's increasing articulateness."[42] Her letters show Richardson caught between a desire for total inner realism and artistic practicality. She writes about *Oberland* (novel 9): "I agree about 'slightness'—& am fully aware. It is due partly to the need to condense that grows with each vol. & partly to M's becoming more out-turned really living. . . . The difficulty with *Ob.* was to keep the balance, that was her balance, between the profundities of the enchanted fortnight & the People. Each episode could have filled a single volume in the old manner—but I should have been in my grave before M's fortnight was at an end."[43]

The genre's compulsion to repeat is evident in its expositions; they not only establish background for the narrative, but they also reiterate, even from the beginning, slipping into the mode of the "middle." Trollope, Richardson, and Powell all use techniques of double or multiple exordiums, undermining the validity of a first exposition by following it with a second (or, in Richardson's case, a third), intimating that any point of initiation is subject to revision and reiteration and is, therefore, arbitrary. This technique, similar to that Genette perceives in Proust's *Recherche*, "mimic[s], as it were, the unavoidable *difficulty* of beginning the better to exorcise it."[44] Trollope's, Richardson's, and Powell's *romans-fleuves* reflect an understanding of the arbitrary nature of introductory and concluding events. It is for this reason that their expositions are oblique, sprawling, and reiterative and that their closures are diffused rather than climactic. They cope with the problems inherent in framing the copious middles of the *roman-fleuve* with arbitrary introductions and conclusions and, in the process, exemplify a narrative resembling, to various degrees, an *écriture féminine*.

The French term *roman-fleuve* suggests the combination of qualities that create the genre's affinity with *écriture féminine*: as both a *fleuve*, or fluid narrative, and a *roman*, a genre associated specifically with women readers and writers, it resembles those elements of fiction traditionally defined as feminine. Antithetical to end-oriented narratives such as the romance, mystery, or adventure novel, the expansive and discursive multivolume *roman-fleuve* rejects the climactic progression that is often considered a masculine model for narrative. Instead, the seemingly digressive narrative is uniquely characterized by a tension between continuation—each volume both contains its own story and continues a more comprehensive plot—and termination, since each volume and ultimately the work itself must end. The extensive vacillation of its narrative, moving forward with new characters, situations, and events, moving backward with reiterations and parallels of previous paradigms, creates a dialectical strain: the narrative oscillates and teases, subverting expectations for an "ejaculatory" discovery or release. Joseph Boone, who coined this usage, notes the association between the "traditional love-plot" and the "male-oriented norm of sexuality [which] foster[s] the illusion that all pleasure (of reading or of sex) is ejaculatory."[45] The tension inherent in this narrative is expressed by the juxtaposition of the French nouns: the *fleuve*, the free-flowing impulse of the narrative, is constrained by the *roman*, which structures and limits the *fleuve* through selectivity.

Descriptions of *écriture féminine* offered by the French feminists reveal an inherent similarity to the features of the *roman-fleuve* I have defined here.[46] Perhaps the most obvious common characteristic is that of the fluid narrative; fluidity is often associated with women's bodies both traditionally and by many of the French feminists. Although this kind of "biologism" has been rejected by some feminists, and although it admittedly risks returning to essentialist definitions of women, which could support the antifeminist backlash, the revalorization of such physiological and narrative features is part of the French feminist project. The nonlinear, discursive, often digressive narrative is also characteristic of both the *roman-fleuve* and an *écriture féminine*; the central feature of these kinds of narrative is their lack of closure. Rachel Blau DuPlessis has demonstrated that this is a feature of the work of twentieth-century women writers,[47] but as the next chapter will show, it is also a narrative characteristic latent in Trollope's proto-*roman-fleuve*. These narratives reject the "ejaculatory" climactic narrative proposed by narratologists from Aristotle to Brooks. Susan Winnett critiques Brooks's model and finds an exclusively male bias: "A narrative based on the oedipal model would have to be profoundly and vulnerably male in its assumptions about what constitutes pleasure"; through her analysis of narrative alternatives to this teleology, such as Mary Shelley's *Frankenstein*, she offers the possibility of a multiplicity of patterns other than the climatic one assumed to be the norm.[48]

Unlike the "ejaculatory" narrative, the *roman-fleuve* terminates without achieving the singular, definitive climax that often characterizes more highly plotted and direct narratives. Although some feminist critics have viewed the narrative of *écriture féminine* as multiclimaxed, suggesting women's orgasmic potential, narrative dynamics in the *roman-fleuve* are more often anticlimactic, deliberately rejecting any kind of narrative peak. Both the *roman-fleuve* and *écriture féminine* are forms that create narrative gaps, though in feminist works the gaps are more obviously ideological, revealing women's social oppression—for example, the gaps of silence that represent experiences traditionally either considered irrelevant because outside the patriarchal sphere or censored because they reveal women's oppression. Although Richardson's narrative best illustrates these gaps (which she exploits both as a modernist and as a feminist), the *roman-fleuve* is a form with an inherent propensity to use this narrative device because of its frequent, multiple divisions, including the conventional novel's divisions between chapters as well as the genre's unique intervolume gaps. Whereas in Richardson the gaps are used to suggest the female protagonist's repressed emotions and experiences, in Trollope's and Powell's *romans-fleuves* two major female characters are killed off in these gaps, keeping the stories of the male protagonists on track.

My preference for the French terms derives from a wish to respect difficulties in translation and to profit from the evocativeness of the language in which these forms originated. The terms are in many ways parallel: just as *roman-fleuve* suggests the tension between form and narrative dynamics, *écriture féminine* evokes the tension between women and writing, an activity historically forbidden or discouraged for women.

The translation of *écriture féminine* as "women's writing" is inexact if the French term is used, as I use it, to designate a kind of gendered narrative rather than writing produced by women. Further, as Cixous has noted, not all women produce an *écriture féminine*. The adjective "feminine" in English is often used with negative connotations; however, inherent in a feminist argument that women may write a different language from men are both the premise that this language is in no way inferior and the desire to reevaluate feminine language.

✣ An Anatomy of Serial Reading and the Ideal Reader of the *Roman-Fleuve*

Through its mode of publication the *roman-fleuve* is associated with installment fictions, particularly the *roman feuilleton* and the Victorian serial novel. The emergence of the *roman-fleuve* in the mid-nineteenth century is clearly indebted to the influence of installment publication: it is not coincidental that Balzac, its first practitioner, published in serial form. Other characteristics of the genre, such as its deemphasized ending, may be traced to nineteenth-century publication modes: "Publication in installments over many months or years inspired a reading with numerous pauses but less sense of an ending. . . . Victorians, in fact, looked forward in their reading toward endings that only provided jumping off places to more and other stories."⁴⁹ In both its length and its division into discrete subunits, however, the *roman-fleuve* clearly emulates—and exceeds—the Victorian serial.

The experience of reading in installments is what might be termed a "variant" or "flexible" characteristic of the genre, which differs substantially for those who read the *roman-fleuve* as first published, volume by volume, over a protracted period of composition, and for later readers who have the option of minimizing the temporal gaps between volumes. Likewise, the Victorian serial had enforced breaks between installments for its contemporary readers that are marked in later editions. Consumers of soap operas are limited to installment viewing, but the recent video publication of television series like "Northern Exposure," "Cheers," and "The Mary Tyler Moore Show" suggests that a continuous experience may someday be possible in this medium also.

While subsequent readers can attempt to recreate the original serial reading, it is more likely they will read without observing the interruptions, putting down the text only to meet the exigencies of real life, which will not permit a reading of a twelve-volume novel in one sitting. Large temporal breaks for the original installment readers were significant in allowing time for "processing" by the individual; as a critic of the soap opera notes, "the reader's own extratextual horizons might change during the course of reading a narrative text."[50] Interludes are also important in allowing communication with others, including colleagues and reviewers. Victorian serial novelists were notably concerned about readers' reaction to their works. The stories of how Dickens considered the responses of his serial readers and how Bulwer-Lytton convinced Dickens to provide a more optimistic ending for *Great Expectations* have become proverbial. Such considerations are probably more common than we know, as Dickens, for example, also influenced the final form of Bulwer-Lytton's serial work.[51]

The *roman-fleuve*, like its predecessor the Victorian serial, may be reviewed repeatedly, often with different evaluations, as the various parts are published. Mary Hamer notes that reviewers could influence consumers and enhance purchases: "Journals did not comment only once, as on the appearance of a new work in three volumes, but referred briefly but frequently to the novel as it progressed. So members of the reading public who previously might have bought neither novels in hardback nor the flimsy monthly parts had their attention drawn to fiction and began to buy it."[52] Publishers were aware of the different experiences offered by various modes of publication. When George Smith was preparing Thackeray's *Henry Esmond* for publication, he sent Charlotte Brontë the novel volume by volume so that her response might anticipate that of lending library readers.[53]

The issue of *how* the *roman-fleuve* is read is crucial, as the examples here suggest. Although it would seem unlikely that the massive *roman-fleuve* would ever be read aloud in the family circle as the Victorian serial was, John Cowper Powys wrote to Richardson that he and his wife read *Pilgrimage* aloud to each other, *backward*, working toward the first volume.[54] Curiously, Richardson was fascinated by the multiple ways of reading a *roman-fleuve*, which she demonstrated in her own reading of Proust. As she received the volumes of *A la recherche* from Bryher, Richardson recorded her reactions in a series of letters: "I cut all those 5 vols piecemeal, leaving them all over the room, and read them in the same way, taking up the first handy vol. and opening at random. At last the whole hung and hangs, a tapestry all round me." In another letter from the same year she claims, "Again with trembling fingers I'm cutting Prousts. Complete now all but the last two volumes, not yet out I think. When we get to Trevone I shall read him straight through." A letter from 1928 describes yet another fashion of reading Proust: "I am now in my third year of reading him—two volumes at a time now one from each end to meet presently in the middle. A change from reading all over the series haphazard, and then from beginning to end and then from end to beginning."[55] This erratic and multiple fashion of reading seems totally eccentric until one learns that Powell received fan mail from readers who also experimented with reading *A Dance to the Music of Time* out of sequence, "deliberately reading it backward."[56]

Another characteristic (and macabre) difficulty of the *roman-fleuve* as a serial mode is that since it is frequently published in fragments, parts, or works-in-progress, the author may expire before completing the whole, just as Victorian serial writers Dickens, Gaskell, and Thackeray all died with novels uncompleted. Often the last segment—or an early version of it—is published posthumously. Although in 1946 Richardson published extracts of *March Moonlight* as work-in-progress (not identified as part of *Pilgrimage*) in *Life and Letters*, the final "chapter," much shorter than previous installments, appeared only posthumously, as part of the 1967 edition.[57] Proust's *Jean Santeuil*, an early version of his *roman-fleuve*, appeared in 1952. He was still revising the last three segments of *A la recherche*, titled in English *The Captive (La Prisonnière)*, *Sweet Cheat Gone (Albertine disparue)*, and *The Past Recaptured (Le Temps retrouvé)* at the time of his death in 1922. They were published unrevised in 1923, 1925, and 1927. Thus, the reading experience may be controlled not only by readers, writers, and publishers but by circumstance—Fate—as well.

The mode of publication may also influence aesthetic evaluation by readers and critics. Accordingly, since the plan of the *roman-fleuve* may not be evident from any one portion of it, especially if it is not identified as a sequence novel, the critical assessment of one volume can differ markedly from that of the whole. The challenge of evaluating a work in installments is especially complex in the case of Trollope's Pallisers, first published in serial installments, then as library editions of individual novels, and finally as a collected edition—the "Parliamentary" novels.[58] Hamer argues that Trollope constructed his serials to exploit the rhythm of gaps in installment publication and that the form itself actually stimulated his "imaginative activity" and artistic development.[59]

This view produces a Trollope radically different from the one attacked for suspenseless, plotless novels, yet the difference is not in the critics but in the various perceptions of the work created when it is read in installments, as a novel, or as a series. Henry James's review of the first volume of the Pallisers demonstrates the impossibility of evaluating a *roman-fleuve*—especially one not recognized as such by author, publisher, or reviewer—before its completion.

In his review of *Can You Forgive Her?* in the *Nation* on September 28, 1865, James criticized the novel for anticlimax resulting from the titular forgiveness asked for Alice Vavasor: "The gradual publication of 'Can You Forgive Her?' made its readers familiar with the appeal resting upon their judgment long before they were in a position to judge. The only way, as it seems to us, to justify this appeal and to obviate the flagrant anti-climax which the work now presents, was to lead the story to a catastrophe."[60] The serial publication of the novel, James would seem to imply, exacerbated the slightness of the reader's interest in Alice's marital indecision. From this one volume James could not have known that Alice has the larger function of acting as a prototype of female discontent that will be developed throughout the following novels. Furthermore, James goes on to criticize Trollope's handling of the Glencora plot in a way that clearly would have been obviated had he known that it would be continued in subsequent volumes: "To a real novelist's eye, the [Glencora] story on which it depends is hardly begun; to Mr. Trollope it is satisfactorily ended."[61] Although there is no certainty that Trollope intended at this time for the Glencora plot to be developed as extensively as it eventually would be, later volumes such as *The Prime Minister* reveal that James's opinion was ultimately validated. If he had read the Pallisers as a *roman-fleuve*, some of his objections might have been forestalled.

The manner in which a *roman-fleuve* is published—incrementally, volume by volume, or in sets that combine three or four novels in omnibus fashion—may have a profound effect on sales. Richardson wrote her editor at Dent, "There have been, uniformly, of late years, rather more sales of *Pointed Roofs* than of the subsequent volumes, clearly indicating that a proportion of new readers falls away after reading this small crude chapter. I am not alone in believing that these, if they had read the first three volumes in one cover, would have gone on to the rest."[62] Richardson's comment suggests that publication in collected editions both encourages readers to continue beyond the initial volume and enforces a larger purchase. The serial modes that offer incentives of price (as with the Victorian serial), or of convenience (as with the soap opera), have a distinct advantage over the *roman-fleuve*, which makes the most rigorous demands on the time, intellect, and pocketbooks—of readers, writers, and publishers alike.

The *roman-fleuve* appeals to persevering serial readers who enjoy the thrill of recognition as they see the similarity between incidents that may be separated by an enormous gap of time or space. In the case of *The Music of Time*, published over a period of twenty-five years, eighteen years separate the reader's first and last reception of parallel incidents such as those in which Jean Duport greets Nick in the nude at the Rutland Gate flat in *The Acceptance World* (1955), or Billson, the Jenkinses' parlormaid, appears naked in the drawing room in *The Kindly Ones* (1962) (actually a flashback to the period of Nick's childhood), or Pamela Widmerpool is discovered naked at Bagshaw's in *Temporary Kings* (1973). Ideal readers of the *roman-fleuve* recall hundreds of similarly parallel incidents, which are interrelated more than interdependent; their recognition integrates the various narrative subunits into a sort of encyclopedic collation, just as the individual volumes are collected, in the *roman-fleuve*, into one extensive novel. Iser suggests that it is the protracted blanks of serial reading that make readers prefer it; they believe "a novel read in installments to be better than the very same novel in book form."[63]

❧ The *Roman-Fleuve* and the Canon: This Impenetrable but Fecund Form

While the length of the *roman-fleuve* would seem the major obstacle to its popular success, reviews of specific exemplars suggest that it is actually the perception of feminine features that negatively affects the genre's reception. The adverse criticism of all three of the writers under discussion reveals a gender bias: Trollope, Richardson, and Powell have each been criticized in language that suggests a lack of virility, an ambiguous gender, impotence, or, strangely in the case of Trollope, a woman's sexuality—all deviations from the male "norm." James, for example, who develops gendered metaphors extensively in his verbal portraits of writers, denigrates Trollope with terms usually applied to women, characterizing him as a grotesque earth mother, charging that his "fecundity was prodigious" and his "fertility was gross." Even when James praises Trollope for his "complete appreciation of the usual," he associates this attribute with the genre of "English fiction" more generally and again echoes female reproductive metaphors, describing the genre as one "in which the feminine mind has laboured so fruitfully"—that is, the domestic tradition.[64] Furthermore, in his "facility of composition," James compares Trollope with George Sand and Mrs. Oliphant, linking him with the productivity of women writers as they rose to commercial prominence in the nineteenth century, clearly a backhanded compliment.

James's female-gendered denigration of Trollope is especially significant in light of his male-gendered exaltation of Balzac. Beyond the obvious and conventional use of gendered terms to indicate positive and negative values, they also function, according to Leland Person, to reveal James's efforts to construct a pluralistic conception of masculinity and a reassuring multiple masculine identity for himself, located between Balzac and Sand—"between male and female masculinity."[65] Most problematic is why Trollope's textual "fecundity" seems "gross" to James whereas this same quality in his French predecessor in the *roman-fleuve* is described as "productive force."[66] He explicitly contrasts Trollope's and Balzac's productivity in his essay on the latter in *French Poets and Novelists*, using terms that associate positive literary values with potent (phallic) masculinity: "There are writers in the same line who have published an absolutely greater number of volumes. Alexandre Dumas, Madame Sand, Anthony Trollope, have been all immensely prolific; but they all weave a loose web, as it were, and Balzac weaves a dense one. The tissue of his tales is always extraordinarily firm and hard; it may not at every point be cloth of gold, but it has always a metallic rigidity."[67] James's metaphors clearly associate tight narratives with tumescence, looseness with female fertility.

It is ironic, however, that although James belittles Trollope's fiction for a lack of organic form, the metaphors he uses against Trollope emphasize the organic process of (female) sexual reproduction. Elsewhere in the same essay, he again unfavorably contrasts Trollope and Balzac: "All this in Balzac's hands becomes an organic whole; it moves together; it has a pervasive life; the blood circulates through it; its parts are connected by sinuous arteries. We have seen in English literature, in two cases, a limited attempt to create a permanent stock, a standing fund, of characters. Thackeray has led a few of his admirable figures from one novel to another, and Mr. Trollope has deepened illusion for us by his repeated evocations of Bishop Proudie and Archdeacon Grantley.

But these things are faint shadows of Balzac's extravagant thoroughness —his fantastic cohesiveness. A French brain alone could have persisted in making a system of all this."[68] James refers to Balzac's "system," described in the author's introduction to *La Comédie humaine*, dividing his early *roman-fleuve* into "Scenes of Private Life," "Scenes of Provincial Life," "Scenes of Parisian Life," and so forth. The essential differences James establishes between Balzac and Trollope seem to be the French novelist's exalted scientific plan, as opposed to the British novelist's domestic appreciation of small things, and, mysteriously, some supposed lack of masculinity in Trollope's quality or tone. Regarding Balzac's life work, James comments, "One would really scarce have liked to see such a job as *La Comédie humaine* tackled without swagger."[69] James would have us believe that Balzac can, by sheer machismo, achieve more coherence in twenty-three octavo volumes than Trollope can in six (James refers to Trollope's Barset series). Although the differences between Balzac and Trollope that James perceives are elusive, the narrative features that James designates as feminine are clearly what lessens the English novelist's value for him.

Curiously, Trollope is defended by Richardson, who speaks in her letters of her own "conversion" into a Trollope fan.[70] She also mentions Trollope—"the half-truths of poetry are not for him"—when she recounts a conversation in which she and a female friend compare notes on writers they would take along if stranded on a desert island: Trollope is included "for masculine companionship." This praise of Trollope, when other classics were readable only "in editions fully annotated by women,"[71] suggests that Richardson considers Trollope a sensitive, feminized man. Strikingly, although James condemns Trollope and Richardson praises him, both place him through inference in the female tradition of novelists. For both, the connection is with the creation of domestic novels that pay tribute to the "usual." Richardson herself both exemplifies and defends this emphasis in *Pilgrimage* (as I show in chapter 3). Furthermore, in creating compelling and highly credible women characters, in contrast to his male contemporaries, most notably to Dickens, Trollope places himself in league with creators of women characters of psychological depth and veracity such as Charlotte Brontë and Jane Austen, gaining Richardson's approval and lessening James's.

Critics' responses to Richardson have often been explicitly "phallic," to use Mary Ellmann's well-known term for sexist denigrations of women writers, but it is even more significant to note the sexual connotations of the terms used to describe Richardson's "failure." Lawrence Hyde, for example, regretted her lack of a "passionate driving force" and the absence of a "laceration, any shattering of the outer force" in her work.[72] Leon Edel, who was interested enough in Richardson to begin preliminary work on a biography of her, described *Pilgrimage* as a sort of virginal ice queen, claiming, "The true difficulty of *Pilgrimage* lies in its impenetrability." The metaphor of the reader as lover continues as Edel contemplates being "inside" or "outside" the text: "A reader can easily achieve a relation with a novel when he is on the outside, watching the story unfold; it is another matter to be 'on the inside' looking out—and especially 'on the inside' of an adolescent girl, in the first sections." It seems that Edel is threatened by the prospect of entering the text he describes as "impenetrable"; his conclusion confirms this impression and again evokes a failed penetration as he describes her *roman-fleuve* as one appealing only to women: "Few men—few critics of their sex—have been willing to climb into Miss Richardson's boat."[73] In describing critics' reaction to the inconclusiveness of the final volume of *Pilgrimage* when it appeared in 1938, Richardson writes to E.B.C. Jones about her less friendly critics: "The others, those of them, the new lads & lassies, who don't just 'dip' & express astonishment over the comments on the cover, triumphantly crow 'I told you so! This endless chronicle led nowhere & now just peters out.' "[74] The flaccid verb must have seemed particularly apt to Anthony West, who repeats it when describing *Pilgrimage* in *Aspects of a Life*, his own chip-on-the-shoulder biography of his father and Richardson's friend, H. G. Wells. West also notes Richardson's inability to give *Dimple Hill* a "climax," which resulted in her symbolic castration at the hands of the publisher Dent, which took over the rights from Duckworth and "brought down the blade of the guillotine" by issuing the penultimate twelfth novel as the conclusion to *Pilgrimage*.[75]

The final volume of Powell's *A Dance to the Music of Time* received a warmer reception, but even the more enthusiastic reviewers expressed reservations. Charles Michener describes Powell's style in ambiguously gendered terms, "something like masculine needlework."[76] Robert K. Morris leaves the final judgment to "Time," but seems disappointed in the "recurrence" suggested by the final passage: "There is no apocalypse or apotheosis; it does not end with a bang or a whimper; it does not give us any final message about time, the dance or the dancers."[77] Similarly, mixing metaphors, Anatole Broyard complained: "If the author is implying that this is what England is coming to, his apocalypse is small beer."[78] The apocalyptic ending had already been appropriated by Doris Lessing in *The Four-Gated City* (1969), the final volume of her *roman-fleuve*, *Children of Violence*. However, characteristic of the genre, Lessing places the "Catastrophe," some kind of mysterious release of radioactive material or nerve gas over England, in the gap that separates the ending of the novel from the letters that conclude *The Four-Gated City*, revealing the fates of the characters in Victorian fashion through letters written in their exile after the disaster. A survey of critics' reception of the *roman-fleuve*, their desire for a "big bang" and disappointment in not receiving it, reveals a gender bias and an Aristotelian expectation of and preference for climactic narratives.

The subsequent three interlocking chapters on the *romans-fleuves* of Trollope, Richardson, and Powell explore the various interrelations of genre, narrative, and gendered discourse. While I certainly do not propose to give wholly new readings of three massive *romans-fleuves* within the confines of my essays on each, I do hope, nevertheless, that my structuralist analysis of these texts as examples of the *roman-fleuve* and as narratives with an affinity for an *écriture féminine* will illuminate the novels themselves and previous interpretations of them. In chapter 2, for example, I demonstrate that *The Eustace Diamonds*, a novel frequently omitted from the Palliser series, serves a function within the Pallisers when it is properly viewed as part of the digressive middle, customary in the *roman-fleuve*. My discussions of Richardson, often denigrated for her inability to finish *Pilgrimage*, and Powell, criticized for the kind of ending imposed, reconsider their closures, providing different criteria by which to assess their purpose and success. The Pallisers, *Pilgrimage*, and *A Dance to the Music of Time* exemplify the genre's evolution through three periods in literary history. Trollope's Victorian proto–*roman-fleuve* initiates narrative features most fully developed in Richardson's modernist *roman-fleuve*, whereas in the mid-to-late twentieth century Powell creates an exemplar poised between the conventionally narrated and the postmodern novel, revealing that genres do not always move to ever-greater experimentation.

Chapter Two

The Palliser Novels:

Trollope's Nineteenth-Century
Proto-*Roman-Fleuve*

Far too often the lengthy Victorian novel is viewed as the antithesis
rather than the wellspring of modern narrative innovations despite the
"ground-breaking contributions made by those later Victorian and early
modernist novelists" and their "experiments with form and closure."[1]
The innovative features of Trollope's narrative—synchronic development,
contested closure, and the avoidance of a linear movement toward a
climactic resolution—anticipate those of an *écriture féminine*. These
narrative features have a significance beyond the merely structural, for
as Maria Minich Brewer notes, "narrative would be seen not so much as
a form through which ideology and its representatives are reproduced,
but rather as that which itself produces them."[2] The formal tensions in
Trollope's novels and the significance they have in revealing his ambivalent sympathy toward feminism as a political movement and toward
women in general have recently been analyzed by critics such as Jane
Nardin and Deborah Morse in their studies of his female characters.[3] If
narrative does indeed produce ideology, such discussion of the feminine
features of Trollope's discourse contributes to an understanding of his
feminism. There are inherent difficulties in arguing for the relationship
of a feminine narrative and a feminist ideology, which are exacerbated in
focusing on a nineteenth-century text by a male writer, yet Trollope's
Pallisers indicate how narrative and ideology might reinforce each other.
Even a critic who opposes the notion of a feminist aesthetic concedes that
the presence of feminist themes may change the stakes of the argument
"if, for example, the text seeks to undermine an obviously patriarchal
ideological position."[4] The congruence of a nascent *écriture féminine* and

an incipient feminism in Trollope's Pallisers presages Richardson's later development of a modernist aesthetic she views as feminine.[5]

This chapter approaches Trollope's experiments with narrative and genre from several critical angles. The first section classifies the Pallisers as a proto-*roman-fleuve* and answers recent attacks on the notion of genre. The subsequent sections examine Trollope's strategies for opening, developing, and terminating his novels in the context of nineteenth-century narrative conventions. Primarily a structuralist analysis of the Palliser novels as a *roman-fleuve*, the chapter establishes the features of the genre and the nascent *écriture féminine* in Trollope's experiments with the novel form, which will be more fully realized in the twentieth-century exemplars discussed in chapters 3 and 4.

❧ Genre in Search of a Historical Context

Recent defenders of genre criticism have noted that genres are best understood in retrospect, from the enlightened vantage point of subsequent literary evolution. Because of their diachronic modification over time, some genres may not be recognized until they have evolved into their paradigmatic forms; only with hindsight can the genre be traced back to the prototype. As Alastair Fowler comments, our perception of the genre is based on its "most inclusive conception," and this is more likely to be a later than an original example of the form, although the prototypes of such elusive and fluctuating artifacts as genres may only be speculated upon rather than discovered.[6] Tracing genres diachronically clarifies traditions and interrelationships between genres and allows "historical localizations" of them.[7] A genre in search of such a historical context is the *roman-fleuve*. Despite the twentieth-century proliferation of such examples as Richardson's *Pilgrimage*, Proust's *A la recherche du temps perdu*, Anaïs Nin's *Cities of the Interior*, Lessing's *Children of Violence*, and Powell's *A Dance to the Music of Time*, as well as the popular series such as Mazo de la Roche's Jalna saga, the historical generic antecedents of these works have generally been ignored. Generic classification not only locates a work in the context of literary history but may also elucidate the work itself, "the relations among its parts."[8] Because of the genre's uniquely complex form, elucidation of the relationship between the individual volumes and the entire collection of a particular *roman-fleuve* is more apropos than in genres that lack division into clearly defined and often separately published parts.

Trollope's proto–*roman-fleuve* represents an inaugural stage in the development of the British genre: the evolution from Trollope to successors such as Richardson, Nin, Lessing, and Powell is a varied one; modern and contemporary examples reveal both the persistence and the transformation of characteristics evinced in their nineteenth-century precursor. Viewing the Pallisers as a nineteenth-century prototype of the genre not only clarifies critical problems of the individual Palliser novels but also creates a context for discussion of the genre's historical evolution and its resemblance to an *écriture féminine*. Massive in scope, Trollope's *roman-fleuve* suggests the encyclopedic impulse and plenitude of *écriture féminine*. The Victorian "baggy middle" of the Pallisers also prefigures the indirect, digressive, and synchronic development of Richardson's modernist exemplar of the genre. Between the individual novels of Trollope's *roman-fleuve*, narrative gaps, in which significant undramatized events occur, presage the silence and gaps of women's censored experience. The conflicted double resolution with which Trollope ends the last novel of the Pallisers, *The Duke's Children*, as well as his articulation of his dissatisfaction with nineteenth-century closural techniques, foreshadows the feminist distrust of linear narratives that end with conventional closure.

It is not my purpose here to offer a new reading of the Pallisers, yet discussion of these novels as a proto–*roman-fleuve* that prefigures characteristics of an *écriture féminine* provides a new context for discussing the functions and interrelations of the volumes, which, taken singly, evoke a variety of critical problems generally contributing to negative criticism of Trollope's art. One such problem is whether the six novels comprise a cohesive group, a necessary assumption for definition as a *roman-fleuve*. Although these novels have traditionally been regarded as one unit—*Can You Forgive Her?*, *Phineas Finn*, *The Eustace Diamonds*, *Phineas Redux*, *The Prime Minister*, and *The Duke's Children* have been published as a series in the Oxford World's Classics edition—some critics would omit certain volumes from the group. By implication, those who deny that the novels are a unit would probably not accept the classification of these novels as a *roman-fleuve*. John Halperin argues that although the Pallisers are not as obviously a unified group of novels as the Barsetshire series, we should accept the grouping of the six Palliser novels proposed by Michael Sadleir.[9] However, critics such as Steven Wall believe that the novels form a series and should be read as such in order to experience the "full humanity of these novels" and the "effects of time and character."[10] While the critical work on Trollope's Parliamentary novels lacks any substantial discussion of their genre, the group has been variously classified as a sequence novel, a sequel, or a *roman-fleuve*.[11]

Trollope's statement in his autobiography about how these novels should be read shows that his conception of them is consistent with the characteristics and requirements of the *roman-fleuve*:

> In conducting these characters from one story to another I realized the necessity, not only of consistency,—which, had it been maintained by a hard exactitude, would have been untrue to nature,—but also of those changes which time always produces. . . . It was my study that these people, as they grew in years, should encounter the changes which come upon us all; and I think that I have succeeded. The Duchess of Omnium, when she is playing the part of Prime Minister's wife, is the same woman as that Lady Glencora who almost longs to go off with Burgo Fitzgerald, but yet knows that she will never do so; and the Prime Minister Duke, with his wounded pride and sore spirit, is he who, for his wife's sake, left power and place when they were first offered to him;—but they have undergone the changes which a life so stirring as theirs would naturally produce. To do all this thoroughly was in my heart from first to last; but I do not know that the game has been worth the candle. To carry out my scheme I have had to spread my picture over so wide a canvas that I cannot expect that any lover of such art should trouble himself to look at it as a whole. Who will read *Can You Forgive Her?*, *Phineas Finn*, *Phineas Redux*, and *The Prime Minister* consecutively, in order that he may understand the characters of the Duke of Omnium, of Plantagenet Palliser, and Lady Glencora? Who will even know that they should be so read? . . . I look upon this string of characters,—carried sometimes into other novels than those just named,—as the best work of my life.[12]

Trollope's omission of two of the Palliser novels would seem to undercut the argument that the six belong together as a series. As Halperin points out, however, Trollope's own groupings of his novels are not only infrequent, but contradictory at that.[13] Moreover, *The Duke's Children* (1879–80) had not been written when Trollope made this statement in his autobiography.[14] Trollope's description of the creation of a "string" of recurring characters who change over time shows that he regarded these novels as a cohesive interrelated group. In addition, the development of the panoramic technique of extending his subject over "so wide a canvas," the emphasis on time and organic natural process, and the accent on the extended experience place Trollope's description of the Palliser novels within the genre of the *roman-fleuve* defined in the previous chapter. The passage also reveals that he believed that the volumes must have individual integrity, must stand on their own as novels, because the public would not be capable of reading them together— although they would be best read consecutively and as a group. Trollope's emphasis on the process of character evolution and the novel sequence undercuts the traditional emphasis on plot. Viewing these novels as a *roman-fleuve*, generic classification, contributes to a historical understanding of the way that audience and publication concerns—in this case Trollope's probably accurate estimation of his readers' limitations— may restrict the development of a full repertoire of new generic features. The trait of individual integrity of novels within a *roman-fleuve* is probably more developed in the nineteenth-century *romans-fleuves* of Balzac and Trollope than in those of Richardson and Powell because the nineteenth-century works are addressed to a mass audience of serial readers. As Ralph Cohen observes, "Generic transformation reveals the social changes in audiences."[15]

Trollope does not, to my knowledge, anywhere describe the Pallisers by using the term *roman-fleuve* or sequence novel. However, within the novels, he often refers to them as "chronicles" and to himself as the "chronicler," as in *Phineas Redux* (2:57) and *The Eustace Diamonds* (1:19 and 2:117). The term is also used by James Kincaid to refer to both the Barsetshire and Palliser novels; he describes the way any Trollope novel may "suddenly invade the territory of another," creating "an illusion of continuance."[16] The Pallisers do resemble a chronicle in that they depict historical events in a generally chronological order. They also correspond, in terms of their content, to a more precise definition of the form: "The chronicle also has a central subject, the life of an individual, town, or region, some great undertaking, such as a war or crusade, or some institution, such as a monarchy, episcopacy or monastery."[17] Trollope's work has such a central subject, if the subject may be defined in terms of a complex and interwoven fabric: it depicts the life of Plantagenet Palliser, his rise to power and fall from the position of Prime Minister. His life story, furthermore, is foregrounded against the institution of the British Parliament during a period of significant political change.

However, Trollope has written something more than a chronicle because the Pallisers conclude; they do not comprise a work that could be added onto indefinitely. According to Hayden White's definition, "The chronicle, like the annals but unlike the history, does not so much 'conclude' as simply terminate; typically it lacks closure, that summing up of the 'meaning' of the chain of events with which it deals that we normally expect from the well-made story."[18] Trollope's *roman-fleuve* achieves closure, albeit in a complex and contested fashion, with the circular structure of *The Duke's Children*, which retells the earlier love conflict of Glencora, Burgo Fitzgerald, and Palliser in the corresponding triangle of Mary Palliser, Tregear, and Popplecourt. Furthermore, this repetition is one of a multitude that give the larger work its structure. A distinction by Scholes and Kellogg further undermines Trollope's use of the term: "The diarist or chronicler may simply record specific data, but the autobiographer or historian seeks a pattern which drives him in the direction of generalization."[19] Trollope does not just record the lives of the Palliser family or the period in which they live; he finds patterns in their lives and in those of other characters in other social strata. Like the historian, his narrator not only interprets data through generalization, but he also editorializes.

Despite Trollope's label, then, the Pallisers are closer to a history than to a chronicle. His choice of the term is significant, nevertheless. "Chronicle" has an archaic sound to it, and by using this term, Trollope creates the impression of a naive narrator, since the writer of a chronicle does not intervene; he details the facts in the order in which they occur. This is the nineteenth-century view of the role of the historian, who assumes that facts can be objectively and passively received, and who values their objectivity, what Henry Carr calls the nineteenth-century "fetishism of facts."[20] This function is more hypothetical than actual, as noted by Ricoeur: "A complete description of an event should therefore register everything that happened, in the order in which it happened. But who could do such a thing? Only an Ideal Chronicler could be such an absolutely faithful witness and absolutely sure about this entirely determined past. This Ideal Chronicler would be gifted with the faculty of being able to give an instantaneous transcription of whatever happens, augmenting his testimony in a purely additive and cumulative way as events are added to events."[21] It may be that the use of the term "chronicle" is an effort to add credibility to Trollope's narrative stance, reflecting his desire to create a persona who guilelessly recounts the history of a period and the individuals within it.

More significant, however, is the way the definition of the Pallisers as a *roman-fleuve* facilitates understanding of the interrelations among the novels within the series. The function of two novels that are usually omitted from the group because they do not focus on the Palliser family, *Can You Forgive Her?* and *The Eustace Diamonds*, may be reevaluated when they are considered as integral components of a larger *roman-fleuve* rather than simply novels within a series with recurring characters. Although Trollope's omission of *The Eustace Diamonds* from his list of Pallisers is problematic, Halperin argues convincingly for the inclusion of this novel in the series because in it Trollope is concerned with the social environment of politicians and because it tells the stories of characters who move forward the plots of other novels in the series.[22] John McCormick maintains that *The Eustace Diamonds* (as well as its sequel, *Phineas Redux*) is necessary to fully understand the characters, among them Lizzie Eustace, in *The Prime Minister*.[23] Kincaid believes that the novel has an essential function for the *roman-fleuve* as a whole: "By itself, [*The Eustace Diamonds*] is a static novel, almost an essay, but it works forwards and backwards in the series, which it, in one sense interrupts, almost as if it were the key to a secret code, revealed to us when we are half-way through the message"; between the two Phineas novels, *The Eustace Diamonds* "breaks in with a commentary which in the end goes to establish the unbroken unity of the Phineas novels. It tells us how good luck and bad luck are finally the same."[24] Moreover, the inclusion of *The Eustace Diamonds* is supported by Bradford Booth simply because Glencora and Plantagenet Palliser appear in the novel.[25]

The inclusion of *Can You Forgive Her?* in the Palliser series may be questioned because its multiplot structure diverts emphasis from the central Palliser plot—the marriage and political career of Plantagenet Palliser—by presenting in two subplots the marital adventures of Alice Vavasor and Mrs. Greenow, parallels to the Glencora plot. However, the initial focus on Alice Vavasor does not presage the emphasis of the entire novel; by the latter part of the volume the interest has shifted to Glencora and the Palliser plot. As Peter Garrett remarks, the Glencora story "displace[s]" the Alice plot.[26] With the birth of the heir, Lord Silverbridge, the Pallisers are established as the central family to be depicted in the *roman-fleuve*. However, the "false start," an opening that focuses on subplot rather than major plot or on secondary characters rather than the protagonist(s), is characteristic of the Victorian novel's asymmetrical structure; a similar introduction is used in other novels of the period such as Charlotte Brontë's *Villette*. In a related technique, a novel without one clear center, such as *Our Mutual Friend*, may use several introductory chapters to present the different worlds of the novel. The "false start" of the Pallisers is a feature of the Victorian novel that is refined in twentieth-century examples of the form such as Richardson's *Pilgrimage*, in which each of the first three novels begins with the heroine's various assays into teaching, a profession she finally rejects, or Proust's *A la recherche du temps perdu*, which also opens with a plot that focuses on a character other than the eventual protagonist, as Marcel narrates Swann's story. The use of a first-person narrator in this and other examples of the modern and contemporary *roman-fleuve* often modulates a potentially unrelated opening by providing a unifying voice, contributing to a more highly developed unity in the later examples of the genre.

The novel that is often considered entirely digressive in the series, *The Eustace Diamonds*, functions as an inversion of the Palliser world, adding variety and presenting the major characters from different vantage points than other novels in the *roman-fleuve*. The centrality of the Palliser family is not evenly developed throughout the series; rather it is produced by the accumulation of portraits throughout the six volumes. For example, in *Phineas Finn*, Plantagenet Palliser is seen primarily through the eyes of young Phineas, who views Palliser as a successful politician to emulate. This contrasts to the presentation of the dull politician as seen from Glencora's point of view in the previous novel, *Can You Forgive Her?*, and the sometimes ineffectual but always dedicated politician campaigning for decimal coinage in subsequent volumes. Glencora is viewed in a similar manner as her rise to power is dramatized from outside her immediate circle. Glencora Palliser, Violet Effingham, and Madame Max Goesler, major characters in *Phineas Finn*, function as a chorus of marginal characters in *The Eustace Diamonds*, commenting on Lizzie Eustace, a major character in this novel. However, their judgments gain credibility because the reader knows them intimately from the previous volume of the series. The shifting importance of characters in the *roman-fleuve* emphasizes the community, its organic complexity and overlapping network of lives variously interconnected. Further, the variable focus anticipates the multiple points of view used in the contemporary "multivalent" *roman-fleuve* such as Durrell's *The Alexandria Quartet*.[27]

The digression from the Palliser plot also gives the impression of a realistic passage of time even as it skips over the tedious and uneventful periods in the family's evolution. While the narrative (reading) time of the lengthy Parliamentary novels is unusually extensive, the narrated (fictional) time is less than twenty-five years, no longer than that of a bildungsroman that takes a protagonist from birth to maturity. The interlude focusing on a different social class allows a jump in time that permits Phineas to leave London and return to his country bride, impregnate her, and lose her in childbirth—all offstage, so to speak. Although *The Eustace Diamonds* breaks up the fluid forward narrative progression, it is less jolting than the transition between *The Prime Minister* and *The Duke's Children*, which covers roughly the same time period but which shocks the reader because of the sudden death of Glencora, a major character, between volumes. Trollope's creation of this kind of gap anticipates the feminist gaps that Richardson employs in *Pilgrimage* to suggest women's unutterable experiences.

Considering *The Eustace Diamonds* as an integral part of the larger *roman-fleuve* also clarifies the function of Lizzie, an atypical Trollopian heroine, as a dark parallel or shadow to Glencora. Just as Glencora hosts the political elite, Lizzie is a willful and calculating hostess to the elite manqué. Within the larger frame of the Pallisers, this novel and its protagonist provide a narrative that contests the reluctant and problematic Victorian self-renunciation of heroines such as Glencora and Alice Vavasor. In this as in other narrative techniques (such as problematic closure), Trollope anticipates an *écriture féminine*. *The Eustace Diamonds* articulates a different discourse than the other novels in this series, creating a double-voiced quality in the whole. Lizzie's rebellion "acts out" the repressed desires of Glencora, the protagonist of the series. As Susan S. Lanser points out, "The condition of being woman in a male-dominated society may well necessitate the double voice."[28] This need for a covertly subversive discourse may account for the contradictions between the narrator's antifeminism and the poignant stories of repressed women's ambitions he dramatizes. Although Glencora clearly articulates her discontent in *Can You Forgive Her?* her dissatisfaction appears to be quelled by motherhood and a political career (as hostess) of her own. In the *roman-fleuve* as a whole, Lizzie's subplot diffuses the impact of Glencora's dissatisfaction, keeping the plot on track until this trait surfaces, first in *The Prime Minister*, where Glencora is associated with much of the vulgarity previously attributed exclusively to Lizzie, and then again in *The Duke's Children*, where her covert rebellion against her own marriage is revealed through her support of her daughter's alliance with Frank Tregear.

Lizzie Eustace, the female rogue, is not dropped from the series after this volume; one of a new class of socially marginal parvenus, she keeps surfacing in drawing rooms, emerging out of the lower social underworld. In *The Prime Minister*, for example, Lizzie is a member of the vulgar society Emily Wharton is drawn into because of her husband Lopez (who proposes to Lizzie that she run away with him). It is also Lizzie who tells Quintus Slide that Palliser paid Lopez's electioneering bill, leading to Palliser's political demise and providing another connection between the two plots. The doubling of Glencora through the Lizzie plot adds a psychological dimension to the series. In the modern and contemporary *roman-fleuve* this device is transformed as secondary characters take on a more direct psychological significance for the central narrator-protagonist, as for example Richardson's Miriam Henderson and Amabel, the friend who initiates her into the feminine, or Powell's Nick Jenkins and his nemesis, Widmerpool.

Analysis of the function of *The Eustace Diamonds* in the Pallisers provides a revised perspective on the structure of this novel, which not only functions as a digression from and inversion of the major plot but is also structured as an inset within the larger frame of the Palliser *roman-fleuve*. As an inset, *The Eustace Diamonds* presents a subplot that is subordinated, except in this one novel, to the *roman-fleuve* as a whole. The Lizzie plot functions as a story within a story when the account of her plight is recounted to the Duke of Omnium for his entertainment by Glencora and others in her social circle. Through simultaneous reported narration, the two plots are juxtaposed at the end of the novel, and her wedding is merely mentioned in a sentence about Glencora's entertainments: "On the 8th Lizzie and Mr. Emilius became man and wife, and on that same day Lady Glencora Palliser entertained a large company of guests at Matching Priory" (2: 370). Although the Lizzie plot predominates throughout the narrative of *The Eustace Diamonds*, it is repressed at the end of the novel as the frame of the major plot reduces Lizzie to an item of discussion at Matching; she is no longer dramatized but only spoken of by the major characters.

The title of the last chapter of the novel, "What Was Said about It All at Matching"—"it" referring to Lizzie's diamond fiasco—contributes to the impression of a concluding frame to the story within the larger structure. All the central Palliser characters discuss Lizzie's story in *The Eustace Diamonds*, and the last chapter of the novel provides a transition back to the main story of the Pallisers. The Duke of Omnium has the last word on Lizzie's fate as he prophesies, "I'm afraid, you know, that your friend [Lizzie] hasn't what I call a good time before her, Glencora" (2: 375). The departure from the Palliser story in much of *The Eustace Diamonds* temporarily shifts the perspective of their family life from an interior to an exterior point of view, the perspective used to introduce the family in *Can You Forgive Her?*, augmenting the complex presentation of Glencora and Plantagenet. *The Eustace Diamonds* represents both a dark inversion of the Palliser world and a digression from the central Palliser story, but it is a digression with links to the major motifs, themes, and plots of the series as a whole.

The *Eustace Diamonds* is also linked to other novels in the series by motific repetition, a device that provides continuity in the *roman-fleuve*. The Duke's interest in Lizzie and her diamonds provides the major connection between the central story of the Palliser novels, of which the old Duke of Omnium is a fairly major figure, and the Lizzie plot, subordinated to the Palliser story in the *roman-fleuve* as a whole. The primary connection is symbolic, and in a form as protracted as the *roman-fleuve*, the continuity provided by recurrent symbols, motifs, and themes is essential. In the Palliser novels, jewels, and diamonds in particular, are synecdochic: they represent the quality of legitimate rank. Lizzie's acquisition of the Eustace diamonds suggests an improper usurpation of social status since she seizes rank and wealth for which she is disqualified by her breeding and essentially false nature; by her conniving, Lizzie causes the Eustace family to lose the diamonds, a symbol of their heritage. The jewel motif, established in *The Eustace Diamonds*, is repeated throughout the rest of the series, most significantly in *Phineas Redux*, the next novel in the sequence, as the Duke's interest in Lizzie's jewels is followed by his own legacy of pearls and diamonds to Madame Goesler in *Phineas Redux*; Madame Max's refusal of the Palliser jewels, however, is antithetical to Lizzie's "theft" of the Eustace diamonds. Marie Goesler wisely turns down the Duke's jewels (and his title) in favor of a more appropriate and satisfying social position—friend to the Duchess of Omnium and wife to Phineas Finn. The jewels, or more precisely the income from them, pass to Palliser's niece Adelaide, who is entitled to them by her birth, though no worthier of them on the basis of character than Marie Goesler.

The motif recurs in *The Duke's Children* as Plantagenet Palliser, now Duke of Omnium, gives Isabel Boncassen a diamond ring that belonged to Glencora, signifying that he accepts her as a daughter-in-law, an acceptance won with difficulty only after she convinces him that she will not marry Lord Silverbridge unless she is willingly received by the British aristocracy. Lady Mabel Grex handles the gift of a large and valuable diamond from Silverbridge as clumsily as she handles his marriage proposal, leaving the ring on a garden bench after she has jokingly and inappropriately demanded it from him; her inability to accept Silverbridge's suit graciously leaves her a spinster and, as a result, the Grex heritage, its rank and name, is lost.[29] Although this motif is one of the abundant repetitions that connect *The Eustace Diamonds* to the rest of the series, creating the network of associations characteristic of the *roman-fleuve*, its introduction does not occur until the third volume. Trollope thus exploits this unifying feature of the genre less extensively than many of his twentieth-century successors. Richardson's *Pilgrimage*, for example, is unified by the quest motif inherent in Miriam Henderson's search for self-awareness, introduced in the opening of the first volume and developed throughout the entire text. In Powell's *A Dance to the Music of Time*, a motific network is initiated on the first page of the work through an extensively developed image referring to Poussin's painting of the same title, establishing constituent motifs of dance, music, and time that recur throughout the twelve volumes. It is because of the comparatively primitive development of unifying characteristics such as this that I term Trollope's Pallisers a proto-*roman-fleuve*.

As a *roman-fleuve*, the Palliser novels follow the nineteenth-century model of Balzac's *La Comédie humaine*, a sequence in which, as Kerr observes, the plan is not evident in any single novel; she calls Trollope "the first author to follow in Balzac's footsteps."[30] *The Eustace Diamonds* functions in the Pallisers much as a novel like *Le Père Goriot* does in *La Comédie humaine*: each contributes to the larger work of which it is a part although the connections are evident only in retrospect. Kerr is not alone in comparing Trollope's *roman-fleuve* to that of Balzac; Walter Allen comments on the impression of reading a collection of Trollope novels: "It is that of the creation of nothing less than a world. With no theory behind him, and with only a modest ambition, Trollope produced a *Comédie humaine*, and though it would be absurd to set him up against Balzac the fact remains that the world he created is almost as capacious as Balzac's and as solid in its reality."[31]

The focus of Trollope's *roman-fleuve* is blurred because of his asymmetrical plots and the digressive progression of narrative. Brooks compares the uneven progression of the nineteenth-century narrative to Freud's description in *Beyond the Pleasure Principle* of the "vacillating rhythm" of instincts rushing forward, jerking back; Brooks's own description delineates the rhythm of the *roman-fleuve* in general, and that of *The Eustace Diamonds* in particular: "A highly plotted nineteenth-century novel will often leave one set of characters at a critical juncture to take up another where it left them, moving this set forward, then rushing back to the first, creating an uneven movement of advance, turning back the better to move forward. As with the play of repetition, and the pleasure principle, forward and back, advance and return interact to create the vacillating and apparently deviant middle."[32] As a digression, *The Eustace Diamonds* has the form of a "deviant middle" in the Palliser novels, contributing to the "baggy" structure that makes Trollope's *roman-fleuve* a hyperbolic version of the Victorian novel. At the same time, his oblique and uneven development foreshadows the indirect narrative and gap-filled stream of consciousness narrative developed by Richardson and other modernists.

The nineteenth-century *romans-fleuves* of Balzac and Trollope do not achieve the comparatively smooth and even development of models such as *The Music of Time* though in this respect they foreshadow Richardson's gap-filled, digressive exemplar of the genre. They are nevertheless characterized by a degree of formal and thematic unity. The unity of Trollope's Pallisers results more from a complex network of repeated characters, settings, and scenes than from that created by theme, symbol, or motif. The development of a single unifying theme is complicated by the vast scope of the *roman-fleuve* and its varied focus on different characters, attributes that demand a comprehensive theme. Trollope suggests the theme of the Pallisers in his autobiography when he describes the depiction of the changes time creates in his characters, requiring a multivolume structure and a narrated time that encompasses a period sufficient to develop the characters' changes, as well as a reading, or narrative, time that makes these changes seem credible and realistic. The movements from exterior to interior perspectives, as the characters shift from principal to marginal status, contribute to the development of their rich and complex evolution. Since the organic nature of Trollope's work integrates the individual's fate into that of his or her society, the portrayal of a changing society is essential to the depiction of characters' evolution.

Although Trollope's work achieves unity through its reliance on the consistent voice of the intrusive narrator and the thematic focus on the effects of time on character, the uneven development of Trollope's *roman-fleuve* forms a link between the Victorian novel form, also exemplified by Balzac's nineteenth-century French *roman-fleuve*, and the modernist novel. Characteristics such as this narrative "bagginess" obscure the generic identity of Trollope's Pallisers, contributing to an ambiguity of form that makes its classification as a *roman-fleuve* more tentative than that of subsequent, more fully developed examples of the genre. However, even if genres are conceived of as mutable and evolving, the prototype should nevertheless be classified within the genre; furthermore, inclusion of the prototype establishes a context for discussion of the evolution of the modern and contemporary *roman-fleuve*. It remained for Trollope's successors, from Richardson to Powell, to refine and perfect the sustained focus through a series of volumes by using a first-person narrator.

Definition of the *roman-fleuve* is usually based on such twentieth-century exemplars, selecting as representative what may be the culmination of the genre's development, ignoring previous or lesser manifestations of it. Limiting the definition of a genre by insisting that it include the traits of the genre's most fully evolved exemplar creates the critical impasse that has led critics to reject genre classification, to concede to generic nihilism. Although each genre is in some way "its own genre . . . *a new genre*,"[33] the persistence of generic criticism and the undeniable similarity of works having characteristics, especially formal ones, that significantly overlap testify to the legitimacy of genre criticism. Fowler argues that "to reconstruct the original genre, we have to eliminate from consciousness its subsequent states."[34] In lieu of this unattainable virgin literary consciousness, diachronic study of genres may suggest possible prototypes, such as Trollope's Palliser novels, facilitating synchronic discussion by broadening definition of genres such as the *roman-fleuve*. Although Trollope's Palliser series does not exhibit the entire repertoire of traits evident in later examples of the *roman-fleuve*, considering it as a member of this genre elucidates the historic origins of the *roman-fleuve* and suggests conventions and narrative features that prefigure those of the more representative twentieth-century successors. The retrospective recognition of genres and their evolution, which I have emphasized in this section, is significant for a discussion of narrative and gender as well. Continental theorists themselves most often trace the literary roots of an *écriture féminine* to modernist male writers: Joyce, Artaud, Céline, and so forth. Nevertheless, intimations of a modernist or feminine discourse may also be found in the nineteenth-century novel.

✤ The Victorian False Start and Evasion of Origins

The extraordinary length of the *roman-fleuve* places particular demands upon the narrative structure, creating difficulties in the exposition of the *roman-fleuve* that exceed those of the ordinary novel. In addition, the *roman-fleuve* confronts the problem of exposition repeatedly, not only at the beginning of the series but also at the start of each volume. In its depiction of historical process or personal development, both extended sequences of events, the *roman-fleuve* is unable to isolate well-defined points of initiation and termination. The most obvious presentation of process would be through linear chronology, yet Trollope undermines the teleology of the highly plotted novel by opening with an oblique and diffused exposition. This choice leaves Trollope vulnerable to charges of plotlessness usually brought against experimental women writers who disdain the forward thrust of the masculine adventure plot. Meir Sternberg, for example, takes Trollope to task for "the lengths he is prepared to go in order to ensure that the reader's mind should be neither pitched forward to the narrative future nor pulled back to the past but left free to dwell on the succession of narrative presents."[35]

Although the static exposition for which Sternberg criticizes Trollope is to some extent characteristic of the nineteenth-century novelistic tradition, Trollope's expository technique in many ways foreshadows that of his successors who write an *écriture féminine*. The attacks on Trollope for his use of narrative features associated with an *écriture féminine* are reminiscent of James's caricature of the writer as a grotesque earth mother. Regarding this kind of "phallic" denigration of women writers, Susan S. Lanser suggests: "If again and again scholars of women's writing must speak in terms of the 'plot*less*' (usually in quotation marks, suggesting their dissatisfaction with the term), then perhaps something is wrong with the notions of plot that have followed from Propp's morphology. Perhaps narratology has been mistaken in trying to arrive at a single definition and description of plot."[36] Since it is the feminine features of Trollope's plots that have traditionally been attacked (their lack of forward-looking suspense in particular), we should reexamine the conventions against which he is evaluated in the context of reevaluations of women writers' adaptation and variation of narrative conventions.

The introduction to the Pallisers exemplifies the multiple and indirect approach of feminine texts, which reject expositions that introduce a narrow, univocal plot propelled toward a climax and a (pre)determined, highly resolved ending. The introduction to *Can You Forgive Her?* is oblique and diffused because Trollope at first refuses to distinguish his major from his subordinate plots. Further, the major plot in *Can You Forgive Her?* may or may not presage the focus of the *roman-fleuve*; this difficulty is an inherent feature of the genre, comprised of both individual novels and the collective whole. Trollope begins with one set of characters and one situation: Alice Vavasor, her father, and her two suitors as well as the details of her social situation and upbringing. The exposition to this one novel, background concerning Alice's situation, takes up two short chapters, approximately twenty pages, before the action proper begins as she breaks off her engagement to John Grey. In addition to its function as exposition to *Can You Forgive Her?*, however, the Alice plot also introduces paradigms that are developed throughout the Palliser series, delaying initiation of the central Palliser plot—the marriage of Plantagenet Palliser to Glencora M'Cluskie and the career of "Planty Pall"—in order to provide the thematic framework within which this plot may be considered. Mr. Vavasor is both the man-who-marries-an-heiress and the man-who-neglects-his-estate. Alice is the prototype for the discontented female. Within this one novel, the Alice plot presents the pattern of a woman torn between two lovers, as has been frequently noted by critics writing about the parallel plot lines of *Can You Forgive Her?*

As in other examples of the *roman-fleuve*, the excitation of desire is devious, its agents undermined. Alice vacillates between the "worthy man," John Grey, and the "wild man," George Vavasor, but cannot definitively localize her desire in either man. She first rejects Grey because she fears life at Nethercoats with him will be dull, but at the same time he apparently stimulates in Alice a physical attraction that frightens her, in particular the attraction of his sensual mouth, a "mouth like a god," whose "beauty comprised firmness within itself" (1: 113). McMaster argues that Trollope is suggesting women's sexual response when he euphemistically uses "imagery of worship, as he does in the case of Alice and Grey as elsewhere in his work."[37] Alice turns to the romantic but violent Vavasor, who inspires sexual repulsion in her. Trollope's narrator undermines Alice's dilemma and ridicules her pursuit of self-realization: she thinks too much about love, he assures us; it is her "undefined ambition [that makes] her restless" (1: 110). As recent Trollopian critics have pointed out, however, there is often "a tension between the narrator's stance and the implications of the tale he tells."[38] This tension impedes both thematic resolution and the forward movement of the narrative, extending, instead, the expository narrative foreplay. The contradiction inherent in this kind of tension (one of several techniques Nardin discusses with reference to Trollope's feminism) suggests the feminist implications of narrative features that represent an alternative to conventional patriarchal patterns.

Any desire stimulated by the Alice plot is further diffused and frequently displaced, most often by the protagonist of what initially seems to be the secondary plot, Glencora Palliser, but also by the heroine of the tertiary plot, Arabella Greenow. These women vacillate between men who more clearly dichotomize the choice between dull comfort and dangerous romance—and its formulation as a dichotomy reveals the narrow range of women's choices. It takes Trollope about 800 pages to establish Glencora as his agent in this novel, and her role as such is undermined by the final predominance of her husband, Plantagenet Palliser, as protagonist of the *roman-fleuve* as a whole, although he is not discernible as such until the final novel, *The Duke's Children*. This predominance is achieved, however, only by means of Glencora's death, the same technique used to suborn Mrs. Proudie in the Barset novels. Although he is one of Trollope's most sympathetic and complex characters, Palliser is a weak and ineffectual image of desire, bumbling his way through the prime ministry, hampered by reservations of conscience that would not hinder a Rastignac or a Sorel, agents of the masculine plot of adventure and intrigue. The oblique introduction stimulates desire sufficiently to move the plot forward, but it functions less to introduce conflicts than to establish the pattern of oscillation that characterizes the middle of the *roman-fleuve*.

The Alice plot not only delays the development of the major plot, however, but also effects a transition into it. Ending with chapter 21, "Alice Is Taught to Grow Upwards, Towards the Light," the first exposition both prefigures and introduces the major Palliser plot; thus, the background concerning Alice Vavasor functions as exposition not only to *Can You Forgive Her?* but also to the entire *roman-fleuve*. Glencora and Plantagenet Palliser are introduced one-fourth of the way through the novel; the preliminary exposition occupies less than one-twentieth of the sequence. The length of this exposition, which is much shorter than it would have been had Trollope immediately introduced all the Palliser characters, not to speak of other marginal characters, is justified by its paradigmatic significance to the whole, for, as Sternberg notes, "owing to the selectivity of art, there is a logical correlation between the amount of space devoted to an element and the degree of its aesthetic relevance or centrality, so that there is a good prima facie case for inferring the latter from the former."[39]

Trollope's expositions also delay and deform time through prolepsis, presenting a micronarrative that evokes an event to take place at a future point of the major plot. In *The Eustace Diamonds* the proleptic tale, in which Lizzie contrives to keep the jewels that Harter and Benjamin seek to repossess for debt, postpones the major exposition of the novel with a story external to the time frame and narrative of the novel. Here Lizzie claims she does not have the jewels, just as she will do after the attempted theft later in the novel. She finds a husband, Sir Florian Eustace, in order to protect them, just as she later courts Lord Fawn, Frank Greystock, and Lord Bruce Carruthers to protect the Eustace diamonds. In both the prolepsis and the major narrative, an attempted theft of the jewels is unsuccessful. This technique disrupts the exposition's linear chronological presentation by anticipating the major plot and delaying it at the same time, creating a tension and vertical development congruent with the general synchronic nature of the Palliser novels and a major feature of self-consciously feminine narratives such as Richardson's *Pilgrimage*.

Trollope's expository methods are, at least in part, justified by his priorities, foremost of which is characterization, as noted in my discussion of his development of the *roman-fleuve* as a vehicle to present the change in characters over time. The deficiencies Sternberg sees in Trollope's expository technique are aggravated by his consideration of the Palliser and Barsetshire series as individual works rather than as interconnected novels, an emphasis on the parts rather than the holistic form Trollope created. Sternberg criticizes the opening of *The Eustace Dia-*

monds for "tedious" exposition, not recognizing that four chapters placed in the third novel of a 4,000-page work are not as cumbersome as they would be at the outset of one 600-page novel: it is a question of proportion and placement. Furthermore, because the exposition to a *roman-fleuve* is necessarily lengthy, the writer of this genre often exploits it for other functions than merely presenting background information. For example, there is more going on in the first four chapters of *The Eustace Diamonds* than the function Sternberg acknowledges, the introduction of four dramatis personae.[40] Trollope not only creates interest from the start in this novel by beginning with a subjective characterization, reporting what Lizzie's numerous enemies say about her, but he also launches immediately into a proleptic tale, the account of the jewels given Lizzie by her father, which anticipates the story of the diamonds given to her by Sir Florian Eustace, the primary plot in the novel. In this novel, as in *Can You Forgive Her?*, Trollope's expositional strategy prefigures the indirect, multiple beginnings of *écriture féminine*, which, since they do not rush headlong toward climactic revelations of some mystery or suspense, often linger to introduce a multitude of themes and plots.

The expository structure of *Can You Forgive Her?* establishes the "premise to the proposition," the motivation for Alice's indecision and vacillation as well as that of other females in the Palliser sequence; it presents concerns and problems that are typical of the entire Palliser series—integrity in the choice of a spouse, the conflict between private and public life, the proper roles for females, and so forth. In privileging features of the suspense plot—curiosity frustrated by delay—as the forces that motivate the reader, Sternberg overlooks the dynamics motivating Trollope's exposition: the narrative of the Pallisers is not pulled forward to a climax by curiosity but moves backward and forward through a teasing movement that subverts the phallocentric pattern of desire. Nardin, for instance, describes Trollope's position as "a degree of unresolved ambivalence" rather than as unqualified sympathy for women's dilemma. In her analysis of *Can You Forgive Her?* she finds an inconsistency within the novel: "The narrator fails to resolve most of the interpretative issues raised."[41] By establishing patterns and parallels that delay the forward movement of plot, in the exposition of each volume and of the *roman-fleuve* as a whole, Trollope creates an oscillating narrative that anticipates the dynamics of an *écriture féminine*. For this reason those who argue that Trollope is a feminist, albeit an ambivalent one, focus on the formal tensions in his work.

❧ The Fertile Middles: Trollope Marshals Fecundity

The deployment of reproductive metaphors, that of pregnancy in particular, to denigrate Trollope's extensive literary production suggests that critics such as James perceive a resemblance between the expansive "middles" of the *roman-fleuve* and the pregnant female form. The use of such a figure, simultaneously describing a narrative and the human body, corroborates critics who postulate a narrative erotics. Further, the form of the pregnant woman is traditionally perceived as one that, if it arouses, incites an illicit desire. Thus, the *roman-fleuve* inscribes the female body and arouses desire in an oxymoronic fashion, again suggesting the tension inherent in the genre. James is not the only one to describe the prolix quality of the novel in metaphors that suggest sexual reproduction; his condemnation of Trollope's "gross" fertility and "prodigious" fecundity is echoed in the form of another such metaphor, as Irving Buchen defines the aesthetics of the novel by claiming, "The key to the artistry of the novel is managing fecundity."[42] Hence, a more appropriate metaphor would focus on channeling desire. The essential challenge for the fecund and libidinous middle of the *roman-fleuve* is organization because, as Kermode points out, "We can perceive a duration only when it is organized."[43] The reader of the *roman-fleuve* is like Kermode's man "in the middest," uncertain about his end but seeking the brackets, the "tick" and "tock," that will both isolate and render significant his experience.

Critics have often defended Trollope against the charge that his novels are loose and sprawling by pointing to his use of repetition. Perhaps the most precise defense comes from Jerome Thale:

> A painting may be united through the repetition, echoing, contradiction, balancing, of such structural features as color, line, mass. In something of the same way, the Trollope novel depends upon parallels, contrasts, repetitions with slight variations. These things, which are present to some extent in any novel, become in Trollope the method of organization. In a Trollope novel, a large number of characters respond differently to the same situation, or do the same things for different reasons. Half a dozen or a dozen people may fall in love and say "yes" or "no" in the same way but for different reasons, or in different ways but for the same reason.

Thus the Trollope novel is the very opposite of the long comic strip, purely episodic; it is like a vast mural, one of those comprehensive images that cover walls, crammed with figures and united spatially.[44]

Thale's contrast between the episodic development of a comic strip and the spatial unity of a mural reinforces my argument that the narrative of Trollope's *roman-fleuve* is synchronic rather than diachronic.

Although Trollopians have often noted the repetition in individual novels, few have noted the way this technique works in Trollope's groups of novels, such as the Palliser *roman-fleuve*. For example, the parallels between Palliser and Lopez in *The Prime Minister* are discussed by Garrett and Klinger, yet they do not find parallels beyond this single novel (although the adventurer Lopez is prefigured by Emilius in *The Eustace Diamonds* and Palliser is paralleled by a variety of figures throughout the *roman-fleuve*). Thale refers to novels such as *The Way We Live Now*, *He Knew He Was Right*, *The Last Chronicle of Barset*, and *The Duke's Children*, but he does not extend his argument beyond the parallels in a single individual novel. Elizabeth Epperly calls Trollope a "master of repetition" and discusses a variety of techniques—including not only textual and narrative reiterations but also "literary allusions, cliches, speech tags"—that he uses to organize his novels. Although her focus is on repetition within individual novels, she discusses the function of political reiterations that occur in two of the Palliser novels: *Phineas Redux* and *The Prime Minister*.[45]

One technique of repetition uniquely developed in the *roman-fleuve* is that of recurring characters: within one or several volumes of the *roman-fleuve* the same characters reappear in the plot and/or the subplot, but they shift in importance. As noted in chapter 1, James comments on this technique, which he attributes to the influence of Balzac and Thackeray. Wall disagrees with the theory that Trollope was influenced by Thackeray's use of this technique, and he adds, furthermore, that Trollope probably did not derive his practice from Balzac; he finds Trollope's use of recurring characters to be inferior to Balzac's because he lacks a "system"; unlike Balzac, Trollope does not use reappearing characters as types to depict social evolution.[46] Although Wall is correct that Trollope is more interested in individuals than in types, Trollope does indeed create a highly complex picture of a society linked through the interrelations of characters, even those who occupy different strata of society. Further, an interconnected society is suggested when characters recur even outside a given *roman-fleuve* as, for example, in the overlapping of characters in the Barsetshire and Palliser novels and the recurrence of some of these characters in Trollope's later novels (such as Dolly Longstaff/Longestaffe in *The Way We Live Now*); but this is a device seldom used, and it functions more as a manifestation of Trollope's worldview than it serves any major structural function.

Like the other forms of repetition, the use of recurrent characters gives the middle of the *roman-fleuve* an oscillating movement; it carries the narrative backward as it recalls the character's previous identity and forward as it shows how the character has changed. Trollope explains his goal in respect to the forward function in *An Autobiography*:

> In writing *Phineas Finn* I had constantly before me the necessity of progression in character,—of marking the changes in men and women which would naturally be produced by the lapse of years. In most novels the writer can have no such duty, as the period occupied is not long enough to allow of the change of which I speak. . . . But I do not think that novelists have often set before themselves the state of progressive change,— nor should I have done it, had I not found myself so frequently allured back to my old friends. So much of my inner life was passed in their company, that I was continually asking myself how this woman would act when this or that event had passed over her head, or how that man would carry himself when his youth had become manhood, or his manhood declined to old age.[47]

Trollope hints at the advantage of the *roman-fleuve* for this kind of character development when he distinguishes the "period occupied" in his novels from that of "most novels." It is not so much the length of time covered in the *roman-fleuve*, the narrated time, however, as the Pallisers depict the passage of only twenty-five years, a shorter period of time than many novels of fewer pages; rather, it is the length of the reading time that allows dramatization of change in character. Wall points out that the use of recurring characters gives the novels a "fictional interconnection that [is] as much spatial as sequential."[48] As characters appear and reappear, evolving through a cumulative process but acting in accordance with an identity firmly developed through the block exposition that begins the novel, they contribute to a development that is more synchronic than diachronic. To develop variations on a theme with details is to move vertically rather than horizontally. Both Trollope's spatial narrative and synchronic development are characteristics of an *écriture féminine* that provide an alternative to the linear movement of the phallocentric narrative.

One of the most successful presentations of character evolution is that of the Pallisers' female protagonist, Glencora. In *Can You Forgive Her?* she is depicted as youthful, impulsive, romantic, and immature, but by the time of her last appearance in *The Prime Minister* she has matured into a cunning and powerful social figure. Even in those novels where she has only a minor function, Trollope is careful to indicate how time is gradually changing Glencora. For example, in *Phineas Finn*, she is only a marginal character, and the economical references to her contrast with her presentation in the first novel. Yet when she appears at the party at Saulsby the narrator says that Glencora, "still a young woman, and a very pretty woman, had taken lately very strongly to politics, which she discussed among men and women of both parties with something more than ordinary audacity" (1: 115), ironically recalling an earlier scene in *Can You Forgive Her?* when Palliser lectures Glencora on politics and the British Constitution as she yawns into her handkerchief. At that time Palliser said, "But I fear I shall never make you a politician" (2: 17), and Glencora admitted that she was ignorant about politics. The reader's mental juxtaposition of these two scenes treating the same subject, one technique through which the *roman-fleuve* creates a complex intertext, reveals Glencora's political education and social evolution. Further, Palliser's statement takes on an ironic cast as Glencora becomes a politician in many ways; indeed, by the time of *The Prime Minister*, Palliser fears it is she who is the more effective politician.

This view of Glencora's evolution and Trollope's use of recurring characters is disputed by Kincaid, who argues that the characters are inconsistent from novel to novel: "Even the characters who recur both are and are not the same. They are called by the same names, but they also serve the special and unique demands of the novel in which they appear." More specifically, he asserts that Glencora changes to suit her function in the various novels.[49] Kincaid may overstate the case for inconsistency of character, however; although the recurring characters naturally serve the function of the novel in which they appear, the changes are never inconsistent; they depict characters' evolution in response to their environments. Glencora is as audacious and impulsive in *The Prime Minister* as she was in *Can You Forgive Her?*, disobeying her husband in both novels as a result of these traits. However, the mature woman is more interested in social success and in the engagement of her daughter than in any personal romance; therefore, she acts in the same way in a different situation. Palliser is depicted as dull and old-fashioned in his confrontations with his two lively sons in *The Duke's Children*, just as earlier, in *Can You Forgive Her?*, he was a dull young man. Trollope is most interested in process, the "state of progressive change" as he calls it, and his depiction of a character's response to experience always moves forward, in anticipation of a character's mature self, as well as backward, to a character's embryonic self, established in an initial portrait.

It is a mark of Trollope's genius that his major characters are unique individuals and, at the same time, paradigms of human emotions and behavior. He uses the paradigms to structure the *roman-fleuve* by suggesting parallels, a technique termed "reiteration" by McMaster, who notes that Trollope uses variations with different characters to emphasize theme.[50] A major example is the paradigm of female discontent. Trollope's handling of this issue is not ambiguous: his narrator sympathizes with women's frustrations and feelings of uselessness but not with the feminist movement or feminist solution.[51] Trollope's interest is in the psychology of the dissatisfied women. Kate Flint has noted the way Alice's question in *Can You Forgive Her?*, " 'What should a woman do with her life?' " introduces a paradigm that "is echoed by the presence of every other woman in the novel."[52] When the Pallisers are considered as a *roman-fleuve*, it is clear that this feminine dilemma is carried through not only the first but all six novels.

Introduced with Alice Vavasor in the first novel, the paradigm is one explanation for the extended and extensive exposition in *Can You Forgive Her?* Alice's articulation of her frustration and dissatisfaction reverberates throughout the series: "What should a woman do with her life? There had arisen round her a flock of learned ladies asking that question, to whom it seems that the proper answer has never yet occurred. Fall in love, marry the man, have two children, and live happy every afterwards. . . . Alice Vavasor was ever asking herself that question, and had by degrees filled herself with a vague idea that there was something to be done; a something over and beyond, or perhaps altogether beside that marrying and having two children;—if she only knew what it was" (*CYFH?* 1: 110). Trollope's narrator ridicules the feminist solution to the problem by his use of the ornithological metaphor, the alliteration in the "learned ladies," and the last clause: Alice has no idea what she should do. The rest of the Alice plot demonstrates that there is nothing else but for her to agree with the narrator since her efforts to engage in politics vicariously through George Vavasor end up only eroding her finances and her self-respect. Yet the novel asks us to sympathize with her struggle to find a vocation. Her increasing subordination to Glencora in the plot, combined with her virtual disappearance from the rest of the series, dramatizes the fate of the compliant Victorian woman.

What is significant for the form of the *roman-fleuve* is the way Trollope uses the detailed examination of Alice's plight as exposition for a more general situation that affects most of the other major female characters in the series. Mabel Grex, who is unable to bring herself to play the marriage game, asks "What is a girl to do?" (*DC* 82) and near the end of the final novel muses: "A girl unless she marries becomes nothing, as I have become nothing now" (*DC* 614). Lady Mary Palliser, who marries the man Lady Mabel truly loved, exclaims, "How I do wish I were a man!" (*DC* 228) and "I have got nothing but him [Tregear]. . . . But it is I that have the suffering in all this. A man can never be like a girl" (*DC* 509). In *Phineas Finn*, Violet Effingham, eventually one of the most happily married of the Palliser women, complains, "I wish I could be something, if it were only a stick in waiting, or a doorkeeper. It is so good to be something" (*PF* 2: 196). Glencora Palliser expresses political ambitions: "I wish I were in Parliament. I'd get up in the middle and make such a speech. You all seem to me to be so much afraid of one another that you don't quite dare to speak out" (*PF* 1: 116). Impetuous as she is, one wonders if a dose of Glencora's determination might have made her husband a more effective politician. Finally, an exchange between Lady Laura Standish and Phineas Finn reveals the melancholy lesson learned by several women in the Palliser *roman-fleuve*:

Laura: "I am beginning to think that it is a great curse to have been born a woman."

Phineas: "And yet I have heard you say that a woman may do as much as a man."

Laura: "That was before I had learned my lesson properly. I know better than that now. Oh dear! I have no doubt it is all for the best as it is, but I have a kind of wish that I might be allowed to go out and milk the cows." (*PF* 1: 301)

What is striking in this small sampling of statements is the similarity of the language of dissatisfaction despite the differences in the women's personalities and their individual situations. The complaints focus on being, identity, action, and speech. Although Trollope suggests a varying degree of success for each individual, none of these articulate, intelligent, and energetic women is able to reach her full potential. The repetition also functions as an internal link, providing continuity between the different volumes of the *roman-fleuve*. Yet each situation, and each novel, retains its own integrity because each presentation is placed within a unique and personal context. When Lady Laura and Mabel Grex speak these words they portend tragedy; Glencora and Violet speak them with irony and self-knowledge; Mary is realistic and hardheaded. Trollope's detailed characterization allows him to use this technique advantageously to suggest, simultaneously, the universality of human emotions and the individuality of response. Furthermore, the device is efficient: the universal situation once explicated through Alice's story, the narrator's judgment made and confirmed, this material need not be repeated in the variations; each case refers back to the original, moving forward with a new exemplum. While the example above is a major one, the Pallisers are resonant with repetitions of paradigmatic human behavior. There is the paradigm of the monied suitor pursuing the eligible younger woman as Cheesacre courts Mrs. Greenow in *Can You Forgive Her?* or Mr. Spooner pursues Adelaide Palliser in *Phineas Redux*. Again, the characters are all fully individual—there can be only one Mr. Cheesacre—but their words and reactions emphasize the commonality of their motives.

Although a complete tally of these recurrent situations in the Pallisers would be tedious, it should be emphasized that this type of repetition exists within both individual novels and the *roman-fleuve* as a whole. The parent-child dispute introduced by George Vavasor and his grandfather in *Can You Forgive Her?* is repeated by Chiltern and his father in *Phineas Finn* and by Mary and Silverbridge with their father in *The Duke's Children*. A brother brings home a friend who becomes an unsuitable suitor for his sister when Everett Wharton introduces Lopez to Emily in *The Prime Minister* and when Silverbridge introduces Tregear to Mary in *The Duke's Children*. Men without fortunes, Lopez and Tregear expect to profit from the wealth of their fathers-in-law. A woman, usually a sister, gives a man money, often to run for office, as Alice and Kate finance Vavasor's campaign in *Can You Forgive Her?*,

and many women offer men their fortunes, usually for political purposes: Madame Max to Phineas, Lady Laura to Chiltern. Critics have
pointed to these repetitions in other contexts. For instance, Ruth
apRoberts uses the repeated situations in *Phineas Finn* as an example of
Trollope's delineation of moral choices in various predicaments: "All
these related anomalous situations comment on one another, and together constitute a cogent form for the novel."[53]

These and other types of repetition are so prevalent in the *roman-
fleuve* as to comprise a contrapuntal organization, a common method
of structuring this genre. The best-known definition of this technique
comes from a character in Huxley's *Point Counter Point*: "A theme is
stated, then developed, pushed out of shape, imperceptibly deformed,
until, though still recognizably the same, it has become quite different.
. . . All you need is a sufficiency of characters and parallel contrapuntal plots. While Jones is murdering a wife, Smith is wheeling the per-
ambulator in the park. You alternate the themes. More interesting, the
modulations and variations are also more difficult. A novelist modulates by reduplicating situations and characters. He shows several people
falling in love, or dying, or praying in different ways—dissimilars solv-
ing the same problem. Or, *vice versa*, similar people confronted with
dissimilar problems."[54] Critics have noted Trollope's techniques of coun-
terpoint and elaboration in individual novels, but contrapuntal structure is most vibrant in the entire Palliser sequence.

In a passage from *An Autobiography*, Trollope describes, without actually using the term, the goals and difficulties of contrapuntal technique in the Parliamentary novels:

> That [Palliser's] character should be understood as I understand it—or
> that of his wife's, the delineation of which has also been a matter of
> much happy care to me—I have no right to expect, seeing that the opera-
> tion of describing has not been confined to one novel, which might per-
> haps be read through by the majority of those who commenced it. It has
> been carried on through three or four, each of which will be forgotten
> even by the most zealous reader almost as soon as read. In *The Prime
> Minister*, my Prime Minister will not allow his wife to take office among,
> or even over, those ladies who are attached by office to the Queen's Court.
> "I should not choose," he says to her, "that my wife should have any du-
> ties unconnected with our joint family and home." Who will remember
> in reading those words that, in a former story, published some years be-
> fore, he tells his wife, when she has twitted him with his willingness to

clean the Premier's shoes, that he would even allow her to clean them if it were for the good of the country? And yet it is by such details as these that I have, for many years past, been manufacturing within my own mind the characters of the man and his wife.[55]

Trollope again reveals his preference for the ideal or "zealous" readers, those who not only read the Pallisers in sequence but also recall in detail what they have read; more important, the passage describes the advantage of the contrapuntal technique in giving coherence to the work on all levels—episode, chapter, and volume, as well as the entire *roman-fleuve*. The multitude of repeated details forms a dense network that structures the *roman-fleuve* on a subconscious as well as a conscious level since the length of the work makes an intellectual perception of all of the parallels difficult. On a thematic level, contrapuntal technique works through juxtaposition, an accumulation of well-placed significant parallels.

In the Pallisers the juxtaposition works simultaneously on various levels: parallels may juxtapose two or more novels, chapters, or simultaneous narrations; they may draw parallels on different levels of society, or in different modes (comic and ironic), or in different generations, or in the plot and subplots, or in dramatized and narrated portions of the text. A large-scale juxtaposition is that of the two Phineas novels, which together form a diptych, a unique structure within the Pallisers. Although *Phineas Finn* continues the themes and plots already established in the series, it also forms the beginning of one extensive subplot. Halperin stresses the importance of this novel and its continuity with the political theme of the series: "[*Phineas Finn*] is a pivotal novel in the Palliser series. It both develops themes more mutely present in *Can You Forgive Her?* and introduces us, in its examination of the beginnings of a political career, to a number of motifs that are to be threaded throughout its successors."[56] McMaster comments on this structure when she notes that the second novel is more a "complement" than a "sequel": "[Trollope] has the events, though literally different, closely parallel those in the first novel, so that Phineas seems to be going through it all again; only it has all turned sour."[57] Trollope himself called *Phineas Redux* a sequel and admitted he intended to bring Phineas back.[58] Despite the inauspicious marriage of Phineas and Mary Flood Jones at the end of *Phineas Finn*, Trollope's open conclusion affirms his intention to take up the Phineas plot again shortly: "What was the nature of his reply to Lord Cantrip the reader may imagine, and thus we will leave our hero an Inspector of Poor Houses in the County of Cork" (2: 356). It is evident that a hero who is only "left" may be retrieved at any time. *Phineas Redux* retells the story of *Phineas Finn* with a twist. In the Phineas novels, the repetition and the diptych structure are used propitiously as the accused criminal retraces the steps of the naive youth, creating a structure that juxtaposes innocence and experience, a common pattern in the bildungsroman. However, this pattern is also a reiteration of the more comprehensive initiation of Plantagenet Palliser, which begins in *Can You Forgive Her?* and is completed in *The Duke's Children*. Critics have often noted the way the love triangle of Palliser-Glencora-Fitzgerald in the first volume is repeated in that of Popplecourt-Mary-Tregear in the last.

The parallel initiations of Palliser and Phineas Finn, two politicians from different social backgrounds, are also examples of the way Trollope uses contrapuntal structure to connect the different levels of society, always emphasizing, however, internal emotions over social events. In discussing Trollope's multiple plots, Mizener comments on this facet of the Trollopian community: "Trollope had an extremely sharp eye for social differences; perhaps no English novelist has had a sharper one. But he knew very well that vanity, fear, and lust, unselfishness, courage, and love are much the same everywhere."[59] This particular use of contrapuntal technique is, of course, established in *Can You Forgive Her?* as the three female protagonists represent three levels of society: aristocracy, gentry, and merchant class; their dilemma is similar despite their various class affiliations. In another parallel, the Pallisers are threatened by intermarriage with a lower class of society in *The Duke's Children*, just as the middle class is threatened by Emily Wharton's marriage to Lopez in *The Prime Minister*.

Trollope also draws parallels in different modes (in Frye's sense of the term), parodying characters by constructing likenesses to inanimate or inhuman entities for a comic or ironic purpose. The most obvious example of this technique is the parallel between Palliser and that of the racehorse Prime Minister, who parodies the protagonist's political fate. As Palliser's political prospects look brighter in *The Duke's Children*, so does the fate of Silverbridge's racehorse.[60] Ironically, Major Tifto, Silverbridge's partner, attempts to use his success with racehorses, Prime Minister in particular, to elevate his position in society, just as Glencora attempts to raise hers through Palliser's success in *The Prime*

Minister. However, as the horse is lamed by Tifto, so Palliser is socially "lamed" by Glencora's political meddling, and Prime Minister's racing career ends as ignominiously as Palliser's political career. Another horse, named Coalition, "fail[s], as Coalitions always do" (*DC* 130). The ironic parallels connect the main plot with higher as well as lower levels, comparing individual relations to international ones. When Laura begrudges Finn's subsequent attachments to Violet Effingham and Marie Goesler, her sentiment is paralleled on a national level as Marylebone is said to begrudge Canada to America (*PF* 2: 169). This ironic connection is suggested by juxtaposition as Laurence Fitzgibbon breaks the news about Marylebone in the same conversation in which he tells Phineas that Violet has quarreled with Chiltern, suggesting a further parallel since Phineas himself does not at this time want Chiltern to marry Violet.

While these parallels represent ironic similarity, others represent variation; as Trollope draws parallels between characters in different generations, the themes of time and social change are emphasized. One such parallel is the similarity between Palliser and his chosen son-in-law, Popplecourt. In addition to the similarity of their situations as husbands chosen by the families of heiresses in love with more attractive but less monied suitors, Palliser and Popplecourt resemble each other in their beginnings as unostentatious politicians and unprepossessing young men. In *The Duke's Children*, Popplecourt is described as "that generally silent young nobleman Lord Popplecourt" (245), recalling the first description of Palliser in *The Small House at Allington* as a man who "in society was quiet, reserved, and very often silent" (250). Like the youthful Palliser, Popplecourt possesses a large estate, comes from an old family, and has prospects of "something higher in rank" (*DC* 271). However, Popplecourt does not achieve Palliser's advantageous arranged marriage because of changes in society's ideas about marriage.

A more surprising resemblance, despite their blood ties, is that of Lord Silverbridge to his great-uncle, the old Duke of Omnium. Silverbridge not only resembles the Duke in his physical appearance, but he also in many ways responds to the attraction of an idle aristocratic way of life his own father shuns. Silverbridge drives a coach and four (much to his father's disapproval), and he cares more for dissipated entertainments like the Derby than about winning the seat at Silverbridge (*DC* 77). In his resemblance to his great-uncle, Silverbridge is linked to the old way of life, but in his marriage, his language, and his disdain for the old ways of life, he represents the future. Other characters suggest social evolution as they represent cumulative variations in each generation. For example, most of the female characters receive some opposition to their choice of husbands from their fathers, but as time passes and society changes, each subsequent woman finds more freedom to marry as she chooses. Glencora is compelled to marry by her family, while Alice marries the man her father approves of after some vacillation (CYFH?). Emily Wharton marries a man her father disapproves of, but she gets a second chance to marry the man he prefers after her first husband's death (PM). Mary Palliser is the only woman to marry against her father's wishes and then to bring him around to her view of the marriage (DC).

The Victorian novel is often compared to Elizabethan drama as a genre that makes extensive use of plot and subplot.[61] More specifically, Kincaid argues that Trollope's multiple plot structure may have been influenced by his reading in Elizabethan and Jacobean drama.[62] The long Victorian novel has often been viewed as a structure comprised of many plots apparently subordinated to a whole. In his discussion of the Victorian multiplot novel, however, Garrett argues that there is often no subordination that makes it possible to find a single center in these works. Opposing those critics who find that subordination of subplots to a major plot gives unity to the novel, he finds that "the form of these novels is neither single- nor multiple-focus but incorporates both, and it is the interaction and tension between these structural principles which produces some of their most important and distinctive effects." Thus, the form of these novel results from "dialogical tensions."[63] Garrett rightly insists, however, that subordination of subplot to plot is uneven in Trollope.

The obvious advantage of Garrett's argument is that he manages to have it both ways, leading him to conclude that the Victorian novel has an open-and-closed form, an issue I will take up in the discussion of closure that comprises the last section of this chapter. However, it should be recognized that Trollope's narrative innovation is to eschew the hierarchy of a major plot, prefiguring the shifting emphasis of multiple plots in modernist fiction and écriture féminine. On a narrative level, Trollope augurs the syntactic style that was fully developed by Richardson, one that has been defined by contemporary theorists as a feature of a feminist aesthetic: "On the discourse level, we find a discursive, conjunctive style instead of the complex, subordinating, linear style of classification and distinction."[64] The unevenly developed Palliser plot, even when viewed as the major plot in this *roman-fleuve*, is nevertheless frequently displaced as the Phineas Finn, Lizzie Eustace, or Emily Wharton subplot takes temporary preeminence.

Trollope's subplots are necessitated by the length of the genre: the sustainment of one unified plot focusing on one small group of characters would threaten the work with an obsessive and tedious self-enclosure; indeed, egotism is one of the main charges made against Richardson's *Pilgrimage*, a text that rejects a hierarchized narrative in favor of other devices. Even a work as ostensibly ego-centered as *A la recherche du temps perdu* abandons the focus on the protagonist to take up the story of other characters, Swann, for instance. These multiple lines of development not only create diversity but, like the more conventional subplot, maintain the energy that propels the narrative: "The development of the subplot in the classical novel usually suggests (as William Empson has intimated) a different solution to the problems worked through by the main plot, . . . assuring the main plot will continue through to the right end."[65] This diffusion of energy provides one explanation for the disunified or digressive portions of the Palliser sequence. However, Brooks's assertion that the use of a subplot enables the main plot to reach its "right end" assumes the hierarchy of a linear narrative and a (pre)determinate closure, assumptions challenged by Trollope's ending to the Pallisers, which rejects a climactic narrative, prefiguring the defiance of twentieth-century practitioners of an *écriture féminine*, who often choose plots that, as Rachel Blau DuPlessis terms it, "write beyond the ending."

❧ Contested Closure in the Ending of the Palliser Novels

As the *roman-fleuve* exaggerates the formal characteristics of the ordinary novel, it intensifies the inherent challenges of the genre. A narrative problem unique to the *roman-fleuve*, however, is to achieve closure at the end of each novel in order to close, satisfactorily, that constituent part and at the same time provide an opening to the next volume in the sequence. The ability of each subsequent volume to resume a former story suggests the contradictory nature of a provisional closure that terminates the inner novel of a multivolume work. Thus, the *roman-fleuve* exemplifies a recurrent search for and evasion of resolution. Because an expectation of continuation has been established, the ending of the final volume is particularly problematic; the final motionlessness of closure is antithetical to its flowing narrative.

These narrative dynamics manifest an affinity between the *roman-fleuve* and an *écriture féminine*: both demonstrate, as their primary and distinguishing feature, a resistance to or even rejection of closure. This is the one characteristic of *écriture féminine* that all of its proponents emphasize. Christiane Makward designates as feminine an "open, non-linear, unfinished writing," while Cixous describes "a female textual body" that is "recognized by the fact that it is always endless, without ending: there's no closure, it doesn't stop, and it's this that very often makes the feminine text difficult to read. For we've learned to read books that basically pose the word 'end.'"[66] In *écriture féminine* and in the novel without end, the evasion of closure is ideologically significant as well since, if we believe Kermode, the ending is that which grants meaning to the whole. As DuPlessis argues, "One of the great moments of ideological negotiation in any work occurs in the choice of a resolution."[67] The choice, conscious or unconscious, of an unresolved ending is perhaps the most emphatic rejection of the "ejaculatory" narrative a writer can make. The resolution of Trollope's Pallisers exhibits both a concession to the Victorian conventions of ending a novel and a gesture toward the "endless" feminine text.

Although problematic closure is often considered to be characteristic of the Victorian novel, Trollope chooses the lengthy subgenre that poses the greatest challenge for satisfactory closure. Torgovnick argues that critics dismiss Victorian endings as unsophisticated without perceiving "disruptive, distancing, or parodic elements in endings, inadequately recognizing that such devices pointed to a discomfort with endings based on a host of possible reasons."[68] Of all the major Victorian novelists, Trollope most candidly reveals his misgivings about conclusions, often disrupting the final passages of his narrative with intrusive comments about the problematic ending. His experimentation with the *roman-fleuve* form and the overlap of his novels, particularly that of the Barsetshire and Palliser series, attest to his sophisticated awareness of alternatives to the seemingly arbitrary and artificial traditional closure. Moreover, this feature of *écriture féminine* in his text, while not fully realized, suggests Trollope's nascent feminism.

The resolution of Trollope's *roman-fleuve* demonstrates the precarious closure inherent in this genre. The final Palliser novel, *The Duke's*

Children, has a dual closural function—it must begin and end, as all novels do, and it must, at the same time, terminate the six-volume sequence in such a way that the reader expects no continuation. To the extent that its diffuse and multifarious narrative has a definable plot, Trollope's *roman-fleuve* may be said to dramatize two major stories—a bildungsroman plot, tracing the personal and political development of Plantagenet Palliser (and the parallel social career of Glencora), and a societal plot tracing the evolution of British culture during a period parallel to the protagonist's lifetime. (That this *roman-fleuve* is referred to as both the Palliser series and the Parliamentary series suggests this dual focus.) The personal story of Plantagenet Palliser and his political world is closed with his recalcitrant acceptance of his own ineffectuality in *The Duke's Children*, but the future of the next generation, his progeny, and the evolution of his society, changed as it may be, continue open and unrestricted. The title of the last volume of the series, *The Duke's Children*, emphasizes this continuation of the generations, subverting the terminal force of the conclusion to Plantagenet Palliser's own story. The societal plot, in its affinity with the narrative flow or *fleuve*, also undermines any closure suggested in the bildungsroman plot. The resolution of the series must suggest that outside the restriction of the *roman*—the covers of the novel—the *fleuve* (of history and "real" life) continues unharnessed. This conflict of dual demands is inherent in the form itself; thus, the Palliser series achieves a closure that is only as conclusive as the form permits.

In the Pallisers, as in the Barsetshire chronicles, Trollope chooses a form that, by reiterating character and situation, moves forward while referring backward, working against anticipation of finality and thus against closure. D. A. Miller argues that reappearing characters work against conclusion and compares Trollope to Balzac in his use of a "double vision of closure": "There is no better way of having, and not having, one's closure than the device of the *retour des personnages*, where what is most importantly 'returned' are not the characters, but the narratable desires they have sponsored. Closure coexists with the possibility of going beyond it in Trollope's Barsetshire and Palliser novels as well."[69] In *The Duke's Children* many characters—particularly Plantagenet Palliser and Mrs. Finn—take their final curtain calls, appearing for the last time. However, the characters who premiere in this volume (the Palliser children played no major roles as characters in previous novels although the birth of Silverbridge effected a major change in the plot) in many ways reiterate their predecessors.

The clearest instance of reiteration is found in the characters of Mary Palliser and Tregear, who resemble Glencora and her youthful lover, Burgo Fitzgerald, in both character and situation. Tregear physically echoes the handsome Fitzgerald, and Mary herself is "very like her mother," not only in appearance, but also "in having exactly her mother's tone of voice, her quick manner of speech, and her sharp intelligence" (*DC* 11). The final volume circles back to the first, *Can You Forgive Her?*, in which Glencora rebelled against an arranged marriage that demanded that she sacrifice romantic love, as her daughter rejects her father's choice of the unromantic Lord Popplecourt. Although Glencora's daughter achieves the romantic love she was herself denied, Mary's marriage does not satisfy and resolve the larger problem of women's discontent posed in the series. The combination of Glencora's disappearance as a living character and her reappearance as a major force in the plot, posthumously subverting patriarchy in the form of her husband's expectations of domestic power, undermines the closure of Palliser's own story and reintroduces the theme of women's discontent in the *roman-fleuve* as a whole.

McMaster's examination of Trollope's manuscripts shows that he intended the series to be even more circular, that there was a "fairly extensive reference" to Alice in the uncut draft of *The Duke's Children* that was omitted to keep the novel to a three-volume format.[70] In this instance, a modification to an individual novel, because it is the crucial final volume, changes and blurs the shape of the entire *roman-fleuve*. Had Trollope retained the references to Alice, he would have achieved a stronger circular ending, one of the most common techniques for conclusions. Given the vast proportions of this work, the location of its resolution is particularly elusive. Can one expect a simultaneous resolution of the diverse themes, diffused plots, and multitudinous characters of a six-volume *roman-fleuve* in the form of one unified and decisive finis? When does the denouement begin? What constitutes the "end" of the series? Torgovnick distinguishes between *ending*, "the last definable unit of the work—section, scene, chapter, page, paragraph—whichever seems most appropriate for a given text" and *closure*, "the process by which a novel reaches an adequate and appropriate conclusion."[71] The Palliser *roman-fleuve* reveals how problematic the application of even the first part of this distinction can be. Is the ending the last chapter of *The Duke's Children*, describing Mary and Tregear's wedding? Or is it the last two chapters, each dealing with the marriage of one of the Duke's children? Does the *roman-fleuve* reach "appropriate conclusion"? Does it have a "sense of an ending," as Kermode puts it? The ending of this *roman-fleuve* may be variously located in the denouement, the last volume, and the concluding passages of *The Duke's Children*, but each location contains different implications for the conclusion. The Palliser series self-consciously achieves closure, especially in resolving the fate of individuals, but the oscillating momentum of the *fleuve*, especially as it is evident in social themes, undermines the neat closure imposed on the work.

The scope of the *roman-fleuve* necessitates an extensive and staggered resolution of the numerous events and multitudinous characters' stories. In one sense, the denouement begins in the first volume, inasmuch as the end is contained in the beginning: the fates of individuals are predetermined by their essential natures; as Christopher Herbert argues, Trollope is aware of change but demonstrates through characters such as Plantagenet Palliser that "personality is essentially monolithic."[72] In a more literal fashion, however, the denouement may be said to begin with Plantagenet's political demise in *The Prime Minister*—after the climax of the Duke's political career and Glencora's parallel social triumph, about halfway through the fifth novel of the Pallisers. To an extent, the whole of *The Duke's Children* is anticlimactic, a concluding bracket to the series. Although the Duke regains office, his position as President of the Council in Mr. Monk's Cabinet is neither as prestigious as the Prime Minister's nor as useful as that of the Chancellor of the Exchequer. Glencora, we learn in the final volume, occupied her last days after the Duke's resignation encouraging Frank Tregear's courtship of her daughter Mary, vicariously reliving her own unresolved youthful romance with Burgo Fitzgerald.

The Duke's Children also functions to dramatize, subsequent to the resolution of his public life, the denouement of the Duke's personal life: his efforts to adapt to life without Glencora and to tolerate, if not accept, the new values advocated by his children. The undramatized death of Glencora, occurring in the margins of the work (in the gap between the penultimate and final volumes), gives the concluding novel the flat taste of anticlimax, diminishing the force of its closure. The narrative energy aroused by Glencora and her "discharged" story is neither resolved nor allowed to continue but simply, seemingly arbitrarily, cut off. Despite the focus on Palliser's career, it is Glencora who is the primary agent of social change and the motivator of plot. Her efforts to create a political salon, though ultimately unsuccessful, motivate the events that lead to her husband's political demise. More significantly, Glencora's actions portend the social forces that will change the aristocratic society Plantagenet represents. Indifferent to lineage, Glencora sponsors arrivistes such as Lopez and Tregear, effecting their entrances into the gentry and the aristocracy respectively, an infiltration that suggests an increasingly larger and more general social devolution as the series continues and the parvenus marry into the Palliser family. Even after her death, Glencora's machinations motivate plot in *The Duke's Children* as Palliser discovers in this novel that his wife approved Mary's engagement to Tregear without informing the Duke or obtaining his consent. However, without Glencora's dynamic presence the impact of her schemes is diminished. The intervolume death of Glencora, a major agent of social change, ensures that the focus on Plantagenet be uncontested, but it detracts from the impact of closure in the subsequent volume.

The Duke's Children is replete with the conventional terminal motifs of marriage and death. However, since the form of Trollope's *roman-fleuve* has established an expectation of continuation antithetical to closure, the efficacy of these terminal motifs is subverted: the oscillation, which works against the expectation of closure, is evident in the formal devices that suggest sequence rather than an inherent "termination point." Closure is a phenomenon closely tied to expectation: "We tend to speak of conclusions when a sequence of events has a relatively high degree of structure, when, in other words, we can perceive these events as related to one another by some principle of organization or design that implies the existence of a definite termination point. Under these circumstances, the occurrence of the terminal event is a confirmation of expectations that have been established by the structure of the sequence, and is usually distinctly gratifying. The sense of stable conclusiveness, finality, of 'clinch' which we experience at that point is what is referred to here as closure."[73] The strongest evidence for determining the strength of closure in this *roman-fleuve*, its "sense of an ending," resides in the final passages of the last volume, describing the two marriages of Palliser's children. Just as the Palliser series opens with multiple beginnings, the juxtaposed marital dilemmas of Alice Vavasor, Glencora Palliser, and Arabella Greenow in *Can You Forgive Her?*, so it is buttressed at the end with double conclusions—the marriages of Palliser's heir to an American and of his daughter to a penniless younger son. The endings are in tension, but the tension may be elucidated by examining their conflicting functions: closing both an individual novel and a multivolume *roman-fleuve*.

An ending that juxtaposes two weddings in two final chapters would seem to provide a tightly bound, well-knotted finish. The chapters resolve plot and subplot in parallel fashion, focusing on the details of each wedding ceremony and "disposing" of two of the Duke's children. The marriages are analogous, as both Lord Silverbridge and Lady Mary choose mates outside their class: the heir is wed to a woman he himself describes as "an American girl whose grandfather had been a porter" (351), and Mary to a member of the English gentry, a younger son with neither title nor wealth. Silverbridge's and Mary's prospective spouses represent similar challenges to social hierarchy, as is evident in the companion statements that they themselves make to justify their marital aspirations. Isabel claims, "I think myself good enough for the best man God ever made" (388), while Frank announces, "I believe myself to be as good a gentleman as though my father's forefathers had sat for centuries past in the House of Lords" (402). Analogous as the two hymeneal chapters may be, however, each marriage suggests a different outcome for the story told in the Palliser novels.

While it is true that the marriage of the major plot, that of Silverbridge and Isabel Boncassen, represents the kind of comic plot Northrop Frye defines, and while the Duke must realize that his children cannot and should not live his life, Plantagenet is a far more sympathetic character than the youngsters. The usual terminal function of marriage, which forestalls future expectations for the courtship plot, is undermined by the focus on reiteration with variation—the suggestion that this marriage represents a *renewal* of the aristocracy. The union suggests the continuation of aristocratic values that harken back to the old Duke of Omnium (Plantagenet's uncle). Silverbridge, despite his youthful indiscretions and initial political apathy, shows a proclivity to undertake aristocratic duties that his father disdained—maintaining the Trumpington Wood for hunting and so forth. In keeping with the aristocratic rank of Silverbridge, the wedding is "one of the most brilliant remembered in the metropolis" (629); all the Palliser family attend and it is "celebrated by special royal favor" (624). The description of the wedding also works against closure, echoing as it does the extravagant and somewhat vulgar social occasions hosted by Glencora in the previous volume, *The Prime Minister*. At the height of her social triumph, Glencora was accused of turning the family estate at Gatherum into an "inn," numbering the rooms that housed her numerous guests. The chapter describing Silverbridge and Isabel's wedding makes reference to a newspaper's report of the cash value of the wedding presents. The narrator makes it clear that the American Boncassens are not to be held responsible for this vulgarity; it is the inevitable result of an ostentatious public wedding. Moreover, as Isabel resembles Glencora in her spirit and wit and even uses Glencora's language in predicting a "Darby and Joan" sort of life for herself and her husband (574), the recurrence of the former protagonists is suggested by the marriage of their son and an American Glencora.

Before the Duke is aware of his son's interest in Isabel, he tells her, "Our peerage is continually recruited from the ranks of the people, and hence it gets its strength" (390). However, although Isabel is American—presumably an agent of change and new blood, a *natural* aristocrat—the novel suggests that when she assumes her role as Lady Silverbridge she will be, in effect, a conservative force, maintaining the privileges and duties of rank. An "apt scholar" who agrees to read the Duke's pamphlets on decimal coinage and who listens attentively as he lectures her on "the mysteries of the House of Lords" (422), Isabel accepts many of his aristocratic values (albeit with a mocking wit) and is willing to adopt his sentiment of noblesse oblige. The wedding ceremony itself, which takes place in spring, on the Wednesday following Easter, presages continuance in the possible birth of new Pallisers. The account of Silverbridge and Isabel's wedding also leaves open the possibility of a sequel detailing the success of their marriage and the story of *their* children.

The Mary/Tregear marriage, placed in the last chapter of the final volume of the series, directly follows the chapter detailing Silverbridge's extravagant marriage. By devoting the final chapter, the position of greatest closural force, to the resolution of the subplot rather than to the major plot, Trollope further undermines any effect of closure achieved in the first marriage. Moreover, in contrast to the previous ceremony, everything about Mary and Tregear's marriage is subdued and elegiac: they are married in the fall, in November, "not altogether an hymeneal month" (630), and the wedding takes place at Matching, the family residence, near the romantic ruins where Glencora is buried. R. C. Terry finds the priory ruins "symbolic of [Glencora's] physical needs."[74] The ironic "presence" of the dead Glencora and the reminder of her sexual and romantic frustration suggest that despite her daughter's success, the mother achieved, at best, only a vicarious and posthumous satisfaction of her own desires. The ceremony is simple and the prospects of the couple are modest in comparison with those of the heir and his American: "There had however been a general feeling that the bride of the heir of the house of Omnium should be produced to the world amidst a blare of trumpets and a glare of torches. So it had been. But both the Duke and Mary were determined that this other wedding should be different. It was to take place at Matching, and none would be present but they who were staying in the house, or who lived around,—such as tenants and dependents. Four clergymen united their forces to tie Isabel to her husband, one of whom was a bishop, one a canon, and the two others royal chaplains; but there was only to be the Vicar of the parish at Matching" (631–32). The passage intimates that Tregear and Mary represent the beginning of the end of the hierarchical class distinctions that prevailed at the opening of the Pallisers in the arranged marriage of Glencora and Plantagenet, a muted but appropriate conclusion for the series.

There are, therefore, two kinds of bifurcation or contradiction within this resolution of the series. First, there is a contradiction between the two marriages. Second, the narrative energies of Glencora's story are split between two younger female protagonists, both expertly crafted by Trollope yet lacking the force of Glencora, his finest creation in the Pallisers. Glencora's spirit continues through the characters of Mary and Isabel, yet since each embodies only part of her traits, there is a sense of diminution as well. These contradictions provide the uneasy resolution of nineteenth-century narratives that DuPlessis has described as prefigurations of those by twentieth-century women who "write beyond the ending" of marriage or death. Glencora is an example of a female hero who "seems always to exceed the bounds that the plot delineates"; she is a disruptive force who undermines closure, the embodiment of "the repressed element [that] is [always] present in shadowy form."[75] Although Trollope does not actually write beyond the ending as Du Plessis defines the phenomenon, he exhibits an uneasiness with the marriage resolution.

The Duke's Children provides the end of Palliser's own story, the finish of his dreams, and his recalcitrant acceptance of the irrevocable impact of time and social change.[76] The work achieves closure—but with difficulty. The difficulties of this closure—at once terminating a novel and a *roman-fleuve*—illustrate the stipulation that closure will be "minimal when the structural forces of continuation are not arrested or overcome . . . when the last allusions are to beginnings or to unstable events, and when concluding assertions are qualified and tentative."[77] The two marriages do not doubly bind the ending of Trollope's *roman-fleuve*; they undermine each other, presenting two futures for the society he depicts. As resolution, they cancel each other out, suggesting even in the final passages the recurrence of the narrative pattern of the *roman-fleuve*, the oscillation of the same-and-the-different.

Critics have often found that although marriage is a conventional closing event in the novel, Trollope's terminal marriages work against closure. According to apRoberts, these marriages provide only tentative closures: "Trollope's last-chapter marriages are generally quite probable, and though they seem like conclusions they do not necessarily make conclusive endings. It is because his endings are not generally "conclusive" that his characters can turn up in sequels, still breathing, aged to the proper degree, still unmistakably themselves."[78] With a few exceptions, apRoberts is correct: the depiction of Silverbridge and Isabel's marriage leaves open the possibility of a sequel. Kincaid maintains that it is the irony of the narrator that subverts the closure usually associated with a marriage: "When a Trollope novel comes to its concluding chapter, there are almost always a few remarks on the general nature of concluding chapters, some wry, even surprisingly bitter comments on the marriages taking place to the effect that marriage is a great anticlimax to what has gone before, and some jocular apologies for boring us all with this conventional detailing of everyone's future. Just as the closed pattern is about to snap shut, the narrator pries it apart here and there, protesting against the notion of fulfillment itself as stagnant and repressive, suggesting that real life has very little resemblance to such neat patterns."[79]

The narrator's protests indicate both his discomfort with nineteenth-century narrative and his latent recognition of the problematic nature of marital fulfillment as closure for his female characters. Moreover, Trollope's technique of reappearing characters allows Lady Laura Kennedy or Marie Goesler Finn to reemerge after seemingly "terminal" marriages: these female characters grow and change and serve new functions in new plots after their marriages. (One significant exception is Alice Vavasor, who is never dramatized after her marriage but referred to only as Mrs. Grey, and who drops out of the subsequent novels.) As with so many of Trollope's independent women, the Palliser females are associated with the *fleuve*, the impulse of continuity in the narrative, resisting closure and termination, the teleology of the masculine plot.

Critics have reacted variously to the conclusion of *The Duke's Children*; a few, like John Hagan, find the ending not "inconclusive and anticlimactic" but believe that when the Duke finally consents to the marriage of Lady Mary and Frank Tregear, he "has exorcised the ghosts of his past forever."[80] For the most part, even those satisfied with the novel's ending find it to be problematic. McMaster, for example, argues that "both the older generation and the younger move hopefully but faithfully forwards towards a future that is filled with promise"; however, in the outcome of Mabel's plot—remaining a spinster and leaving the Grex family, even more ancient than the Pallisers, without issue— she also finds a troubling contrast to the weddings in the two final chapters.[81] Morse, in her feminist reading of the Pallisers, finds that the stories of both Mabel and Glencora undercut an otherwise comic ending: "The sense of comic fulfillment at the end of the series is undermined not only by the tragic fate of Mabel Grex, but by the memory of Glencora, whose dissatisfied ghost broods over the weddings of her children."[82] Although the resolution of Mabel Grex's story is in tension with the happy endings of the other youthful protagonists' plots, this tension is also a component of the two Palliser marriages, each suggesting in a different way the diminution or transformation of the aristocracy. Indeed, not only is the society presented infiltrated by foreigners and gentry, but British aristocrats such as Mabel lack the vitality even to sustain their order without renewal. Mabel's story confirms the Duke's realization that an aristocracy "of the very best" must undergo modification if it is not to degenerate as do the Grex family and estate.

The ending to the Palliser *roman-fleuve* is inconclusive because of the narrator's recalcitrance, the double ending, and the Duke's own ambivalence. It is Palliser's reassessment of Tregear (and of the introduction of nouveaux—Americans or penniless English gentry—into the aristocracy) that constitutes the final passage in *The Duke's Children*: " 'But now I will accept that as courage which I before regarded as arrogance' " (633). McMaster finds evidence of the Duke's change in his "hilarity" at Mary and Tregear's wedding: "He has been able to change and progress from the middle-aged widower obsessed with the need to repeat his past to the tolerant father-in-law who will make a benign and even jocular grandfather," while Morse believes the statement "surely must indicate a kind of thematic closure to the novel, and perhaps to the entire Palliser series."[83] However, although the end of the series depicts Palliser's acceptance, the tone of his acceptance is bitter and the value of what he accepts is dubious. One must question the narrator's interpretation of the Duke's behavior at the second wedding. The mood of Plantagenet Palliser, an almost tragically sober man dedicated to blue books and given to discourses about the value of pattens, is never, throughout the six Palliser volumes, described by such an epithet as "hilarity." The narrator is either mistaken (and the pronouncements of Trollope's narrator have often been questioned)[84] or he has misinterpreted a forced gaiety.

What Palliser has realized cannot lead him to "hilarity": both politically (in *The Prime Minister*) and personally (in *The Duke's Children*) he has been ultimately ineffectual. His plaint, as he "accepts" Silverbridge's marriage to an American, is that of a man whose humanity and sense of justice yield him no choice: " 'My opinion is to go for nothing,—in anything!' The Duke as he said this knew that he was expressing aloud a feeling which should have been restrained within his own bosom. It was natural that there should have been such plaints. The same suffering must be encountered in regard to Tregear and his daughter. In every way he had been thwarted. In every direction he was driven to yield" (563–64). This eloquent expression of suffering reveals a tragic resolution that contests the novel's comic ending. Moreover, it suggests that characters grow but that the essential self remains constant. As the *roman-fleuve* comes to a close, the outcome of plot events seems predetermined by character: from the opening of the series, Palliser is depicted as an earnest man, acting in good faith, accepting the inevitable, whether it be his wife's romantic indiscretions or his own political demise. As he bows to inevitable social change, represented by his daughter's marriage, Palliser's essential nature prevails.

Trollope's novels often end with chapters entitled "Conclusion," where the narrator protests against "the custom of the thing" all the while he scrupulously adheres to the custom.[85] The "jocular apologies" of Trollope's narrator reveal his insight about readers' reactions to narrative long before the emergence of narratology and reader-response criticism. At the beginning of the last chapter of *Phineas Redux*, the second novel in the Palliser series, the narrator glibly asserts, "There remains to us the very easy task of collecting together the ends of the thread of our narrative, and tying them into a simple knot, so that there may be no unravelling" (357). The conclusion that follows supplies the most typically Victorian closure among all the Palliser novels, as the narrator sums up the future fates of all major characters. When Phineas Finn and Adelaide Palliser are each married off, plot and subplot are resolved; the knot seems securely fastened. However, the last paragraph of the novel subverts a neat closure by presenting the possibility of continuing the larger Palliser story: the new Duke is said to be "on the very *eve* of success with the decimal coinage" and the use of progressive verbs, "his hair is *becoming* grey, and his back is *becoming* bent," suggesting that the process of the protagonist's evolution is ongoing rather than completed (360; italics added). The last line of this novel suggests both the stasis of character identity and the continuation of Glencora's story: "Nothing will ever change the Duchess." This is the narratorial self-subversion that Torgovnick finds in many Victorian novelists, who "have a curious way of dismissing the endings to their novels even as they unroll."[86]

The narrator's subversion of his own conclusion in *Phineas Redux* suggests not only the provisional closure necessary for an inner volume of the *roman-fleuve*, but also a dissatisfaction with conventional closure: a marriage (or even two) is not an ending in real life; more important, ending itself is antithetical to the narrative "desires" the novelist stimulates. For Trollope it is *sustaining* the narrative that is a challenge: "What novelist, what Fielding, what Scott, what George Sand, or Sue, or Dumas, can impart an interest to the last chapter of his fictitious history? Promises of two children and superhuman happiness are of no avail, nor assurance of extreme respectability carried to an age far exceeding that usually allotted to mortals. The sorrows of our heroes and heroines, they are your delight, oh public: their sorrows, or their sins, or their absurdities; not their virtues, good sense, and consequent rewards. When we begin to tint our final pages with *couleur de rose*, as in accordance with fixed rule we must do, we altogether extinguish our own powers of pleasing."[87]

Trollope, thus, evinces both his frustration with affirmative Victorian endings and his awareness of the dynamics inherent in reading narrative: it is conflict that stimulates readers, not resolution. Closure (especially the happy ending) is static and, ultimately, extrinsic to narrative. The impossibility of an organic and stimulating ending is evident in the extensive *roman-fleuve*, revealing a problem with narrative endings more generally: "The suspensive and dispensive logic of narrative is such that an effective closure—no matter how naturally or organically it emerges from the story—always stands in a discontinuous (or negative) relation to it."[88] Since traditional narrative is sequential and forward-moving (if not always linear and chronological), then closure, the termination of that sequence, must be external to it. The discontinuous nature of closure is especially problematic in the *roman-fleuve*, a genre motivated by an oscillating and reiterative narrative. The difficulty the *roman-fleuve* finds in closing is seen in its tendency to repeat, even at its end, as it does from the beginning.

Moreover, the contesting relation of the two concluding passages at the end of *The Duke's Children* reveals a dissatisfaction with conventional closural devices (such as marriage), a dissatisfaction that is inherent in the *roman-fleuve* itself, as it is in an *écriture féminine*. In affixing two endings, Trollope attempts to counteract the process orientation of the *roman-fleuve* by imposing boundaries, however arbitrary, on a narrative. The problematic resolution in the stories of Mabel Grex and Laura Standish demonstrates that Trollope can conceive of female endings other than marriage or death. Except for Mabel, the women do indeed marry or die, but the presentation of multiple and contrasting options suggests the "both/and vision" DuPlessis has associated with the Etruscans, an enigmatic and pluralistic feminine discourse. Transcending the "either/or dichotomized universe," it subverts binary oppositions. Trollope does not "write beyond the ending," as DuPlessis describes the project of twentieth-century women writers, yet his self-contesting endings do "say different things, not settle on one, which is final," as characteristic of DuPlessis's Etruscan language.[89]

Trollope's problematic endings reveal his proclivity to break with the teleology of the traditional linear plot. As in Victorian novels by women writers, such as Charlotte Brontë's *Jane Eyre*, his ending also reveals a text that is ideologically unstable. This instability produces an inconclusive ending, but one that is appropriate for the theme and form of the Pallisers. As Ricoeur observes, "An inconclusive ending suits a work that raises by design a problem the author considers to be unsolvable. It is nonetheless a deliberate and a concerted ending. . . . Its inconclusiveness declares in a way the irresolution of the problem posed."[90] Trollope cannot completely reject the conventional novel's resolution, but his contested ending reveals the dynamics inherent in the *roman-fleuve* and foreshadows his feminist successors' ultimate rejection of closure. The convergence of innovative and feminist narrative features often functions to foreground the limitations of his women characters' options and the tragedy of their failure to realize their full potential in society. His deployment of such features to emphasize feminist themes (such as women's dissatisfaction) also points to a significant convergence of gender and genre in the Pallisers.

While Trollope's nascent sympathy for feminism went undetected by most of his early twentieth-century critics, modernist novelist–critics like Richardson and Rebecca West perceived this strain in his novels much earlier: "Trollope was a feminist," West claims.[91] Nardin locates the shift in Trollope's treatment of women in the period concurrent with the beginnings of the Palliser series (1864–65): "between the writing of *Barchester Towers* in 1855 and that of *The Belton Estate* in 1865," leading him to create feminist subtexts in his novels.[92] The reason for Trollope's transformation and his enlightenment, relative to his male colleagues, remains uncertain. Looking to the novelist's biography, it is tempting to argue that it was the example of his capable novelist/ mother, Francis Trollope, or his friendship with the American feminist Kate Flint that made him a secret sympathizer with women's struggles against patriarchy. A psychological explanation might look to an identification rooted in his own painful social marginalization because of his family's poverty and his father's instability, but a similar childhood experience had no such feminist influence on Charles Dickens. Clearly, Trollope exhibits the kind of bisexuality, a highly individualized gender neither androgynous nor unisex, that Cixous advocates: "For there are some men who do not repress their femininity, some women who, more or less strongly, inscribe their masculinity."[93] The source of his narrative innovations is less elusive: Trollope's dissatisfaction with the artificiality and limitations of the conventional novel is explicitly stated both in his novels and in his autobiography. In searching for a form that would write beyond the conventional novel, Trollope detected the potential of those narrative features designated feminine and produced a new form in British literature. Trollope's *roman-fleuve* exaggerates narrative features of the baggy Victorian novel, creating a genre that, paradoxically, points forward to modern fiction. By acknowledging the innovations of Trollope's Pallisers, we unearth a precursor for modernist experiments with narrative in a genre sometimes denigrated for its outmoded conventions.

Chapter Three

Dorothy Richardson's
Pilgrimage
Writing the Consummate Flow

Flooding the boundaries of the novel form, *Pilgrimage*, published over the twenty-three-year period from 1915 to 1938 (with the final install-ment appearing posthumously in 1967), exemplifies a full development of the *écriture féminine* prefigured by Trollope's proto–*roman-fleuve*. Richardson, it has been argued, "not only originated a type of sequence novel but produced the most extreme example of it."[1] She carried the form of the *roman-fleuve*, characterized by scope and flow, to its natu-ral end: stream of consciousness narrative. Significantly, the innovations of Richardson's modernism resemble the features of an *écriture fémi-nine*. DuPlessis argues that there is an inherent connection between mod-ernism, gender, and form: "In women's writing, as in modernist, there is an encyclopedic impulse, in which the writer invents a new and total culture, symbolized by and announced in a long work, like the modern long poem"; Alice Jardine views modernism as "a search for what has been 'left out,' de-emphasized, hidden or denied articulation,"[2] a de-scription that also serves as an apt summary of the aesthetics of *Pil-grimage*. This chapter demonstrates the affinity between the form of the *roman-fleuve* and *écriture féminine* in *Pilgrimage*; each section con-siders some narrative feature(s) of the genre and draws a connection be-tween them and gendered writing. Richardson exploits the formal and narrative characteristics of the *roman-fleuve*—its scope, its propensity for narrative gaps, its reiterative and indirect narrative, and its evasion of beginnings and endings—to create an *écriture féminine*.

In the thirteen volumes of her experimental *roman-fleuve*, Richardson deliberately and self-consciously creates language she perceives as feminine. Ever since Virginia Woolf enigmatically praised Richardson for developing the "psychological sentence of the female gender," critics have sought both to explicate Woolf's statement in relation to Richardson's fiction and to define a difference between the writing of men and women.[3] An *écriture féminine* is created not only by style but also by the form chosen or developed. Contemporary theorists' observation that an *écriture féminine* is not limited to women's writing is anticipated by Richardson in her preface to the omnibus edition of *Pilgrimage*, when she praises Charles Dickens and James Joyce for writing "feminine prose" that is "unpunctuated, moving from point to point without formal obstructions" (12). This observation is relevant to Dickens, Joyce, and Richardson not only because of their preference for the long, multi-claused sentence, but also because it suggests the narrative of the *roman-fleuve*, particularly Richardson's *Pilgrimage*, as it evolved from the Victorian novel. She describes the individually titled volumes as "chapters," emphasizing her conception of the work as an entity—as one massive novel.

Richardson is motivated to create a meganovel by her dissatisfaction with the spatial and temporal limitations of previous novelistic tradition. As with Trollope's narrator, her protagonist, Miriam Henderson, is frustrated with the insufficiency of narrative to communicate the complexity of reality: "Why would people insist upon talking about things—when nothing can ever be communicated?" (*Interim* 306). Both narrators express a contextualist and encyclopedic conception of narrative in that they believe the most satisfactory form would be the most complete, the most comprehensive. Further, the alternative form Richardson creates is motivated by the narrator's desire to fill in the gaps left by the traditional realist novel—which, Miriam makes clear, embodies a tradition she rejects as masculine: "The torment of *all* novels is what is left out. The moment you are aware of it, there is torment in them. Bang, bang, bang, on they go, these men's books, like an L.C.C. tram, yet unable to make you forget them, the authors, for a moment" (*DLH* 239). Miriam often uses the train metaphor to describe the linearity and narrow teleology of patriarchal thought, writing, and narrative. The writing she proposes violates expectations about plot and would more accurately reflect the rich complexity of perception: "Poured chaotically out it would sound to them like the ravings of insanity. All contradictory, up and down, backwards and forwards, all true. The things they would grasp, here and there, would misrepresent herself and the whole picture" (*Interim* 306). Miriam is stymied in her early efforts to write within the patriarchal tradition, but she realizes that any attempt to create a feminine expression will be misinterpreted as disorder and insanity—a legitimate fear, given Richardson's own experience with critics who complained that the writer had an abnormal mind.[4] An anonymous 1938 review in *Time*, evaluating the twelve-volume edition, concluded with the statement that Richardson had "reduc[ed] the stream to a trickle, merely furnish[ing] psychologists with another hard case to work on."[5]

Miriam's distrust of language that reduces reality to a false consistency or to a linear narrative suggests Irigaray's argument that women's writing emerges from their diffuse, multiple sexuality, creating a narrative distinct from the traditional model: "It really involves a different economy more than anything else, one that upsets the linearity of a project, undermines the goal-object of a desire, diffuses the polarization toward a single pleasure, disconcerts fidelity to a single discourse."[6] Although Richardson seems unaware of any physical or sexual basis for this narrative "economy" (many critics and reviewers have commented on or complained about the asexual nature of *Pilgrimage* and its protagonist), she shares with Irigaray the conviction that women must create a feminine form and style. In developing a narrative appropriate to her subject matter, one that would overcome the inadequacies of traditional narrative, Richardson privileges inner reality—an emphasis that suggests a relation between the modernist stream of consciousness narrative and what she defines as specifically feminine qualities of thought and discourse. The insistence on process, on being and consciousness rather than activity, is expressed in the diffuse and flowing style of *Pilgrimage*, exemplifying Richardson's argument that prose should be unpunctuated.

As a writer, Richardson's protagonist rejects the emphasis on plot because it is end-oriented, and in a letter to her sister, Miriam attacks the unsophisticated hoax of suspense narratives: "People thought it was silly, almost wrong to look at the end of a book. But if it spoilt a book, there was something wrong about the book. If it was finished and the interest gone when you know who married who, what was the good of reading at all? It was a sort of trick, a sell. Like a puzzle that was no more fun when you had found it out. There was something more in books than that. [. . .] Then you read books to find the author! That was it. That was the difference . . . that was how one was different from most people. . . . Dear Eve; I have just discovered that I don't read books for the story, but as a psychological study of the author . . . [.]" (*H* 384).[7] This rejection of story or plot (what happens) in favor of essence ("the author") is, of course, the impetus behind modernist stream of consciousness, the narrative technique that Richardson herself pioneered in England. *Pointed Roofs*, the first volume of *Pilgrimage*, was begun in 1913 and published in 1915, a fact often obscured by the more celebrated achievement of Proust, Joyce, and Woolf. Contemporary feminists' new recognition of early women experimental writers necessitates that we redefine the origins of modernism, taking into account achievements such as Gertrude Stein's *Three Lives*, published in 1909—before *A la recherche du temps perdu* (1913) or *A Portrait of the Artist as a Young Man* (1916).[8]

Richardson's aesthetic subverts the forward-moving plot of the traditional novel. Brewer argues that narratologists conceive of plot as a "discourse of male desire recounting itself through the narrative of adventure, project, enterprise, and conquest."[9] Aristotle may have been the first to conceive of narrative as a structure with a well-defined beginning, middle, and end, but it is the nineteenth-century dramatic theorist Freytag whose language most clearly reveals the male model of sexuality behind this pyramidic plot, which begins with tumescent "rising action," peaks in a "climax," and ends with the flaccid "falling action."[10] The narrative dynamics of Richardson's thirteen volumes, however, subvert the phallocentric emphasis on a forward-moving plot and Brooks's idea that we read "*for* the plot," with an emphasis on process rather than destination. This is characteristic of the *roman-fleuve* and evident in the works of Trollope and Powell—but the tendency is most pronounced in Richardson's feminist *roman-fleuve*.

Richardson, like most French theorists today, would reject the appellation "feminist," just as she denied that Miriam Henderson was a feminist.[11] Richardson's denial must be evaluated in several contexts, however. First, this allegation about her protagonist was made on a highly charged emotional occasion. Critics had poorly reviewed *Clear Horizon* because, her husband Alan Odle argued, they took Miriam for a feminist.[12] Furthermore, as Hanscombe remarks, for Richardson the term would have evoked "those who were engaged in the struggle for suffrage and other forms of social and political equality."[13] While Richardson treats this sort of feminist sympathetically in *Pilgrimage* (as Amabel and other suffragettes are jailed), Miriam is obviously a different kind of feminist; Richardson's heroine classifies her own position as an "intermittent feminism" (*DH* 504). Amabel rejects political activism after she marries and becomes a mother, but Miriam, never active in feminist organizations, continues to examine and reexamine what it means to be a woman until the last sentence of *Pilgrimage*. She anticipates what has recently been termed "the woman centered perspective," which views "male experience as different, or even deviant, from what in this view is considered central, or normal."[14] Moreover, Richardson's hostility toward men, as with that of her protagonist, is a response to misogyny, to being devalued as a woman under patriarchy.

The correlation between Richardson's deployment of an *écriture féminine* and a feminist ideology is perhaps best defined by Irigaray: "This 'style' does not privilege sight; instead, it takes each figure back to its source, which is among other things *tactile*. It comes back in touch with itself in that origin without ever constituting in it, constituting itself in it, as some sort of unity. *Simultaneity* is its 'proper' aspect—a proper(ty) that is never fixed in its possible identity-to-self of some form or other. It is always *fluid*, without neglecting the characteristics of fluids that are difficult to idealize: those rubbings between two infinitely near neighbors that create a dynamics. Its 'style' resists and explodes every firmly established form, figure, idea or concept."[15] Thus, the style of *écriture féminine* originates in the positively reconstructed female body, according to Irigaray—the fluidity traditionally associated with women corresponds to their multiple erotic response and is rendered as a synchronous (rather than linear) narrative dynamics. Women's sexuality is autonomously tactile in a different way than men's: "Woman 'touches herself' all the time, and moreover no one can forbid her to do so, for her genitals are formed of two lips in continuous contact."[16] Irigaray's description notes the inherent subversiveness of this prose: it is ever moving, always in tension, engaged in an explosion of traditions. Privileging the sexual and narrative traits designated feminine, Irigaray draws on the deprivileged terms of binary oppositions. Richardson's feminism is clearly aligned with the thinking of Irigaray and Cixous (though she is a late Victorian in her reticence about the body) as she espouses a linguistic feminism—an *écriture féminine*. However, the strategies she advocates, in valorizing the feminine, clearly are political in addressing the fundamental feminist issue of female subjectivity.

After years of neglect and deprecating "phallic criticism," several excellent studies of Richardson in the 1980s and 1990s examine her feminism and/or take a feminist approach to her work. DuPlessis's chapter on Richardson, Hurston, and Walker in *Writing Beyond the Ending* shows how, as a twentieth-century women's novel, *Pilgrimage* creates an alternative "ending" for its protagonist, beyond the destinies of marriage or death reserved for nineteenth-century female protagonists of women's novels. Hanscombe's *The Art of Life* emphasizes the way Richardson's "perception of the distinctiveness of female consciousness in turn gave rise to the evolution of an experimental technique of fiction"; Hanscombe is concerned, as I am, with the genre of *Pilgrimage*, which she defines as an example of "autobiographical fiction," a genre that overlaps with the *roman-fleuve*; as subgenres of the novel they are not mutually exclusive. Hanscombe also analyzes Richardson's use of a feminine language, and defines what she calls Richardson's "Bi-polar world view," resulting from the disparity of male and female consciousness.[17] The first critical studies to situate Richardson in the context of an *écriture féminine* are Ellen G. Friedman and Miriam Fuchs's *Breaking the Sequence* and Friedman's "'Utterly Other Discourse': The Anticanon of Experimental Women Writers from Dorothy Richardson to Christine Brooke-Rose"; the book-length study places Richardson in the "first generation" of twentieth-century women writers whose experimental texts develop "radical forms—nonlinear, non-hierarchal, and decentering," which constitute "a way of writing the feminine."[18] In their introductory chapter, Friedman and Fuchs note the similarity between the project of these writers and the writing called for by French feminists who promote an *écriture féminine*. Jean Radford also views Richardson as a "precursor of *écriture féminine*" and finds "a series of remarkable correspondences, theoretical and stylistic, between the text of *Pilgrimage* and Cixous's writing." However, Radford does not find the *roman-fleuve* a true example of the writing promoted by the contemporary French feminists because it does not "explicitly engage in psychoanalysis."[19]

Specifically informed by the work of French feminists as well as narratology and reader-response theory, this chapter provides further theoretical contexts for discussing Richardson's gendered discourse and genre. No published study to date analyzes in any detail Richardson's place in the development of the *roman-fleuve* and her use of the narrative resources of this genre. Although Richardson's form has not always been perceived as ideologically charged, she creates and advocates a position that would clearly be considered feminist today, though not by any means one that all feminists would support. Richardson's *Pilgrimage*, which may be read as a discourse on difference as well as an experimental novel, explores the implications of gender in language and society.

✥ Inscribing the Flood of Female Plenitude

I am spacious, singing flesh.
—Hélène Cixous, "The Laugh of the Medusa"

The scope and massiveness of the *roman-fleuve*, which make it a form especially conducive to the profuse, expansive style of an *écriture féminine*, facilitate Richardson's extensive colloquies and exemplifications of gendered discourse. She associates women's intellect with images of plenitude and magnitude: "The knowledge of women is larger, bigger, deeper, less wordy and clever than that of men" (*Tun* 188). Her male and female characters and their respective discourses throughout *Pilgrimage* embody a contrast between the reductive cleverness of men and the capacious, intuitive understanding of women. Miriam criticizes male language for reductiveness; it does not expand thought but binds by moving "from *word* to *word*" (*RL* 278). This critique of patriarchal discourse is a corollary to Richardson's analysis and rejection of the traditional dynamics of plot. The feminine narrative (like Woolf's "psychological sentence of the female gender") is characterized by comprehensive and synchronic development. In contrast to the fragmented view of men, whose "lives are passed among scraps," women are able to see "everything simultaneously" because they "see in terms of life" (*RL* 393).

Richardson's aesthetic illustrates Cixous's claim that woman's language "does not contain, it carries; it does not hold back, it makes possible"; her "writing can only keep going, without ever inscribing or discerning contours."[20] Even the ironically depicted Eleanor Dear, who uses her femininity in a predatory fashion, demonstrates a superior creativity in her "power of creating an endless present"; it is in this respect that Miriam dubs her "a great artist" (*RL* 284). One of the best examples of the phallocentric narrative dynamics that Richardson rejects is found in the lecture on Cervantes prepared by Mrs. Bailey's French boarder, Lahitte. When asked to critique his intonation, Miriam is horrified: "The sentences grew in length, each one climbing, through a host of dependent clauses, small sharp hammer blows of angry assertion, and increasing in tone to a climax of defiance flung down from a height that left no further possibility but a descent to a level quiet deduction. [. . .] But the succeeding sentence came fresh to the attack, crouching, gathering up the fury of its forerunner, leaping forward, dipping through still longer dependent loops, accumulating, swelling and expanding to even greater emphasis and volume" (*Deadlock* 116). Miriam's evaluation collapses terms traditionally used to describe male sexual response with those used to designate plot—"climbing," "increasing," "climax," "gathering," "swelling," "expanding"—and associates this discourse with that of warfare ("blows," "angry," "assertion," "leaping," "defiance," "attack," "crouching," "fury"). Lahitte's presentation is characterized by the same traits as the ejaculatory plot, building to a climax that, in Miriam's imagery, is characterized by an angry violence. Implicitly, this discourse is characterized by the same dynamics at any level—sentence, paragraph, narrative.

In contrast to the aggressive, violent movement of phallocentric discourse, Miriam endorses passivity; she deconstructs the binary opposition activity/passivity. Activity, that forward-driving force she associates with males such as Lahitte and Hypo G. Wilson (Richardson's fictionalized portrait of H. G. Wells), interferes with the receptivity essential to understanding of the self and the world. In her 1938 foreword to *Pilgrimage*, Richardson quotes Goethe's "manifesto" in *Wilhelm Meister* to support her preference for the passive protagonist: in a novel the hero "should be acted upon"; s/he should be a "retarding personalit[y]" (11). It is not only characters, however, but also writers who must be passive and receptive. While correcting the artificial style of Lahitte's vapid lecture, Miriam has a revelation about herself as a writer: "Sitting over there, forgetting, she had *let go* . . . and found something. And waking again had seen distant things in their right proportions. But *leaving go*, not going through life clenched, would mean *losing oneself, passing through, not driving in, ceasing to affect* and be affected. But the forgetfulness was itself a more real life, if it made life disappear and then show only as a manageable space and at last only as an indifferent distance" (*Deadlock* 135; emphasis mine). Miriam privileges passivity and rejects the phallocentric consciousness—aggressively ever driving in, driving forward. It is significant that this passage, associating the masculine thought process with sexual penetration, uses the word "clench," which is also used in a later scene to characterize Miriam's response to her unpropitious sexual union with Hypo Wilson, another kind of attack. Her ability for "living," what Hypo calls her "agreeable loafing that leads no where" is contrasted to his "ceaselessly becoming for" (*DLH* 220), the preposition at the end emphasizing the dangling, futile nature of a goal orientation without the self-awareness and spiritual understanding that Miriam seeks. As she says, "Realization takes time and solitude" (*DLH* 238), a statement that explains her misanthropy, her need for a "clear horizon" free of personal involvement.

Through the dialectical conversations of Miriam and Hypo and through Miriam's response to them, Richardson contrasts the approach and motivations of male and female writers: "Miriam recalled her impressions of the authors she knew. It was true that those were their effects and the great differences between them. How did he come to know all about it, and to put it into words? Did the authors know when they did it? She passionately hoped not. If they did, it was a trick and spoilt books. Rows and rows of 'fine' books; nothing but men sitting in studies, doing something cleverly, being very important, 'men of letters'; and looking out for approbation. If writing meant that, it was not worth doing" (*Tun* 130). Throughout *Pilgrimage*, the word "clever" is invariably used for men's outward-directed efforts to impress. The "clever" male writer, seeking fame, is epitomized by Hypo G. Wilson, the antithesis of the receptive Miriam. In conversation, Wilson's propensity is for "asking questions by saying them—statements" (*Tun* 110). In contrast to this blind assertiveness, Miriam believes that the writer should be intuitive and inward-directed. As Hypo recommends that she write a novel, Miriam's comments reveal her motives for writing and illuminate the formal choices Richardson herself makes in *Pilgrimage*. Women must write to fill in the blanks left in the male tradition of realism: "A lifetime might be well spent in annotating the male novelists, filling out the vast oblivion in them, especially in the painfully comic or the painfully tragic and in the satirists" (*DLH* 240). Although Richardson denies that her protagonist is a feminist, Miriam's critique recognizes the ideological implications of the power structure embodied in discourse. In one of her numerous debates about gender difference with Michael Shatov, Miriam explains the significance of the digressions she associates with women's language: " 'Well, men arguing always look like that, to women. That's why women always go off at a tangent; because they reply not to what men *say* but to what they *mean*, which is to *score a point*, and which *anybody* can do, with practice, and while they hold on to the point they mean to score, they are revealed, under all sorts of circumstances, all sorts of things about them are as plain as a pike-staff, to a woman, and the results of these things; so that she suddenly finds herself saying something that sounds quite irrelevant, but isn't'" (*Deadlock* 170). The digressive, divergent *roman-fleuve* is the ideal form to express the vast inner space within—the seemingly irrelevant that is most relevant, the tangent that addresses the fundamental reality.

As *Pilgrimage* is a bildungsroman and a *Künstlerroman*, the cumulative process orientation of the *roman-fleuve* dramatizes the heroine's gradual and indirect progression to maturity; she moves, circuitously and arduously, as a woman and an artist, from the mistaken desire to emulate men's writing to finding her own woman's voice. Miriam gradually realizes she speaks two languages, anticipating feminist arguments that because women are members of two cultures—they are part of both the dominant male culture and the majority female "subculture"—their writing is often double-voiced, a characteristic of *écriture féminine*. In *The Tunnel* Miriam evokes the Janus figure to reveal the relation between this gender identification and language: "I am something between a man and a woman; looking both ways. But to pretend one did not see through a man's voice would be treachery" (187). Miriam must transcend this divided discourse, however, and develop her own feminine language. Her discovery anticipates the injunction of Cixous and other contemporary French feminists: "Woman must write woman. And man, man."[21] The emphasis on the process of Miriam's gradual acquisition of a feminine discourse explains one troublesome feature of Miriam's character: her hatred of women in the early volumes and her descriptions of herself as a man.

In the first three novels, for example, the protagonist emulates—to varying degrees at different points—the phallocentric discourse that she has acquired from Pater, from whom she seeks approval as she tries to play the role of the much-wished-for son in a family of daughters. The imitation of this voice, however, is at odds with Miriam's feminine being, and until she overcomes the desire to emulate the patriarchal discourse that is both familiar to her as a member of the culture and foreign to her as a *woman* within that culture, she will be in discord with her true nature. As she mentally evaluates her response to the letter of Bob Greville, Miriam reveals this linguistic gender conflict: "He won't expect me to have that kind of handwriting, like his own, but stronger. He'll admire it on the page and then hear a man's voice, pater's voice talking behind it and not like it. Me. He'll be a little afraid of it. She felt her hard self standing there as she wrote, and shifted her feet a little, raising one heel from the ground, trying to feminize her attitude; but her hat was hard against her forehead, her clothes would not flow . . ." (H 418-19). Although Miriam purportedly congratulates herself on her ability not only to imitate this language but also to speak it more forcefully than a man, she has begun to realize that her feminine being resists adopting the discourse of "Pater," her appropriately named dominating father: the conflict is reflected in her involuntary rigidity, a male trait—her clothes will not "flow," her hat feels "hard." In this passage Richardson defines gender distinctions in terms of conventional metaphors of male hardness and feminine flow, acknowledging binary oppositions, while at the same time her protagonist tries to undermine male authority.

Furthermore, Miriam's subversive stance, her desire to disconcert Greville, foreshadows her subsequent rejection of patriarchal discourse. In *The Tunnel*, Miriam's ambivalent double-voiced discourse is revealed in her appropriation of a masculine strategy to demean Hypo G. Wilson after their initial meeting. She describes him in a reductive simile, claiming she no longer fears the "great man" once she has seen him, since he looks "like a grocer's assistant" (110). The name given this character ("Hype-o") also degrades this prototype of male logic; he's a huckster of the type Wells himself satirized in the portrait of Teddy Ponderevo in *Tono-Bungay*. Fromm points out that "hypo" is the fixing agent used to develop a photograph, a derivation that also suggests the static defining quality Richardson associates with the male mind; Showalter notes that the name literally signifies "less than or subordinated to" and connotes "hippos and hypocrisy."[22] *The Tunnel* dramatizes Miriam's increasing awareness that imitation of phallocentric discourse will not raise her above the qualities she despises in women; she realizes that "clever" women are mere parrots, mouthing "things that sounded like quotations from men" (251).

Although Miriam is the work's protagonist and the thirteen novels of the *roman-fleuve* chart her uneven journey to self-awareness, in many ways her friend Amabel is foregrounded as the model for an *écriture féminine*. Miriam encounters a series of women—Fraulein Pfaff, Eleanor Dear, Miss Holland, and Amabel—who function not only as the *roman-fleuve*'s reiteration of cases, the same-and-the-different, but also as avatars of what Miriam might become without the financial security provided by a father or husband, an adaptation of the nineteenth-century female bildungsroman convention. Through her relationship with Amabel, Miriam receives an initiation that teaches her to speak her silenced experience; according to Hanscombe, Amabel "reveal[s] Miriam's inner, unconscious being to herself."[23] She is repeatedly cast into female communities—her home of four sisters, Waldstrasse, Wordsworth School—but it is only after Miriam's encounter with Amabel that she is able to fully appreciate the feminine, making the final renunciation of Pater's misogyny that is necessary to her complete self-acceptance and self-awareness. The relationship provides a woman-to-woman identification essential if Miriam is to discover the value of her feminine self, to transcend the schism of the gendered-Janus figure.

Amabel is an appropriate teacher in this respect because feminine discourse has been "so long already habitual in this girl's young life" (*DLH* 216). Miriam and Amabel intuitively recognize and pay homage to the feminine in each other: "The girl's reality appealing to her own, seeing and feeling it ahead of her own seeings or feelings that yet responded, acknowledged as she emerged from her reading, in herself and the girl, with them when they were together, somehow between them in the mysterious interplay of their two beings, the reality she had known for so long alone, brought out into life" (*DLH* 217). Miriam claims women need this kind of "homage" to become fully developed: "Women [. . .] want recognition of themselves, of what they are and represent, before they can come fully to birth" (*DLH* 230). While the relationship is one of mutual admiration, it is not one of complete equality; at different times the women manipulate (thus attempting to dominate) each other: Amabel initiates and insists upon the friendship; Miriam finally disposes of Amabel by choosing for her a husband, her own former suitor. The friendship is most significant, however, as a landmark in Miriam's progress toward becoming a woman writer; it is defined as a gendered linguistic experience.

One of the most revealing early scenes involving Amabel is in *Dawn's Left Hand*, when Miriam receives a letter from her new acquaintance, a sort of love letter that marks the beginning of this friendship with a visual representation of feminine discourse. The letter exemplifies the gaps of women's silence—that which cannot be spoken. In Amabel's distinctive handwriting each individual letter as well as the strokes of each letter are surrounded by blank space and must be "put together by the eye as it went along" (214), also suggesting the seemingly fragmented visual appearance of Richardson's text. Suzette Henke's description of Richardson's style suggests that the novelist's own syntax is similar to the writing she attributes to Amabel: "If Richardson's style is rife with circumlocutions and suspended participles, it is because her language suggests the mental process of labored self-discovery. Her syntax implies interior distance: it reflects the gulf that divides one person from another, the reader from the author, and the ego from the thoughts that it formulates."[24]

Amabel writes in a genre often considered feminine; her letter is a feminine discourse written for a female audience with the shared knowledge necessary to comprehend a document filled with gaps. In this sense, an *écriture féminine* surpasses the purported completion of conventional writing. Amabel's writing, which Miriam also describes as "hieroglyphs," is nonlinear, creating an image in itself, in contrast to phallocentric writing, which moves "from *word* to *word*." For example, Miriam contemplates her friend's transcription of the word *Egypt*, a word she finds ugly but made beautiful in Amabel's gap-filled script, where the letters do not touch: "Beautiful, yes, and suggesting all its associations more powerfully than did the sight of the word written closely" (*DLH* 216).[25] The gaps in Amabel's handwriting speak by affecting the way the words they surround are perceived. "Between each letter of each word was as much space as between the words they were supposed to compose. Yet each was expressive, before its meaning appeared. Each letter, carelessly dashed down, under pressure of feeling, was a picture, framed in the surrounding space" (215). Miriam's experience reading Amabel's letter provides a sensual and aesthetic revelation of an *écriture féminine* that writes woman's body: "Each word, each letter, was Amabel, was one of the many poses of her body" (215). As Jane Gallop observes, "Love letters have always been written from the body in connection with love"; Radford calls it "a scrutiny of the body of the beloved."[26]

Richardson's *écriture féminine* undermines, reverses, or deconstructs traditional binary oppositions, privileging those qualities usually denigrated because they are attributed to women. Admittedly, this strategy risks instating an oppression of men by women; Domna Stanton, skeptical of a reversal that privileges the feminine, warns of the process whereby "the feminine, the devalued term in phallologic, becomes the superior value, but the system of binary oppositions remains the same."[27] Yet *if* binary distinctions are characteristic of our thought, as Richardson seems to believe, her strategy provides a means of destabilizing and equalizing their hierarchy. Richardson, however, employs the contextualistic and reiterative narrative of the *roman-fleuve* in a subversive fashion. Miriam and Amabel's relationship, for example, suggests *difference-within-sameness*, two distinct psychological orientations (in some ways a contrast between introvert and extrovert) that are complementary within their shared identity as women.

The historical context of *Pilgrimage*, begun in the early phase of the feminist movement, also provides justification for Richardson's strategies. Miriam's reaction to reading *Lovely Women* (a British antifeminist book that sold 100,000 copies in 1903)[28] in the office of Mr. Leyton, one of her dentist-employers, is to criticize the inherent denigration of the qualities that binary oppositions associate with women: "It ought to be illegal to publish a book by a man without first giving it to a woman to annotate. But what was the answer to men who called women inferior because they had not invented or achieved in science or art? On whose authority had men decided that science and art were greater than anything else? The world could not go on until this question had been answered. Until then, until it had been clearly explained that men were always and always partly wrong in all their ideas, life would be full of poison and secret bitterness. Men fight about their philosophies and religions, there is no certainty in them; but their contempt for women is flawless and unanimous. Even Emerson . . . positive and negative, north and south, male and female . . . why *negative?*" (*Deadlock* 50–51). Although Emerson has been influential for Miriam, she cannot accept the implications of his polarities: his thought is, inevitably, phallocentric. This passage, foreshadowing Cixous's criticism of binary oppositions, asks the same question: Why is woman always the devalued, the "negative" term?

One of Miriam's subversive tactics is to reinterpret the hierarchy and/or to deny the denigrated term in certain binary oppositions. An illustration is the pair "civilization-chaos," which is complicated by an elaborate subterfuge seeming to associate women with both the civilizing impulse and the chaos beneath it. (*Heart of Darkness* is the classic example of this pair, embodied in Kurtz's two women, the idealized "Intended," the white civilizing impulse, and the African woman representing, in the context of some readings, chaos and savagery.) However, Miriam recasts this conventional gendered pair when she associates women with a superior inner civilization, while males are associated with a superficial "civilization of the outside world": "The real inside civilization of women, the one thing that has been in them from the first and is not in the natural man, not made by 'things,' is kept out of it. Women do not need civilization. It is apt to bore them. *But* it can never rise above their level. [. . .] [Men] must leave off imagining themselves a race of gods fighting against chaos, and thinking of women as part of the chaos they have to civilize. There isn't any 'chaos.' Never has been" (*Deadlock* 219). Women, then, embody an inherent civilization that cannot be surpassed by an outer (cultural) civilization, of which men presumptuously imagine themselves the god-like guardians.

Further, Miriam denies the association of chaos and women. Elsewhere she shows that the civilizing impulse associated with women is a projection of *man's* impulse, exposing the polarity as a conflict of impulses within man himself: "The chaos that torments [man] is his own rootless self" (*RL* 280). Kurtz's Intended is merely man's idealization of his own impulse to colonize. If, then, chaos is within man, his exalted impulse to civilize it is mere bravado—a narcissistic conflict with the self. Miriam defends her strategy of denial and reversal in a conversation with Dr. Densley reported to Miss Holland in *The Trap*. Densley, influenced by Shaw, had argued that women want to lose the conflict with their husbands in marriage. Miriam recounts her refutation of Densley and claims that she herself "say[s] things like that on principle. Anything to break up addlepated male complacency" (468).

Richardson overturns traditional associations: she not only reprivileges and denies denigrated terms but also draws imagery from the female sphere, parodying conventional images (handled with bitter irony). One of her principal strategies is to expose the phallacy of metaphors that associate engendering a child with the creation of texts. A context for this tactic is established in the scene where Hypo argues that Miriam should become a mother and a novelist—in that order: "*Middles. Criticism*, which you'd do as other women do fancy-work. *Infant*. NOVEL" (*DLH* 240). In his scheme, writing short nonfiction is incidental work to occupy Miriam during her pregnancy, but only after giving birth to a child will she be able to write a major work of fiction. Hypo's sequence places *himself* in the crucial position prior to Miriam's emergence as a novelist: *he* must impregnate her before she can deliver a novel. Ironically, however, unknown to Hypo, Miriam has already engendered herself as a writer; in *Deadlock* her discovery of a method for translating is described in birth imagery. As she translates, Miriam is "giving birth, as one by one the motley of truths urging its blind movements came recognizably into view [. . .] to see, through the shapeless mass the approaching miracle of shape and meaning" (142). Richardson subverts the traditional associations of the metaphor although, typical of the delaying tactics of the *roman-fleuve*, the parodic treatment of the writer-as-inseminator does not become clear until subsequent episodes. While Hypo seems at first to serve as her literary mentor, the satiric treatment of his role in Miriam's emergence as a writer/mother is evident in two later "engendering" incidents involving Hypo: their uneventful tryst in *Dawn's Left Hand* and her supposed impregnation by him in *Clear Horizon*.

In the first episode, Richardson subverts the traditional seduction plot and creates one of the most ludicrously comic love scenes ever written. The mood is not erotic, but analytical, as Hypo tries to seduce Miriam, a prelude to their eventual intercourse in a subsequent episode, while she contemplates the limitations of his mind. She tells Hypo, "I'm preoccupied with one person" (240)—not with him but with Amabel, with whom she can truly communicate. When they undress, Miriam finds Hypo "not desirable" but "pathetic" and instead of the expected seduction we are given a parody in which the lovers are portrayed as mother and son:

> And as gently she rocked him to and fro the words that came to her lips were so unsuitable that even while she murmured "My little babe, just born," she blushed for them, and steeled herself for his comment.
>
> Letting him go, she found his arms about her in their turn and herself, surprised and not able with sufficient swiftness to contract her expanded being that still seemed to encompass him, rocked unsatisfactorily to and fro while his voice, low and shy and with the inappropriate unwelcome charm in it of the ineffectual gestures of a child learning a game, echoed the unsuitable words. (232)

Here the inexperienced virgin nurtures the male seducer, who ironically becomes a child in her arms, imitating *her* language. (The scene also foreshadows the final scene in *March Moonlight* in which Miriam holds the son of Amabel and Michael in her arms.) The sexually suggestive language describing the embrace of "her expanded being" which "seemed to encompass him" evokes an image of vaginal enclosure—without penetration. As a lover, the putative ladies' man is emasculated, as he will be again when their affair is finally consummated after Hypo slips into her bedroom during a visit to his country house in the next chapter.

In an ironic miscommunication in *Clear Horizon*, the humor is again at the expense of Hypo, who misunderstands Miriam's note to him after they have consummated their affair. During a social evening with Miriam and her friend Amabel, he rushes Amabel into a cab, finding her an intrusive third to what he anticipates will be a discussion of Miriam's plight: he believes her to be "booked for maternity," a "postulant mother" (324). In actuality, Miriam informs Hypo Wilson that her pregnancy was a false alarm, that he *did not* impregnate her at all. His misunderstanding of her note only confirms the impossibility of communication between men and women, as Wilson sardonically notes, echoing Miriam's arguments about gendered discourse: "'For I am disappointed, you know, quite acutely. You had lifted me up into a tremendous exaltation. Miriam, you see, is allusive in a way my more direct, less flexible masculine intelligence doesn't always follow; and when you said you had come down from the clouds, I thought you meant you were experiencing the normal human reaction after a great moment, not that you had been mistaken, but that . . .'" (CH 325). Thus, with hindsight it is obvious that Hypo is ultimately impotent in the sexual scenario he has authored: Miriam is able to become a writer without his insemination. In the reiterative and contextual narrative of the *roman-fleuve* these seemingly unrelated incidents form a complex intertext, creating a brutally ironic commentary on the masculinist conception of engendering a text. Critics have seldom appreciated Richardson's humor in this scene and others like it. Horace Gregory, for example, notes but underestimates Richardson's wicked irony, finding that her "effects are almost never witty; yet throughout *Pilgrimage* there are glimpses of quiet amusement that are seldom found in women writers and are usually associated with the masculine trait of British understatement."[29] In *Pilgrimage*, Richardson surpasses this purportedly "masculine" understatement and develops a subversive feminist humor that undermines the privileged moments of the male tradition, seduction and sexual consummation.

❧ The Speaking Silence of Narrative Gaps

The form of the *roman-fleuve* resembles Amabel's letter as it creates narrative gaps that do not represent but that signify important events or emotions censored by or inexplicable to patriarchy. Although the most perceptible gaps are those between volumes, the most significant are undramatized events—the death of Mrs. Henderson and Miriam's encounter with Jean—that are presented primarily in retrospect. This, of course, resembles the technique of intervolume death used in the Pallisers and *A Dance to the Music of Time*, where compelling female characters, such as Glencora Palliser and Pamela Widmerpool, are killed off between volumes when their plots threaten to overpower those of the male protagonists, foregrounding the protagonists' reactions to the deaths, subordinating potential (female) rivals for center stage. Richardson also employs gaps and subordination to move forward her central plot, Miriam's pilgrimage to self-awareness, but she exploits these techniques more extensively than Trollope or Powell. Mrs. Henderson, for example, has been called a "surrogate sufferer," who dies so that Miriam may continue her quest.[30]

Miriam's pain and guilt over her mother's death are repressed in the narrative. The suicide, which takes place in a beach-side boardinghouse, is not narrated but only implied as the landlady tells Miriam, " 'You must never, as long as you live, blame yourself my gurl' " (*H* 489). When she first submitted the manuscript of *Honeycomb* to her publisher, Richardson did not include the final chapter containing Mrs. Henderson's death, and Gerald Duckworth informed her that she must write one more chapter that would form a true conclusion to the novel.[31] The oblique treatment of this event, and Richardson's initial reluctance to include it, may be related to the biographical source of the incident: Richardson's own mother committed suicide under much the same circumstances. Miriam is divided between her guilt over her mother's death and her desire to free herself from responsibility for the unavoidable: her mother was obviously depressed but it was impossible for Miriam to be with her every moment. In *Pilgrimage* the revelation of such events and emotions signals a return of the repressed, the resurgence of crucial experiences that society and the novelistic tradition subordinate to other, supposedly more significant, narrative actions.

Miriam's repressed memory and guilt over the death return periodically throughout the *roman-fleuve*, first in a passage that anticipates the telling gaps in Amabel's handwriting. The seventh chapter of *The Tunnel* consists of only one paragraph, surrounded by blank space, which visually evokes the suppressed trauma surfacing from the depths of Miriam's psyche:

Chapter 7

Why must I always think of her in this place? . . . It is always worst just along here. . . . Why do I always forget there's this piece . . . always be hurrying along seeing nothing and then, suddenly, Teetgen's Teas and this row of shops? I can't bear it. I don't know what it is. It's always the same. I always feel the same. It is sending me mad. One day it will be worse. If it gets any worse I shall be mad. Just here. Certainly. Something is wearing out of me. I am meant to go mad. If not, I should not always be coming along this piece without knowing it, whichever street I take. Other people would know the streets apart. I don't know where this bit is or how I get to it. I come every day because I am meant to go mad here. Something that knows brings me here and is making me go mad because I am myself and nothing changes me. (136)

The blank space surrounding this passage is contextual, a frame of silence, symbolizing unexpressed experience and emotions. In this chapter speaks a voice repressed until this point in the *roman-fleuve*: an unassertive Miriam, who feels entirely passive and out of control, who attributes events to forces and places outside herself, in contrast to the strong and opinionated protagonist of the primary narrative. Her weakness and vulnerability are traits she seeks to keep hidden, traits that, if indulged, will lead her to her mother's fate, an example of Jane Miller's contention that "most women's novels are engaged at some level in extricating their authors as well as their heroines from charges of abnormality."[32]

Until this point in the text Miriam has intermittently and ambivalently continued to identify with her father, particularly in *Pointed Roofs*, where she imitates his misogyny, thinking, "She loathed women." Among the women she mentions are not only her teacher and Eve (who also dies, another undramatized event, in the course of the *roman-fleuve*) but also her mother. In self-justification Miriam explains, "Pater knew how hateful all the world of women were and despised them" (*PR* 22). Thus, the death of her mother may be suppressed in the narrative because Miriam assumes her father's guilt over her mother's death: she is both his agent, in taking care of the ill Mrs. Henderson, and his accomplice, mouthing the attitudes that cause the self-loathing that destroys his wife, Miriam's mother. In discussing Miriam's comment in *The Tunnel* that "all women ought to agree to commit suicide" (221), Showalter argues that suicide may be a "female weapon" to subvert "male dominance."[33] While this may be the only item in Mrs. Henderson's arsenal, Miriam shuns it as an option for herself. Except for the brief resurgent passages on her mother, Miriam represses madness, even during the breakdown that precedes her trip to Oberland. In *Pilgrimage*, suicide represents self-destruction, a negative pilgrimage, the fate Miriam escapes through her will and her struggle against the social order that killed her mother. Suicide surfaces in the narrative to acknowledge this destiny, one possible end of women's experience, but in contrast to Mrs. Henderson or Edna Pontellier, Miriam imagines other options.

The resurgent nature of this chapter also graphically demonstrates the isolated nature of Miriam's feelings: she cannot speak her grief; it cannot be incorporated into her life story, illustrating Irigaray's description of the linearity of patriarchal discourse that denies the feminine: "the teleology of discourse, within which there is no possible place for the 'feminine,' except in the traditional place of the repressed, the censured."[34] The cumulative and reiterative development of the *roman-fleuve*, however, provides an alternative to the teleological narrative and illuminates the significance of Mrs. Henderson's death for Miriam and her ability to overcome, if not openly acknowledge, it. A passage in *Deadlock*, the sixth novel, reveals again a grief repressed in the two novels intervening since the fragmented chapter 7 of *The Tunnel*.

> She saw, narrow and gaslit, the little unlocated street that had haunted her first London years, herself flitting into it, always unknowingly, from a maze of surrounding streets, feeling uneasy, recognizing it, hurrying to pass its awful centre where she must read the name of a shop, and, dropped helplessly into the deepest pit of her memory, struggle on through thronging images threatening, each time more powerfully, to draw her willingly back and back through the intervening spaces of her life to some deserved destruction of mind and body, until presently she emerged faint and quivering, in a wide careless thoroughfare. She had forgotten it; perhaps somehow learned to avoid it. Her imagined figure passed from the haunted scene, and from the vast spread of London the tide flowed through it, leaving it a daylit part of the whole, its spell broken and gone. (106-7)

Here again the hidden "haunted" street provokes a mental crisis as Miriam is carried down into the vortex of her repressed grief, moving inward and backward into memory, through images of womb-like "spaces" and the "pit" of a memory she has "learned to avoid." However, her progress in dealing with the trauma is revealed by her ability to emerge, reborn, though "faint and quivering." As Miriam recognizes and acknowledges her profound identification with her mother, this journey to the depths of her self breaks the "spell" of her repressed grief. However, the problematic nature of her identification is signaled by the ambiguous pronoun "her": Is it Miriam or her mother who passes, an "imagined figure," from the scene? Miriam must identify with her mother if she is to become fully woman herself, but to identify *fully* would be to marginalize herself irrevocably in the real world, to be driven mad, or to annihilate herself.

In *Dawn's Left Hand*, the tenth volume, the significance of the recurrent setting is expanded as it is revealed that Miriam has finally transcended the trauma of her mother's death:

> And *this* street, still foul and dust-filled, but full now also of the light flooding down upon and the air flowing through the larger streets with which in her mind it was clearly linked, was the place where in the early years she would suddenly find herself lost and helplessly aware of what was waiting for her eyes the moment before it appeared: the grimed gilt lettering that *forced me to gaze into the darkest moment of my life and to remember that I had forfeited my share in humanity for ever and must go quietly and alone until the end.*
>
> And now *their power has gone. They can bring back only the memory of a darkness and horror, to which, then, something has happened, begun to happen?*
>
> She glanced back over her shoulder at the letters now away behind her and rejoiced in freedom that allowed her to note their peculiarities of size and shape. (155-56)

Here Miriam is able to articulate her previous reaction to the suicide, her feeling that *she* must serve penance for her mother's death. Finally Miriam is able to experience joy, recurrently symbolized by the radiant light she seeks throughout *Pilgrimage*. Triumphing over the threat of the sudden, intrusive tea-shop sign that represents Miriam's psyche, she now reads and understands, in a telling pun, her "grimed gilt" (guilt). After this last experience, she feels joy and eats an apple "tasting like pineapple" (*DLH* 156): Miriam rejects the Judeo-Christian guilt of the mother Eve, which destroyed her own mother, rejoicing in a more exotic view of feminine nature. Through revisiting a setting, the accumulated reiteration of the *roman-fleuve* dramatizes Miriam's pilgrimage to a mature identification with the mother and transcendence of the snares of madness and suicide, self-destructive escapes from patriarchal dominance.

A second crucial undramatized event is Miriam's relationship with Jean, which occurs in the gap between *Dimple Hill* and *March Moonlight*. Jean is first obliquely introduced in the letter that opens the last volume or "chapter" of *Pilgrimage*. Since the letter is addressed to

"Dick," a character not previously mentioned, it is not clear at first whether Miriam is writing or reading the letter. Although it is subsequently clarified that "Dick" is Jean's nickname for Miriam, it is never explained why. The relationship is a female friendship that surpasses the identification Miriam felt with Amabel. Whereas the relationship with Amabel allows Miriam to acknowledge the feminine part of her self and discover an *écriture féminine*, a stage in her pilgrimage to become a woman writer, Jean seems to embody the object of Miriam's identity quest—a superior, transcendent woman who has achieved spiritual peace: "To return to Jean is to find oneself at an unchanging center" (*MM* 566). Radford also comments on the spiritual nature of this character, suggesting she may be named for John in the Gospels.[35] Jean epitomizes the receptivity that Miriam values; in contrast to Hypo, whose questions are statements, Miriam recalls Jean "only as questioning and listening; never as giving a verdict" (564). The oblique, indirect textual presentation of the letter and the retrospective narration of this relationship through letters and memory suggest there is something unspeakable about it. As with the death of Miriam's mother, the relationship is perhaps too painful to be directly evoked and rendered. Further, these are both woman-woman relationships outside the language of patriarchy:

> If I were less than I am, I should talk about her until my friends would grow to dread her name. If I were more than I am, I should follow her path, the path to freedom. But I forget. Again and again, until something pulls me out into remorse. If only I could remain always in possession of my whole self, something of Jean-in-me would operate.
>
> Good that she is gone. How right are the Catholics in separating within their orders those who grow too happy in each other. To give oneself, fully, to God-in-Others, one must belong to no one. Careful though she was, and in the end taught me to be, to avoid, in public, any revelation of partiality, we yet aroused jealousies. As those last weeks slid away, the glow we created in each other could not be concealed. (612)

The repressed discourse is again signaled by Miriam's emphasis on forgetting and her insistence on a reality that overwhelms her will: "something pulls me out." Although until recently most of Richardson's critics have denied the possibility of homosexuality in Miriam's response to women, the narrative treatment of Jean strongly suggests the possibility of a lesbian relationship. In the context of the feminist implications of

Pilgrimage, it is important to note that Richardson writes many *genders*, despite her (seemingly essentialist) generalizations about men and women, the two sexes.

The issue is complicated by Miriam's ambivalence about sexuality, a separate issue but certainly relevant to her sexual preference. Sydney Kaplan, noting that Miriam's "obsessions with women contain more desire" than the treatment of her relations with men, argues that Miriam should not be considered a lesbian, though she exhibits "latent homosexual feelings"; while Hanscombe argues that Miriam's friendship with Amabel is contrasted to her "erotic" reaction to Shatov and Wilson, indicated by signs of physical "arousal," as the beating of the heart.[36] However, this kind of physical reaction is also present in her response to Jean, where the "heart beat," a cliché of romance, is also used to signal romantic passion. Hanscombe believes that the relationship with Amabel is significantly not erotic because "the commitment of the body entails, necessarily, the exclusion of consciousness, thus defeating her desire to experience her whole self as an integrated part of external reality. She has not found, nor does she believe, that a relationship between a man and a woman can be of this order, since it seems that sexuality must be the preeminent factor."[37] DuPlessis suggests that although there is no conclusive evidence, "for Miriam, the lesbian moment is broadly absorbed as it is refused in specifics" and further suggests, though cautiously, that the Jan-Mag relationship may "appear lesbian" to today's reader.[38]

Miriam and Jean evoke a physical reaction, a "glow" in each other; the mention of the separation of clergy evokes the tradition of latent or overt homosexual attractions in literary depictions of Catholic orders. When Miriam claims that "with Jean, for me, friendship reaches its centre" (613), she suggests a deep, intuitive, and possibly physical, response. Further, whereas most of the characters in *Pilgrimage* are based on people Richardson knew (in fact she sometimes referred to the prototypes by their character names), the original Jean is, as far as I have been able to discover, unknown or nonexistent.[39]

Although their friendship is evidently more physically affectionate than the previous one with Amabel, Jean's kiss might seem insignificant except for the oblique treatment the relationship is given. The kiss, according to Catherine Stimpson, is a convention that encodes lesbianism, a "staple of lesbian fiction . . . with vast metonymic responsibilities"; her speculation about the function of the kiss suggests one kind of female erotics that subverts the linearity of the "ejaculatory" pattern: "Does the kiss predict the beginning of the end, or the end of the beginning, or a lesbian erotic enterprise? Or is it the event that literally embraces contradictions?"[40] Further evidence for viewing Jean's kiss as a possible encodement of lesbianism is the scene involving the erotic postcard Miriam receives from Olga, the Russian girl, sent just before her suicide. Miriam hides the card, a photograph of Rodin's sculpture *Le Baiser* (The Kiss), depicting an aggressive woman in a heterosexual embrace, from Rachel Mary and the Quaker household, fearing it reveals "an unsuspected angle of my being" (643). The ambiguously presented "angle" is never clarified.

Other retrospective revelations of the *roman-fleuve* may also function to encode a lesbian impulse. In *Dimple Hill* Miriam launches into a curious tirade about couples who sit "confronted," across a table in a restaurant, an interpersonal configuration that publicly exposes their inability to communicate. Miriam concludes, "Everywhere, people should be side by side, facing the spectacle, meeting in it. Confronted people can't meet more than once" (534). The significance of this odd observation is elucidated a few pages later when it becomes evident that Miriam is generalizing about heterosexual couples as, despite her disappointment with Amabel, she feels a gendered affinity with her, "side by side, silent, with the whole universe between us, within us, in a way no man and woman, be they never so well mated, can ever have" (545). Although the narrative account of Miriam's relationship with Amabel only ambiguously suggests a lesbian response, the subsequent relationship with Jean indicates that Miriam's gender preference—it being impossible to speak conclusively of sexual preference in light of her seemingly asexual nature—is for women. As Fromm comments, "Miriam's passions will never be strongly sexual in nature. Neither were Dorothy Richardson's."[41]

By the end of *Pilgrimage*, woman-woman bonds supersede those of the heterosexual couple. Miriam's love for Jean may be erotic or merely romantic, falling to one end of the "lesbian continuum" Adrienne Rich describes as a "range of woman-identified experience,"[42] a concept that is useful for discussing gender more globally. Erotic or platonic, Miriam mourns the loss of Jean, "her heart, that so recently had missed a beat in imagining Jean, and Jean's love that was her own passport to eternity, abolished from the universe" (MM 580). Somehow Miriam was deceived in the relationship: perhaps she misunderstood the nature of

Jean's affection for her or perhaps Miriam was, in this particular relationship (and in contrast to the one with Amabel), the one who loved more. She remarks, "Blind, I was, to the drama playing itself out under my nose" (573), a page before Jim Davenport, whom Jean eventually marries, is introduced. The denouement and aftermath of Miriam and Jean's relationship are not revealed. However, as with the death of Miriam's mother, the significance for Miriam surfaces at an unexpected moment, in the very last line of *Pilgrimage* when, as Miriam holds Amabel's child, she wonders, if "Jean's marriage to Joe Davenport brought her a child, should I feel, in holding it, that same sense of fulfillment?" (658). Thus, the final sentence, the most privileged point in the entire *roman-fleuve*, muses about Jean. Richardson's elliptical and metonymic presentation of lesbian love breaks silence about this often unwritten experience at the same time that it avoids the conventional narrative strategies used to represent heterosexual love and romance.

❧ Evasion and Reiteration

From its first pages, *Pilgrimage* evades a point of origination and contests a forward-moving linear progression: instead, the narrative begins in tension. The first volume, *Pointed Roofs*, opens in a "March twilight" (18), while the last volume is titled *March Moonlight*, suggesting that the temporal stretch or movement from the first to the thirteenth volume has been minimal. Although the projected journey to Hanover implies a point of origin, and the title *Pilgrimage* suggests progression, the references in the first chapter are to endings: the repeated elliptical refrain of the chapter is a negation: "No more all day bézique. . . . No more days in the West End. . . . No more matinées . . . no more exhibitions . . . no more A.B.C. teas . . . no more insane times . . . no more anything" (PR 18). The motif of termination suggests at once the close of Miriam's childhood and the assumption of adult responsibilities. Her father's financial crash, not fully realized until the next volume, *Backwater*, generates the freedom and poverty that, as a single working woman, Miriam will experience. As a feminist text, *Pilgrimage* is launched not by male desire but by the fall of the father, whose financial ruin both hinders the daughter's ability to remain in the social class she has been brought up to enter and releases her for the freedom of earning her own way, an equivocal beginning.

Richardson's construction of her protagonist's beginning anticipates

Cixous's view that feminine writing avoids the paternal origins of conventional exposition: "The origin is a masculine myth. . . . The quest for origins, illustrated by Oedipus, doesn't haunt a feminine unconscious. Rather it's the beginning, or beginnings, the manner of beginning, not promptly with the phallus, but starting on all sides at once, that makes a feminine writing. A feminine text starts on all sides at once, starts twenty times, thirty times, over."[43] Although perhaps not as multi-origined as Cixous's feminine text, "starting on all sides at once," Richardson's *roman-fleuve* uses an indirect, multiple beginning, a reiterated false start similar to that with which Trollope begins his proto–*roman-fleuve* in *Can You Forgive Her?*

The first three volumes of *Pilgrimage* present variations on the same event: Miriam's experiences as a teacher, first at Waldstrasse and then at the Wordsworth school, and finally as a governess at the Corries. The three teaching experiences, seeming dead-ends to her subsequent vocation as dental secretary and finally as a writer, each contain, nevertheless, revelations for Miriam. At Hanover she learns to value the aesthetic, whereas at Wordsworth school she learns how difficult it is to live deprived of beauty. Her first two experiences, moreover, place her in communities of women and gradually attenuate the misogyny she has learned from Pater. In the third experience, at the house of the lawyer Mr. Corrie and his wife, Miriam is tempted by her contact with the kind of wealth that makes beauty part of one's everyday life: "Now she knew what she wanted. Bright mornings, beautiful bright rooms, a wilderness of beauty round her all the time—at any cost" (*H* 403). This insight, however, is undermined by a series of painful social occasions at Newlands. At one dinner party Miriam smokes a cigarette and tries to vie with the men in conversation only to realize she is seeking an approval she despises. Finally, she sees that her efforts are futile; in this society men and women are different species: "Why were women there? Why did men and women dine together?" (376).

Near the end of her residence at Newlands, as Miriam observes the married couples, the Corries and the Cravens, she realizes that "these things had been got together only for the use of the men" (376)—that the women are there to serve and the men are there to do or "pretend to do" (388). Although Miriam's residual conflict about her identification with her father continues—"I can't stand women because I'm a sort of horrid man" (404)—she rejects the worldly, ironically named Newlands way of life when she begins to realize that the cost of wealth is acceptance of the patriarchal society that produces a luxury to which women sacrifice their identity: "In that moment Miriam felt that she left New-lands for ever. She glanced at Mrs Corrie and Mrs Craven—bright beau-tiful coloured birds, fading slowly year by year in the stifling atmosphere, the hard brutal laughing complacent atmosphere of men's minds . . . men's minds, staring at things, ignorantly, knowing 'everything' in an irritating way and yet *ignorant*" (H 443). The women are ornamental birds, but because their keepers are males whose foreign minds stare without seeing, the wives are Others who fade, their true selves un-known and unperceived. The insight Miriam gains at Newlands is rein-forced by Mrs. Henderson's despair and suicide in the final chapter of *Honeycomb*. This less advantaged, even more faded woman kills herself because "my life has been so useless" (472).

Since her aesthetic deprivileges teleology, Richardson also rejects a dia-chronic or horizontal narrative movement for one that is synchronic. She justifies this innovation in a biographical sketch she was asked to prepare for a Spanish translation of *Pilgrimage*: "The material that moved me to write would not fit the framework of any novel I had experienced. I be-lieved myself to be, even when most enchanted, intolerant of the roman-tic and the realist novel alike. Each, so it seemed to me, left out certain essentials and dramatized life misleadingly. Horizontally. Assembling their characters, the novelists developed situations, devised events, climax and conclusions. I could not accept their finalities."[44] Richardson's nar-rative, however, is developed vertically, through variation and reiteration, rather than horizontally: each new example of a pattern, instead of mov-ing the plot forward, represents a synchronic development by further in-tensifying the effect and further suggesting insight into the initial experi-ence. DuPlessis also comments on this passage in conjunction with the plot of *Pilgrimage* and the way the term "horizontal" is "a synonym for narrative sequence, chronology, causation."[45] Hanscombe points out that "there is, in other words, a central point rather than a starting point; there is expansion and dissolution, but not development; and there is re-iteration, but not a deductively reasoned conclusion."[46]

One of these recurrent patterns in *Pilgrimage* is that of the protago-nist's encounters with a Chopin nocturne. Miriam first hears this theme at Waldstrasse, the school where she teaches in *Pointed Roofs*. When she again hears the nocturne in *Oberland*, the ninth novel in the series, Miriam observes it more closely: "Its charm she now saw, coming to it afresh and with a deepened recognition, lay partly in the way it opened:

not beginning, but continuing something gone before. It was a shape of tones caught from a pattern woven continuously and drawn, with its rhythm ready set, gleaming into sight. The way of the best nocturnes" (*O* 36). In other words, a narrative, in music or prose, should be evocative; it should direct the reader and writer inward, to discover truth, rather than outward toward superficial events or plots. Moreover, the description of the nocturne, ever continuing, opening without a beginning, suggests the narrative construction of *Pilgrimage*: each volume expands and extends; beginnings and endings are deprivileged.

The nocturne recurs periodically throughout the *roman-fleuve*. Its aesthetic and its spiritual significance are first explicitly revealed in *Honeycomb*, the third novel, as Miriam sings a song in German for the philistine Mrs. Corrie and her guests: "Her listeners did not trouble her. They would not understand. No English person would quite understand —the need, that the Germans understood so well—the need to admit the beauty of things . . . the need of the strange expression of music, making the beautiful things more beautiful" (*H* 374). The nocturne reinforces Miriam's Waldstrasse illumination about the value of the aesthetic, an experience akin to the Proustian moment. In *Oberland*, as Miriam hears the theme in the modest Swiss hotel, it again evokes her initial encounter with this theme in Hanover:

> In the stillness of the room it was like a voice announcing her installation, and immediately from downstairs there came as if in answer the sound of a piano, crisply and gently touched, seeming not so much to break the stillness as to reveal what lay within it.
>
> She set down her teapot and listened, and for a moment could have believed that the theme was playing itself only in her mind, that it had come back to her because once again she was within the strange happiness of being abroad. Through all the years she had tried in vain to recall it, and now it came, to welcome her, piling joy on joy, setting its seal upon the days ahead and taking her back to her Germany where life had been lived to music that had flowed over its miseries. (*O* 35)

Once again the musical theme is associated with joy and spiritual illumination. The nocturne, both a remembered and a new experience, precipitates a simultaneous backward and forward movement in the narrative. It is an epiphany in tension, infusing and undermining the present with the past.

Reiteration in *Pilgrimage* focuses primarily on things, in contrast to Trollope's recurring characters and Powell's use of recurrent situations. Miriam prefers concrete objects to the abstractions privileged by phallocentric logic, as the reaction to her editor's advice about one of her verbal sketches reveals. In response to his comment, " 'If you can describe people as well as you describe scenes, you should be able to write a novel,' " Miriam mentally counters, "But it is just that stopping, by the author, to describe people, that spoils so many novels?" (*MM* 613–14). In part she is, here as elsewhere, rejecting conventions of the nineteenth-century novel, such as the use of block description to introduce characters. The alternative to "masculine realism" she wishes to create is, as Arline Thorn has noted, a reaction against the Balzacian idea of "realism."[47] Nevertheless, Miriam's preference for the literal—things—rather than the abstractions of personalities, leaves Richardson open to the deprecation of a critic who quipped, "Miriam aches always to be alone with a room or a bus or a bicycle."[48]

This emphasis on the literal and tangible, recalling Irigaray's description of feminine style as tactile (quoted at the beginning of this chapter), is problematic because it may reinforce the denigration of qualities traditionally considered feminine; however, as Margaret Homans explains, "Women might, and do, embrace this connection, not for the same reasons for which androcentric culture identifies women and the literal, but for reasons having to do with women's own development and identity. . . . The literal is ambiguous for women writers because women's potentially more positive view of it collides with its devaluation by our culture."[49] Homans traces the association of the male and figuration, the female and literal, to theories of sexual identity formation proposed by Freud and revised by Lacan: "What the son searches for, in searching for substitutes for the mother's forbidden body, is a series of figures: 'someone *like* his mother.' At the same time, language is structured as the substitution for the (female) object of signifiers that both require the absence of the object and also permit its controlled return, something *like* the lost object."[50] As a result of this process, the male develops a figurative language, the female "retains the literal or presymbolic language that the son represses."[51]

In *Pilgrimage* this perspective is evident in Miriam's insistence that spiritual fulfillment is found *through* the beauty of material objects and experiences; this is the lesson reiterated in the first two novels:

She must keep her secret to herself. This Brighton life crushed it back more than anything there had been in Germany or at Banbury Park. In Germany she had found it again and again, and at Banbury Park, though it could never come out and surround her, it was never far off. It lurked just beyond the poplars in the park, at the end of the little empty garden at twilight, amongst the books in the tightly packed bookcase. It was here, too, in and out the sunlit days. As one opened the door of the large, sparely furnished breakfast-room it shone for a moment in the light pouring over the table full of seated forms; it haunted the glittering scattered sand round about the little blank platform where the black and white minstrels stood singing in front of their harmonium, and poured out across the blaze of blue and gold sea ripples, when the town band played Anitra's Dance or the moon-song from the *Mikado*; it lay all along the deserted promenade and roadway as you went home to lunch, and at night it spoke in the flump flump of the invisible sea against the lower woodwork of the pier pavilion. (*B* 318)

Introduced in *Pointed Roofs* as Miriam rejoices in the tangible aesthetic experience in Germany—the *Vorspielen*, the chocolate, the luxury of the room she shares with the German girls Emma and Ulrica—this theme is reiterated throughout the novel. Miriam believes that truth is to be found through the material; she distrusts abstractions and generalizations: "The things they said were worldly—generalizations, like the things one read in books that tired you out with trying to find the answer, and made books so awful . . . things that might look true about everybody at some time or other, and were not really true about anybody—when you knew them" (*Tun* 97).

The prevailing symbol of the joyous aesthetic experience is light, which, while it signals illumination in *Pilgrimage*, is not experienced by Miriam as a Joycean epiphany, a climactic revelation, but as an undercurrent of spiritual experience: the light is ever present, and Miriam's quest is to be receptive, ever aware of it. It is a symbol of the communication between her soul and the outer, material reality. Miriam's emphasis is on everyday experiences, privileging the constant and the quotidian. An example of this priority is her frustration with the disparity between her life at the Wordsworth school and her contact with her family during the holidays. Miriam cannot communicate to her family the ordinary details that are the most significant: "going home like a visitor, and people talking to you about things that are only theirs now, and not wanting to hear about yours . . . not about the little real everyday things that give you an idea of anything, but only the startling things that are not important" (*B* 264–65). Richardson's aesthetic denigrates the climactic epiphany; through this as through other strategies she deconstructs the hierarchy of binary oppositions.

The reiterative and evocative narrative of *Pilgrimage* undermines narrative progression and anticipates Irigaray's description of the dynamics of women's discourse: "We need to proceed in such a way that linear reading is no longer possible: that is, the retroactive impact of each work, utterance, or sentence upon its beginning must be taken into consideration in order to undo the power of its teleological effect, including its deferred action. That would hold good also for the opposition between structures of horizontality and verticality that are at work in language."[52] Richardson's narrative frequently exemplifies Irigaray's "retroactive impact" as she withholds information at crucial points in the text. Characters speak before they are introduced; some details are never revealed—for example, the nature of the operation Miriam's mother undergoes, or the details of her suicide, or the cause of Eve's death. Others are postponed until their significance has passed, as with the suggestion in *March Moonlight* that Ted, Miriam's suitor in *Backwater* (who never reappears in subsequent volumes), may have abandoned Miriam not because of her flirtation with Max but because of the loss of the Henderson income, or the revelation that Miriam's bicycle accident in *Interim* was nearly fatal. The impact is not that of the "deferred action" characteristic of the suspense plot because Richardson does not build to a climactic revelation or action.

Richardson chooses the form of the *roman-fleuve* for aesthetic and ideological reasons; as Jean Radford notes, "The 'excessive length' is thus a symptom of the search for a new feminine form and is crucial to Richardson's poetics of the novel."[53] However, through her protagonist she rejects the reductive Jamesian emphasis on the unity of lengthy fiction. In her ambivalent evaluation, Miriam describes James's "hopelessly complacent masculine ignorance"; yet she also attributes to him "the first completely satisfying way of writing a novel" (*Trap* 410).[54] When Miriam hears her opinionated protégé, Michael Shatov, enthusiastically praise the novel *Anna Karenina* for being a "masterly study of a certain type of woman," she protests: "Why must a book be a masterly study of some single thing? [. . . .] But if one never found out what a book was a masterly study of, it meant being ignorant of things every one knew and agreed about; a kind of hopeless personal ignorance and unintelligence; reading whole books through and through, and only finding out what they were about by accident" (*Deadlock* 61). Not only is Miriam alienated by Shatov's reductive view of Anna and the novel form, but she also rejects his dictatorial view of reading, a sort of New Critical conspiracy about the correct meaning of a text.

In contrast to the unity and linearity of conventional fiction, Richardson defends what is usually regarded as digression: during her brief career as a teacher, Miriam's method of instruction permits digression; this procedure is also indicative of Richardson's technique as a novelist: "The children stood at ease, saying whatever occurred to them, even the snoring girl secured from ridicule by Miriam's consideration of whatever was offered. Their adventure took them away from their subject into what Miriam knew 'clever' people would call 'side issues.' 'Nothing is a side issue,' she told herself passionately" (*B* 249). Miriam's teaching style, like the narrative of *Pilgrimage*, is circular, reiterative, and discursive, refusing to drive forward to a resolution. In *March Moonlight*, Miriam has a revelation about what would constitute a specifically feminine narrative: "But the best and, for me, the most searching moment of the afternoon was the sudden perception of what lies behind the 'simple' person's inability to summarize, behind the obvious enjoyment, particularly remarkable in women, of the utmost possible elaboration of a narrative, of what is evoked in the speaker's mind, while in torment one waits for the emergent data" (569). Richardson's narrative tantalizes the reader with a profusion of details, the "utmost possible elaboration," while it refuses to reveal all, holding back information that would bestow a final meaning and thus close the narrative.

⚘ The Oblique Object of Desire

Richardson subverts readers' expectations about the conventional novel. Throughout the protracted reading of the *roman-fleuve* we suspect that despite her reservations, Miriam's *Bildung* will end in marriage and an announcement, perhaps more subtle or sophisticated than Jane Eyre's, that nonetheless, "reader, I married him." In the early volumes, Miriam envisions, hallucinates almost, a husband-savior; and her repeated encounters with suitors—Ted Burton, Max Sonnenheim, Michael Shatov, Dr. Densley, Richard Roscorla, Charles Ducorroy—each suggests a man who may be appropriate in a different way. Even in the last "chapter" of her *roman-fleuve*, Richardson teases the reader with a possible marriage of

Miriam and Charles Ducorroy, hinting as the novel approaches an end that, finally, this is *the* man. Miriam considers the prospect of such a marriage, which even Mary Rachel approves, but is seriously concerned about the need for "shared belief" between husband and wife, and her own need to confess her past. "This I must soon decide," she concludes (*MM* 646–47). As DuPlessis notes, however, Richardson evades the conventional resolution and writes beyond the conventional marriage ending.

The avoidance of the marital ending is a primary example of the way Richardson resists an emphatic treatment of events generally privileged— even fetishized—in the novel tradition. Major plot developments (such as the death of the protagonist's mother or of her sister Eve in *The Trap*) are subordinated and the reader's curiosity about seemingly major events is subverted and directed instead to an inner reality. For example, when Miriam visits the Wilsons in chapter 6 of *The Tunnel*, it is suggested that Miriam has found her destiny as a writer in the literary circle that congregates at their country home. However, the friendship is repressed during *Interim*, the next volume, only to reemerge with an unexpected romantic focus in *Deadlock*, as Miriam is personally both attracted and repelled by Hypo during her month-long visit to the house. When Miriam's ambivalent interest finally leads to sexual intercourse with Hypo Wilson during his furtive nocturnal visit to her room, the event is decidedly anticlimactic. Miriam finds herself on a journey outside her body, watching the "lovers" with detached, wry curiosity: "It was uncanny, but more absorbing than the unwelcome adventure of her body, to be thus hovering outside and above it in a darkness that obliterated the room and was too vast to be contained by it. An immense, fathomless black darkness through which, after an instant's sudden descent into her clenched and rigid form, she was now travelling alone on and on, without thought or memory or any emotion save the strangeness of this journeying" (*DLH* 257). The romantic climax of the traditional novel, the consummation of a love affair, is here a decidedly solitary, tense, and unpleasant experience: "I'm not here," Miriam tells Hypo as he enters and again when he leaves her room. The narrative does not build to a sexual climax, but is instead deflated by the narrator's ironic comment placing Miriam's lover in a ludicrous, clinical role: "The robed figure stood over her like a short doctor" (257).

The scene marks the end of Miriam's interest in Hypo: "His relaxed form was nothing to her. A mass of obstructive clay from which the spirit had departed on its way to its own bourne. Its journey, foolishly undertaken through her fault in hiding, failing to communicate their essential unrelatedness, had been through a familiar pleasure into restful nothingness that presumably would bear the fruit he sought therefrom" (257). Not only is Hypo's body unappealing to Miriam, but the description of his form as "a mass of obstructive clay" suggests that physical love inhibits an ability to transcend the flesh; sensual pleasure is denigrated. The scene emphasizes the disparity between Miriam and Hypo rather than their union. Their failure to communicate erotically only reaffirms their linguistic impasse. Miriam's response to the invasion is to depart into the space within her spiritual being. Her reaction to Hypo's coy evasion of her the following day is anger; she refers to him as a "neatly plump Silenus" (262). The relationship is also anticlimactic in that it follows the relationship with Shatov, seemingly the most serious of Miriam's male suitors, and it is clear that there is no romantic love in the relationship where, Miriam claims, Hypo's love is "nothing for her individually" (191).

In this novel it is Miriam's friend Amabel who displaces the male romantic interest. Amabel, as she kneels to Miriam and scrawls "I Love You" on her mirror, is more passionate and persuasive than Miriam's male suitors; she both parodies and surpasses their methods. As Fromm suggests, "Her success underscores [Hypo's] failure, perhaps even causes it."[55] Miriam's other relationships with women may also parody the conventional romance. DuPlessis comments on the way her friendships with Miss Holland and Eleanor Dear are "grotesque rewritings of heterosexuality"; in her friendship with Eleanor, as Miriam herself notes, she becomes responsible for a "dependent wife."[56] Although the female confidante usually plays a supporting role to the male lover, Miriam's friendship with Amabel is here the privileged relationship. The significance of this friendship is anticipated in a previous passage in *The Tunnel*, when Miriam attends a performance of *The Merchant of Venice* and finds the Portia-Nerissa friendship more meaningful than the play's heterosexual love relationships: "How much more real was the relation between Portia and Nerissa than between either of the sadly jesting women and their complacently jesting lovers. Did a man *ever* speak in a natural voice—neither blustering, nor displaying his cleverness, nor being simply a lustful slave?" [. . .] 'Man's love is of man's life a thing apart . . .' so much the worse for man; there must be something very wrong with his life" (187). The conclusion she draws from viewing the play makes clear that for her the play's protagonist is female: "Woman's wit. Men at least bowed down to that; though they did not know what it was. 'Wit' used to mean knowledge—'inwit,' conscience" (*Tun* 188). Thus the etymology reveals that Miriam places the vast intuitive conscience of women in opposition to the superficiality of masculine knowledge. Any deficiencies in Portia, as a character, result from being "invented by a man." Whereas Hypo's physical presence causes Miriam's alienation, as she hovers outside herself, Amabel's influence becomes part of Miriam and will "remain with [her] for ever" (*DLH* 251). As Hanscombe comments, "Her romantic needs can be fulfilled by women precisely because, since they share its configuration, they do not threaten the integrity of her consciousness."[57]

Richardson's refusal to structure *Pilgrimage* around the romantic courtship plot is, according, to DuPlessis, a deliberate aesthetic strategy: "The enormous lack of a 'story' in this novel is then a serious, deeply held, and justifiable element of Richardson's poetics of fiction, given the fact that 'story' for women has typically meant plots of seduction, courtship, the energies of quest deflected into sexual downfall, the choice of marriage partner, the melodramas of beginning, middle, and end, the trajectories of sexual arousal and release. . . . For kinds of formal patterning involving priority, weight, cause and effect, connection, sequence, and meaning are undermined in a casual but drastic way by *Pilgrimage*."[58] DuPlessis argues that Miriam's story, unlike those of her fictional nineteenth-century predecessors, defies the end-in-marriage, a traditional closural event of the novel.

In *Revolving Lights*, Miriam denigrates the restriction of closure and expresses a preference for duration and process when she complains to Hypo, " 'Things always end just as they're beginning.' " His response characteristically privileges closure and forward movement: " 'Things end, Miriam, so that other things may begin' " (*RL* 364). Richardson not only refuses, emphatically, a particular ending, she rejects closure itself. Her association of closure and the novelistic tradition is evident in Hypo and Miriam's discussion of the genre in *Dawn's Left Hand*. Miriam refutes Hypo's suggestion that the writer's career should culminate in the writing of novels, the "end and aim of a writer's existence" (239). In contrast to Hypo, she rebels against the "dreadful enclosure" that has traditionally characterized the novel. She mentally projects her image of an alternate narrative onto the plot of *Crime and Punishment*: "She saw Raskolnikov on the stone staircase of the tenement house being more than he knew himself to be and somehow redeemed *before* the awful deed one shared without wanting to prevent, in contrast to all the people in James who knew so much and yet did not know" (239). Forestalling the murder and subsequent retribution, Miriam rewrites Dostoevsky's novel, rejecting the forward linear movement of the suspense plot that "encloses" and embracing instead the ever-expanding self-awareness Richardson seeks—for Raskolnikov as for her own protagonist.

Richardson's rejection of closure is most strikingly evident in the publication history of *Pilgrimage*. The appearance of this novel in installments over a period of twenty-three years, further extended by the posthumous appearance of *March Moonlight* in 1967, exasperated her critics: How, after all, can an unfinished novel be evaluated? Gerald Duckworth's comment that the manuscript of her third novel lacked a concluding chapter pointed to a pattern repeated throughout Richardson's work on her *roman-fleuve*. Her publishers, faced with the challenge of selling a work-in-progress that might remain forever unfinished, pushed her to finish her work once and for all. In 1938 Dent published a twelve-volume edition of *Pilgrimage* advertised as "the complete work of twelve parts, including one not hitherto published"; this edition ended with *Dimple Hill*. Fromm claims that Dent was under a "misconception" and that Richardson did not remember ever implying that *Dimple Hill* would be the concluding "chapter."[59] Since Richardson had begun writing *March Moonlight* even before the first omnibus edition was published in 1938,[60] the suggestion could not have been her own. Understandably, critics were puzzled about the lack of conclusiveness in the purportedly final novel. Those previously receptive to the work "passed over *Dimple Hill* in silence," confused by its inconclusiveness; critics previously hostile to Richardson's enterprise were gratified.[61] The publishers' advertisements were undermined when further installments of *Pilgrimage* appeared. Selections from the thirteenth novel or section, *March Moonlight*, appeared in three issues of *Life and Letters* in 1946, but since these fragments were entitled "Work In Progress," readers were given no indication that they were a continuation of *Pilgrimage*.[62] When the entire thirteen-novel work, including the fragment *March Moonlight*, was published in 1967, Richardson's publishers again announced the *final* volume, this time with better authority.

Pilgrimage differs markedly from other examples of the *roman-fleuve* in that it is much more a single meganovel than a series of discrete novels. Whereas Trollope's proto–*roman-fleuve* and Powell's contemporary *roman-fleuve* achieve some degree of closure with each volume, Richardson's volumes often end inconclusively or abruptly. The earlier ones are more self-sufficient, suggesting that Richardson became more innovative, envisioning an ever-larger, ever more fluid form as her writing of *Pilgrimage* progressed. The first three novels, for example, end with the termination of an experience: *Pointed Roofs* with Miriam's dismissal from Waldstrasse, *Backwater* with her decision to quit the Wordsworth school, *Honeycomb* with her rejection of the Corries. This third novel, which is also the end of the first volume of the omnibus edition, concludes with the traumatic, but inexplicit, death of her mother. Increasingly throughout the series, however, novels end with transitions as Miriam leaves one setting for another—a linking ending appropriate for both a multivolume narrative and a work entitled *Pilgrimage*. Whereas critics such as Friedman and Fuchs define *Pilgrimage* as "a fluid chronicle of multiple climaxes and resolutions," a tendency that would seem expected of the *roman-fleuve*, which offers an opportunity for a miniclimax in each volume, increasingly Richardson avoids climax altogether.[63]

Most of her novel-volumes avoid the conventional nineteenth-century dramatic climax, usually a revelation related to plot—the identity of Pip's benefactor in *Great Expectations*, the existence of Rochester's previous wife in *Jane Eyre*. The middle volumes sometimes end with anticlimactic revelations—that Mrs. Bailey will take boarders (*Tunnel*) or that someone in the dining room is reading poetry (*Interim*)—and the subsequent novels often begin without any explanation, a device that resembles the gap-filled, fragmented narrative technique of *Pilgrimage* as a whole. In *Pilgrimage*, evaluations and summaries are undermined as they are repeated, deflating their conclusiveness. For instance, Miriam's revelations about the incompatibility of men and women—and about her inability to marry a particular man—are repeated throughout the volumes of *Pilgrimage*.

Richardson's closural strategies correspond to Cixous's description of the female libido. Jean Radford, who finds the novel a precursor rather than an example of *écriture féminine*, argues that the "body can be 'heard' in *Pilgrimage*, if one reads for it."[64] Thus, the origin of the interrelation between the *roman-fleuve* and *écriture féminine* is placed in women's sexuality: "This is how I would define a feminine textual body: as a *female libidinal economy*, a regime, energies, a system of spending not necessarily carved out by culture. A feminine textual body is recognized by the fact that it is always endless, without ending: there's no closure, it doesn't stop, and it's this that often makes the feminine text difficult to read. For we've learned to read books that basically pose the word 'end.' But this one doesn't finish, a feminine text goes on and on and at a certain moment the volume comes to an end but the writing continues and for the reader this means being thrust into the void."[65]

Critics' evaluations of the final installment of *Pilgrimage* reveal various reactions to what Cixous calls being "thrust into the void." Thomas Staley finds the work's lack of closure thematically appropriate: it "anticipates developments in Miss Richardson's art and preserves the consistency of the open-form novel which reflects Miriam's continuous journey through life"; he sees the final incident as essentially circular: "Thus *Pilgrimage* ends as it had begun: Miriam is about to set out again on another journey."[66] In contrast, other critics have traditionally sought to defend Richardson from charges of inconclusiveness. Gregory, for instance, finds a closure in the last novel; he argues that *March Moonlight* brings together the "loose threads left dangling at the end" of the previous volume and claims that "it seems complete"; however, while he views *March Moonlight* as a "coda to the whole work," he neglects to mention the new element of this work, the enigmatic Jean.[67] Fromm also feels compelled to find some kind of closure: "in spite of its unfinished state—[*Pilgrimage*] bears a stamp of completeness in the unity and philosophic integrity of its vision."[68] While Richardson's biographer provides copious evidence that Richardson faced numerous obstacles in completing *Pilgrimage*—the distractions of the war, her incessant search for adequate housing, the needs of Alan Odle—Fromm's analysis also suggests that Richardson did not feel compelled to finish the *roman-fleuve*. Whatever the uncongenial demands of her publishers and the exigencies of supporting herself and her husband, the unassailable fact is that if she had wanted to give *Pilgrimage* a neat and well-bound ending, she had ample opportunity to do so, both when *Dimple Hill* was published and afterward. More recently, feminist critics Friedman, Fuchs, DuPlessis, and Showalter have viewed the "incompleteness" as a deliberate artistic choice.[69]

The final novel, *March Moonlight*, evades closure through the contested ending characteristic of the *roman-fleuve*—a narrative feature also found in the Pallisers and *A Dance to the Music of Time*. *March Moonlight* provides an ending stalled by a series of tensions. Although another prospective husband, Charles Ducorroy, is eliminated (he backs out when

Miriam confesses her affair with Hypo, and Mary Rachel asks her to leave the house because of Ducorroy's continued interest in her), her feelings about him are ambivalent. The penultimate prospect, Richard Roscorla, was eliminated more conclusively when, as he visited her in her sitting room Miriam refused to give him a sign that she was still interested, that smile of "invitation" that she despises in women (*MM* 622). She claims that since it takes five years to recover from love, she will be over Ducorroy in the autumn of 1915 (657). One of two explicit dates in the entire thirteen volumes of *Pilgrimage*, this is of course the year *Pointed Roofs* was published, suggesting a correlation between the end of this last thought of marriage and Miriam's emergence as a writer. As Miriam is taken in as a lodger by Mrs. Gay, one further possible suitor appears. Although Miriam has specified that she wants to lodge only in a house where she is the sole boarder (either to give her more opportunity to write or to avoid the suspicion of any further entanglements with men), when she arrives at Mrs. Gay's she is greeted by the Chopin piece, that recurrent theme suggesting joy, played by the "unconfessed" lodger, Mr. Noble, a thinly disguised portrait of Richardson's husband, Alan Odle. The ending of the novel does not clearly foreshadow a relationship, but Miriam met three of her most important previous suitors (Michael Shatov, Richard Roscorla, and Charles Ducorroy) through the social atmosphere of the boardinghouse. Although DuPlessis argues that no future relationship is hinted at and that "Richardson avoids for the telos of *Pilgrimage* the transformative act she chose for herself,"[70] because of the possibility of yet *another* suitor, the novel does not achieve the closure of Miriam's certain spinsterhood.

Her relationships with Amabel and Jean provide other resolutions in tension. Although Amabel behaves in a condescending way to Miriam after her own involvement with Michael begins, this does not erase the mutual significance of the relationship. Amabel is smug about achieving the purportedly feminine ideal of marriage; she insistently and wrongly suggests to Miriam that she has won some sort of "rivalry" between them, when in reality Miriam notes, "How thankfully I had given Michael into her hands" (658). The portrayal of Amabel reveals deficiencies in the role she has assumed. Amabel, who believes in "exploiting feminine charm and feminine weakness" (*CH* 343), is shown to degrade both herself and Miriam in viewing them as rivals. In the final scene she is reduced, as Miriam predicted she would be, to a "busy, responsible housewife disposing of an amiably cherished young visitor saying: 'Well, my poppet,' and going on to suggest the disposal of my morning" (MM 658). The idea of "disposing" of time, a precious commodity to Miriam, evokes the character of Alma, Hypo's wife, similarly limited by her role as housekeeper and wife. Amabel's feminism may also be undermined when the previously jailed suffragette claims, "Marriage, and Paul, have swept away all my interest in votes for women" (658). The statement reveals the superficiality of Amabel's previous political stance, in contrast to Miriam's alternative feminism behind the scenes of the suffrage movement. These revelations foreground Miriam as ultimately a more consistent feminist, one of greater integrity, a comparison suggested by their names. Both names contain the syllable "am," both women are in contact with "being"; however, whereas Miriam is able to achieve the "I am" of true identity,[71] her friend is caught in the role prescribed for her by patriarchy, she is (am) a-bel(le).

Despite her ambivalence about Amabel's domestic conversion, Miriam decides that "the essence of our relationship remains untouched" (658), and the final scene—of March Moonlight and of Pilgrimage—attests to the bond between the women. When Miriam picks up and holds Amabel and Michael's child she feels "the complete stilling of every one of my competing urgencies. Freedom" (658). Miriam has achieved maternal fulfillment by bringing together Michael and Amabel, whose limitations make them suited for each other. At the same time Miriam is freed for the self-development impossible for one involved with (and thus limited by) others. This fulfillment, which seemingly sets up a kind of closure, is, however, immediately undermined by a question: "If Jean's marriage with Joe Davenport brought her a child, should I feel, in holding it, that same sense of fulfillment?" (658). There is always another case, another possibility to be explored. Her relationship with Jean, much deeper and never fully articulated in the text, offers another possibility— the unspeakable possibility of lesbian love, which may not hinder self-knowledge in the same way as the male-female relationship.

The last scene is also ironic: any closure that it achieves is accomplished through the freeze-frame technique, presenting a tableau with Miriam as madonna, the "virgin" mother, holding the boy-child that is and is not her own. Hanscombe stresses the alternative posed by this ending, as it suggests "the possibility that female creative energy may issue, not only separately in the production of babies on one hand, and books on the other, but also simultaneously in the production of both, by the manipulation of art to produce life."[72] Hanscombe's reading of this scene suggests yet another subversion of patriarchal engendering of texts. Ironically, Amabel and Michael name their boy Paul, evoking the misogynist apostle. The name recalls an earlier scene in *Honeycomb*, when Miriam finds herself unable to read the New Testament to Mrs. Henderson because "St Paul rhapsodized sometimes . . . but in a superior way . . . patronizing; as if no one but himself knew anything" (486). In the final scene, Miriam cradles the arch-misogynist, recalling that curious love scene in which Miriam maternally embraces Hypo G. Wilson, her "little babe, just born." The patriarchal principle is suborned, reduced to the ineffectuality of a child in his mother's arms. The reiterative and self-reflexive narrative of the *roman-fleuve* invites us to look at the final scene not merely as resolution, inherently outside the narrative, but also within the context of the entire *Pilgrimage*.

The final tableau marks Miriam's triumph in a number of ways. Hanscombe believes it "embodies Miriam's eventual acceptance of her own maternal longings, but with the striking difference from the traditional image that the child she holds is not her own."[73] As DuPlessis argues, it "resurrects the mother-child dyad" while at the same time Miriam has evaded marriage and fulfilled her quest, distinguishing this resolution from those nineteenth-century endings of death or marriage[74] or death-in-marriage. Miriam has achieved a vicarious motherhood through Amabel and Michael's parenthood, which she initiated by introducing them. Her ability, as a surrogate, to give birth suggests she has surmounted her grief over her mother's death in achieving a sort of motherhood herself. At the same time, Richardson seems aware of the problem inherent in an ending that privileges the madonna–boy-child dyad. She forestalls the suggestion that she has engendered a male line, reinstating patriarchy, with the ironic allusion to St. Paul. The ending represents an ideologically charged feminist triumph, but it acknowledges the conflicts and contradictions that are inherent in a dual-sex culture: the constant struggle to dominate and subvert domination are reflected in the ironic final tableau. The ending is the place where these conflicts must inevitably surface: "Any resolution can have traces of the conflicting materials that have been processed within it. It is where subtexts and repressed discourses can throw up one last flare of meaning; it is where the author may sidestep and displace attention from the materials that a work has made available."[75] Although the ending provides a kind of closure, it is a resolution in tension, characteristic of the oscillating dynamics of the *roman-fleuve* and the nonlinear narrative of an *écriture féminine*.

The connection between a form such as the *roman-fleuve* and gendered discourse is suggested by Susan Gubar: "The attraction of women writers to personal forms of expression like letters, autobiographies, confessional poetry, diaries, and journals points up the effect of a life experienced as an art or an art experienced as a kind of life. . . . Many books by women writers (like Dorothy Richardson's *Pilgrimage* and Olive Schreiner's *From Man to Man*) cannot be finished because they are as ongoing and open-ended as the lives of their authors."[76] In *Dimple Hill* Miriam, an emerging writer, wrestles with the problem of form and her rejection of the novelistic tradition. She rejects "these tracts of narrative [that] were somehow false, a sort of throwing of dust that still would be dust even if its grains could be transformed to gold; question-begging, skating along surfaces to a superficial finality, gratuitously, in no matter what tone of voice, offered as a conclusion" (524). Miriam rejects writing that draws the conclusions of a phallologocentrism that feigns knowledge and closure based on "clever" platitudes. *Pilgrimage*, it appears, was not completed because Richardson's aesthetic deemphasizes closure and finality—not, as Showalter suggests, because she associates the ending of her *roman-fleuve* with her own death.[77] Although she, like any other writer, was gratified by the publication and recognition of her achievement, in her 1938 foreword to *Pilgrimage* Richardson makes an important distinction between publication and "participation" in literary innovation; the latter is more important to her than publication, which the very genre and techniques she has chosen may render impossible (10). As long as the writer is experiencing, learning, developing, her work can never be complete. The obsession with closure is part of the phallocentric game.

In *Pilgrimage*, Richardson presents an alternative to phallocentric discourse by defining and representing an *écriture féminine*. Her position is to eschew androgyny as a solution to women's oppression, and her protagonist does not seek to transcend the boundaries of feminine language but rather to exploit the content within. Richardson, however, in this controversial novel seeks to transcend the boundaries of conventions of fiction. In the creation of her lengthy *roman-fleuve*, she is not only the first modernist stream of consciousness writer, but she is also the precursor of those contemporary feminist theorists who would create a woman's language. Hélène Cixous claims that "with a few rare exceptions, there has not yet been any writing that inscribes femininity."[78] In her pioneering experimental novel, Dorothy Richardson is one of those rare writers who advocate and inscribe an *écriture féminine*.

Chapter Four

Anthony Powell's *A Dance to the Music of Time*

A Text of Arrested Desire

Narratologists from Aristotle to contemporary literary critics employ metaphors that compare the progression of plot to a journey, a quest, a stream, a mystery. Perhaps most provocative of all is Brooks's explicitly coital metaphor: the movement from the incitement of desire, through the stimulating detours of narrative subplots, to the climax of revelation is the model of the plots we read for. Powell's *A Dance to the Music of Time*, however, exemplifies the diffusive narrative dynamic of *écriture féminine* as it resists this pattern. Desire functions as both a narrative stimulus and a major theme in this text. Yet the sexuality Powell foregrounds through the erotic response of his characters—impotence, voyeurism, nymphomania, promiscuity, homosexuality, and communal sexual rites—insistently collapses the erotic into patterns of teasing, purportedly deviant desire, desire often designated as feminine.

The neon diver, whose presence seems almost to precipitate Nick's first embrace of Jean Templer Duport, is an emblem of the recursive desire that motivates plot and character in *The Music of Time*: "[She] dives eternally through the petrol-tainted air; night and day, winter and summer, never reaching the water of the pool to which she endlessly glides. Like some image of arrested development, she returns for ever, voluntarily, to the springboard from which she started her leap" (*AW* 64). The "arrested" progression of the diver suggests the oscillating narrative of *The Music of Time* and anticipates its avoidance of climax. Continually reiterating, the narrative, like the neon diver, persistently evades its destination. Each new incident drives the narrative on—to the telos of a new scene, chapter, volume—but as it reiterates, returning to the "springboard," so to speak, it creates a narrative in tension. The accumulation of varied narratives both advances the plot and delays— "eternally," "endlessly"—the culmination of the reading. Repeatedly refusing termination, the extensive reiterations of the *roman-fleuve* ultimately give the various plot lines the wavelike, synchronous progression of *écriture féminine*. This successive advancing and retracting movement produces a tantalizing, incessant narrative foreplay.

Given its reiterative structure, it is surprising that the narrative can progress at all, but *The Music of Time* does, eventually, move forward despite its repeated steps backward. Brooks's description of the pleasure and frustration derived from the "binding" force of repetition suggests the extended foreplay of a sexual tease: "As the word 'binding' itself suggests, these formalizations and the recognitions they provoke may in some sense be painful: they create a delay, a postponement in the discharge of energy, a turning back from immediate pleasure, to ensure that the ultimate pleasurable discharge will be more complete. The most effective or, at the least, the most challenging texts may be those that are most delayed, most highly bound, most painful."[1] This description assumes a more satisfying "discharge" as a result of the delays of repetition, but in this as in other examples of the *roman-fleuve* deferral continually entices the reader without culminating in the narrative ejaculation Brooks proposes.

One would expect that as a contemporary *roman-fleuve*, *The Music of Time* would exhibit many of the traits of its modernist antecedents in the genre, such as *Pilgrimage* and *A la recherche du temps perdu*, and that a later exemplar produced by a writer as well steeped in literary tradition as Powell might push the genetic repertoire of the *roman-fleuve* to a greater experimentation. As Fowler notes, "What produces generic resemblances, reflection soon shows, is tradition: a sequence of influence and imitation and inherited codes connecting works in the genre."[2] Powell is undeniably aware of the Proustian *roman-fleuve*— his narrator Nick Jenkins not only reads *A la recherche du temps perdu* in *The Military Philosophers* and compares himself at one point to Proust's Marcel (121), but he is also elated in this novel to find himself billeted in Cabourg, Proust's Balbec. Furthermore, as I mention in my introduction, Powell discovered Proust while at Oxford. However, when it comes to the form of his own *roman-fleuve*, Powell exhibits, by and large, an indifference to Proust's narrative innovations.[3] Powell's description of his rationale in choosing the multivolume form echoes the passage from Trollope's autobiography in which he describes the form of his Pallisers:

> In practice the term "novel", after every kind of variation has been tried out, has come to be thought of as comprising a work with some sort of a beginning, middle, end, taking up a length of about 80,000 words. Although well disposed in the arts towards discipline in structure (a phrase again to beg all sorts of questions), I have never felt particularly at ease in the eighty-thousand framework as an end in itself. . . . A long sequence seemed to offer all sorts of advantages, among them release from the re-engagement every year or so of the same actors and extras hanging about for employment at the stage door of one's creative fantasy. Instead of sacking the lot at the end of a brief run—with the moral certainty that at least one or two of the more tenacious will be back again seeking a job, if not this year or next, then in a decade's time—the production itself might be extended, the actors made to work longer and harder for much the same creative remuneration spread over an extended period; instead of being butchered at regular intervals to make a publisher's holiday.[4]

Powell, then, conceives of his project as a hyperbolic novel, expressing dissatisfaction not with the form but rather with the restricted length and scope of the conventional novel.

In many ways, Powell's *roman-fleuve* resembles the multiplot Victorian novel, exhibiting many of the characteristics found in Trollope's Pallisers: the shifting emphasis on various groups of characters, the reiterations of plots and subplots, the digressive middle, and the copious flow of a detailed and primarily chronological but often nonlinear narrative. Neil Brennan classes Proust's and Powell's *romans-fleuves* together because of their resemblances to the Victorian novel: "Proust's seven volumes (1913-27) and Powell's eleven to date (1951-73) derive as composite structures from a reactionary tendency in the novel: a return to something like the massive Victorian triple-decker, but they return with greater esthetic control."[5] However, because of the vast difference between the narrative techniques of Proust and Powell, the latter is in many ways closer to his nineteenth-century British predecessor.

At the same time, Powell surpasses the scope of his precursors: although *A Dance to the Music of Time* is closer in length to Richardson's *Pilgrimage*—2,948 pages (Little, Brown edition) and 2,110 pages (Knopf), respectively—than to Trollope's significantly longer 4,413 pages (Oxford World's Classics), Powell's narrative (fictional) time is greater, spanning approximately fifty years in comparison with the roughly twenty-five-year periods covered in the narratives of the Pallisers and *Pilgrimage*. This expanse suggests that Powell exceeds Trollope's and Richardson's encyclopedic and comprehensive conception of the genre and further expands its temporal quality. Although Powell is postmodern more in the chronological sense than in the technical use of the term—his narrative techniques are relatively conventional—a hint of postmodernity is found in the text's point of view, in the irony of Jenkins's self-effacing stance and his skepticism about his role as narrator, which intimate a kind of postmodern consciousness.[6] In general, however, Powell is poised between the Victorian and modern conceptions of the genre. His self-proclaimed "discipline in structure" leads him frequently to rely upon features of the conventional novel in a postmodern exemplar of a predominately modern form. This ambivalence vis-à-vis narrative innovation typifies his efforts to write against the features of the *roman-fleuve*.

Some of the features Powell uses, such as the digressive middle, appear in both the Victorian and the modern *roman-fleuve*. The war trilogy of the third movement of *A Dance to the Music of Time*, for example, breaks with the generally upper-class and bohemian cast of characters, as Nick finds himself an officer in Wales surrounded by men of a different social class, generally Welsh bankers. This world is largely repressed at the end of the third movement as Nick shifts back into the world of civilian life. Characteristically, the structure of Powell's *roman-fleuve* seems to suggest the organization of the traditional novel; however, although the work appears symmetrical, neatly divided into novels of equal length comprising four movements, or subsets, of three novels each, an examination of these parts reveals that the order is less neat and tidy than it seems. The division of *The Music of Time* into twelve titled volumes and four movements suggests both a zodiacal and a seasonal organization, but time progresses unevenly within the four movements; Henry Harrington notes "their temporal asymmetry, covering roughly twelve, sixteen, six, and finally, twelve years."[7] Although the four-volume division corresponds, in a seasonal progression, to stages in the lives of Nick Jenkins and Widmerpool, within the volumes themselves four or five highly integrated episodes generally create a narrative structure that is more fluid than discrete.

Powell's *roman-fleuve* thus exhibits a resistance to certain proclivities of the genre. The episodes, volumes, and movements provide a means for emplotting the *fleuve*, creating a sense of unity, but the primary structural principle is that of a tension between its backward and forward impulses, creating a spiraling or cyclical movement, a fluid narrative that distinguishes the *roman-fleuve* from more highly plotted novels. Although the final novel seems to achieve a neat closure, circling back to reveal that the entire narrative is a flashback, its resolution is actually as conflicted as those of Trollope or Richardson. The tension inherent in the *roman-fleuve*, a dynamics poised between containment and flow, is exacerbated in *A Dance to the Music of Time* by another kind of tension. Powell's novelistic techniques reflect an Aristotelian and Jamesian aesthetic privileging unity and closure, yet these features conflict with the feminine narrative propensities of the genre he has chosen.

✥ The Entrance of the "Exciting Forces"

The ejaculatory paradigm implies that the function of an introduction, once the narrative housekeeping of exposition is completed, is to initiate "the exciting forces," the desire that will dispatch the protagonists in search of their destinies and precipitate the readers forward in a parallel quest for Barthes's "pleasure of the text." Barthes's description of the "deflation" that follows the long-anticipated "erotic scene" in texts of desire[8] is significantly averted in Powell's *roman-fleuve*, which deprivileges the forward momentum toward the forceful climax of the traditional novel and thus forestalls what Barthes describes as an inevitable narrative postcoital *tristesse*. Powell's work as a Hollywood scriptwriter is, according to his own descriptions, an influence on his ideas about exposition, "the necessity of 'establishing' early on in the story circumstances to be used at a later stage. This is a technique to be observed in the books of, say, Proust or Joyce, as much as in any competent detective story."[9] Unlike the expository gaps of film or the detective story, however, which create a forward movement of curiosity, Powell's exposition instead is motivated, almost from the very start, by a backward pull characteristic of the highly developed structural or *roman* elements in his work. The exordium of *The Music of Time* provides the basis for a more pronounced unity in this *roman-fleuve* than in Trollope's Pallisers or Richardson's *Pilgrimage* but, at the same time, it exhibits little forward-moving drive, in keeping with the narrative resistance of *écriture féminine*.

As with other examples of the genre, its vast scope poses a challenge for those who have not read or cannot remember details from previous volumes. Allan James Tucker comments on this problem in conjunction with one of Powell's references to a painting, the Modigliani that disappears and reappears several times in the series: "But not everyone who picks up *Books Do Furnish a Room* will have read *The Acceptance World*; and, to put it mildly, not everyone who has will recall the passing reference to the Modigliani: a twelve-volume *roman-fleuve* bears some matters off to be lost and forgotten in the deep."[10] Powell evinces an awareness of the difficulties that a multi-volume work poses for the readers. In an interview, he evokes "the exigencies of publication" to explain the need to make each volume self-sufficient and remembers that Proust, paying for the publication of *A la recherche du temps perdu* himself, "didn't make the slightest effort to make the thing complete in itself"; at the same time, he concedes that "it's probably quite good for [the writer] to make your 80,000 words intelligible for somebody who hasn't read the others."[11]

Powell, like Trollope, comes up with a solution that addresses the needs of both the casual and the perspicacious reader. When he alludes to an event of a previous volume, the actual reference is usually made without explanation, allowing the ideal reader (the one who reads the work in its entirety) the excitement of recognition. However, a page or so later he usually follows with an explanation, which needlessly interrupts the knowledgeable reader's forward movement in the narrative. For example, in *Temporary Kings* Nick narrates an event he did not himself witness, describing how Bagshaw's father encountered Pamela Widmerpool standing naked in the downstairs hall of his son's house in the middle of the night. Because of its oddity and its similarity to two previous peculiar occurrences, the ideal reader immediately mentally juxtaposes these three scenes, searching for a symbolic link between them. However, Powell apparently fears that the casual reader might not connect the three incidents, because Nick explains the obvious similarity several pages later: "Reflecting on similar instances in my own experience, there was the time (actually not witnessed) when the parlourmaid, Billson, had walked naked into the drawing-room at Stonehurst; more tangibly, when the front door of her flat had been opened to myself by Jean Duport in the same condition. Unlike Candaules's queen, these two had deliberately chosen to appear in that state, not, as the Queen—anyway vis-à-vis Gynes—involuntarily nude" (196).

The explanation is perhaps included to show Nick's reaction to the incidents (comparing the scenes to that depicted on the Tiepolo ceiling), but this too is a comparison the reader could make. Powell's technique is generally to establish explicit rather than implied connections. This kind of narratorial condescension, exhibited by both Trollope and Powell, may indicate a lack of confidence in the memories of their readers, an inevitable problem given the complexity and length of the genre chosen. As originally published, with an average two-year hiatus between each of the twelve volumes, *The Music of Time* may have needed these references to stimulate the readers' memories. (It is unfortunate that any individual reader of the *roman-fleuve* cannot experience a first reading of the text in both installment and collected formats in order to compare the impact of these different kinds of reading.) The genre does, nevertheless, provide a common fund of experiences and knowledge that joins reader and writer in an experience that aspires to the fullness of life itself. Richard Jones comments, "As the work gathers way, the loyal reader picks up the recapitulations and echoes from the past, and these create not only a sense of life lived but of life shared with the writer."[12]

Despite such a compromise in service of the less-informed reader, Powell refuses to begin entirely again (despite his recapitulations) in each volume, a major refinement in the form of the *roman-fleuve* and a contrast to the Victorian expository techniques of Trollope. Each volume of Trollope's *roman-fleuve* commences with exposition that either introduces new characters or brings us up to date on previous ones (as, for example, with Phineas Finn in *Phineas Redux*). The individual volumes of *The Music of Time* usually begin either by circling back in time to the period of Nick's childhood, or by referring back to the exposition of a previous volume, or by combining these two retrospective techniques, contributing to the effect of an expansive meganovel. This technique, also typical of the serial, "is more characteristic of modern than Victorian fiction."[13] The backward movement achieves a link with the past material and gives Powell's *roman-fleuve* a high degree of unity, while it also engenders a staggered exposition by introducing the large casts of characters incrementally, throughout the *roman-fleuve*, rather than in the first volume.

The "dynamic system" of a text, claims Meir Sternberg, "turns on gaps in general and expositional gaps [those created by plunging *in medias res*] in particular."[14] If this were the case in *The Music of Time*, Powell would have created perhaps the longest expository gap in literary history. The initial exposition raises questions that remain unanswered for twelve volumes: "Two thousand nine hundred and forty-seven pages later the reader learns that at the narrative's beginning Nick has just stepped from Henderson's art gallery in the neighborhood of Berkeley Square."[15] This delayed exposition does not provoke the suspense-creating gap that stimulates curiosity, however. The reader of *The Music of Time* is not consumed with desire to know from what vantage point the narrator is watching the street workers or why they are working on the streets. Although there is a gap in the knowledge initially supplied about Nick—we know nothing about his physical appearance, and his family background is scattered piecemeal throughout this and subsequent volumes—because he is so neutral, especially in this first chapter, where he is almost completely passive, Powell's sparse depiction does not stimulate the reader's desire for more information. Two other expository gaps occur in *A Question of Upbringing* as Stringham announces that Widmerpool "got Akworth sacked" (13) and as Nick mentions the "Braddock alias Thorne" incident (35), the major plot event of the chapter, the account of which is postponed for about a page while Nick introduces his two friends Stringham and Templer. The mention of the Akworth affair may stimulate some slight curiosity on the part of the reader, and indeed it does turn out to be a significant detail in *Hearing Secret Harmonies* as Widmerpool does penance for his unjust treatment of Akworth, but it certainly does not initiate the detective genre of suspense.

Although Nick Jenkins does not explicitly mock suspense as Trollope's narrator does, he generally will not condescend to it either, as, for example, in the scene in *At Lady Molly's* when Nick meets Isobel and immediately reveals that he will marry her. (One notable exception to this practice occurs in *Casanova's Chinese Restaurant*, when Nick states that Isobel is in a nursing home but delays disclosure of the reason—that she has had a miscarriage—for over thirty pages.) Because of the device of a retrospective narrator any gaps are, of course, deliberate and contrived: if Nick withholds information it suggests either repression for purposes of suspense (which Nick generally disdains) or his own lack of information about circumstances at a specific point of his life. The latter occurs in the delayed revelations of details about Nick's affair with Jean Duport. At the time of Jenkins's affair in *The Acceptance World*, the reader has no real sense of being denied information because of Nick's habitual reticence about his private life. However, in keeping with the chronological narrative, details about Jean's simultaneous affairs with Nick and Jimmy Brent are delayed until Jenkins learns of the Brent affair through a conversation with Bob Duport in *The Kindly Ones*. In this way the reader shares with Nick the shock of a mistaken conception of a past reality.

Nick's after-the-fact disclosure of titillating specifics about his affair with Jean elicits a similar shock when he recalls, in *Books Do Furnish a Room*, "that sudden hug watching a film, her whisper, 'You make me feel so randy'" (99) or, in *The Military Philosophers*, "those words, those very unexpected expressions, she was accustomed to cry out aloud at the moment of achievement" (235). This suppressed revelation is obviously contrived, as Nick possessed this information from the time of the third volume. Although Powell withholds information, when it is finally revealed it is used to achieve the backward-moving revision of earlier conception (a modernist technique also used by Richardson), rather than the conventional forward-moving drive of suspense. Both writers subvert the momentum toward the climax of traditional narrative, but Powell's narrative seems divided against itself, stimulating curiosity after the fact. Powell undermines the narrative climax, ironically, by revealing that there was a climax that was not offered to the reader: a climactic event is narrated in an anticlimactic fashion. The reader is offered the anticlimax of an event that has already taken place, offstage so to speak.

The introduction of Powell's *roman-fleuve*, like those of Trollope's and Richardson's, disseminates desire in an erratic and uncertain way, typical of the genre's emphasis on process: the narrative *fleuve* conflicts with sharply defined introductions, resulting in oblique exposition. Desire is obstructed at the same time it is incited as the text begins its characteristic pattern of development, repetition, and oscillation—the narrative "dance"—before the necessary introductory functions are completed. Furthermore, as in Trollope's *Can You Forgive Her?*, the protracted exposition, necessitated by the numerous characters and plot lines to be introduced, constantly shifts the focus from one plot and protagonist to another, creating confusion about who, if anyone, will emerge as the real protagonist, the strongest agent of desire. Brooks argues, in Lacanian fashion, that narratives present a story of "desire," but in the introduction of *The Music of Time* that story is difficult to locate. Indeed, *if* Nick Jenkins is the work's protagonist, the male plot of quest and adventure is conspicuously (and significantly) absent.

Powell's *roman-fleuve* works its way through layers of exordia, a staggered presentation that obscures the boundary between exposition and "rising action." The first introduction, an extended metaphoric prologue that compares the street workers Jenkins is contemplating to Poussin's painting *A Dance to the Music of Time*, is a frame narrative that introduces the entire *roman-fleuve* rather than the individual novel in which it appears. The prologue exposition initiates no action; it points not forward, to future events, but backward in time, to "the ancient world—legionaries in sheepskin warming themselves at a brazier" (*QU* 1–2). The forward movement of the major associations of Nick's thoughts is interrupted by embedded comparisons that delay the forward movement of the passage and refer backward, alluding to a seventeenth-century painting, then moving from the mythical to the personal past: "Classical associations made me think, too, of days at school, where so many forces, hitherto unfamiliar, had become in due course uncompromisingly clear" (2). Introducing a metaphor that suggests both a view of human destiny and the narrative dynamics of the *roman-fleuve*, Jenkins describes Poussin's dancers as "human beings, facing outward like the Seasons, moving hand in hand in intricate measure: stepping slowly, methodically, sometimes a trifle awkwardly, in evolutions that take recognisable shape: or breaking into seemingly meaningless gyrations, while partners disappear only to reappear again, once more giving pattern to the spectacle: unable to control the melody, unable, perhaps, to control the steps of the dance" (2). The dancers, like the seasons they represent, move in a nonlinear, circular or cyclical configuration—the dance has no start, no finish—but they step in "intricate measure," just as the *roman-fleuve*, a novel seemingly without end, progresses through succinct narrative units that develop into an increasingly complex interrelation. The work's design, like Poussin's dance, has "evolutions" that take "recognisable shape" only with the terminal frame, which reveals the whole narrative to be a flashback in the mind of the narrator.[16] It is a narrative that, as in *l'écriture féminine*, resists linear progression or immediate comprehension; like the dancers, it "break[s] into seemingly meaningless gyrations," independent, synchronic narratives whose cumulative meaning only gradually coalesces in the mind of the incrementally informed reader.

The prologue, or frame, effects a transition into a second, more conventional exposition to the individual novel, *A Question of Upbringing*, recounting Nick Jenkins's recollections of his days at school, in particular the day that Widmerpool first took shape in his mind, emerging from the fog, jogging clumsily along. The second exposition, however, reiterates the methods, techniques, and themes of the prologue introduction. The dance imagery of the prologue, for example, is evoked in the description of Widmerpool running, "stiffly, almost majestically mov[ing] on his heels out of the mist" (4). The technique of double exordia intimates that any point of initiation is subject to revision and reiteration and is, therefore, arbitrary. The second introduction is a frame within a larger frame: just as the extended metaphor of the street workers brackets the first and last volumes of the *roman-fleuve*, so this exposition recalls the birth of Nick's conception of Widmerpool and anticipates his death in the final pages of *Hearing Secret Harmonies* (where Widmerpool drops dead during a ritual cult run). Although this exposition gradually moves into narrative action, it does not initiate a linear narrative, but instead develops at times diachronically (dramatizing the process of social evolution), at times synchronically (depicting the recurrent pattern of human fate), subordinating forward progression to a spiraling, seemingly digressive comprehensiveness. This vacillation between the linearity of the conventional novel and the synchronous development of *écriture féminine* characteristic of the *roman-fleuve* is typical of *A Dance to the Music of Time*.

Powell's *roman-fleuve* also exhibits a tension between an impulse toward multiplicity, the plenitude of *écriture féminine*, and an impulse to tightly order the wealth of detail. The major purpose of the exposition is not to initiate action but to originate a metaphoric context; it supplies a frame of reference for the narrative to follow, one function of beginnings. As Edward Said observes: "The more crowded and confused a field appears, the more a beginning, fictional or not, seems imperative. A beginning gives us the chance to do work that compensates us for the tumbling disorder or brute reality that will not settle down."[17] The multiplicity of plots and the swarm of characters that comprise *The Music of Time* undoubtedly constitute a "crowded field." The initial exposition, as has been noted by Powell's critics, implies that life and history are patterned rather than chaotic,[18] imposing an image of order upon the variety of the diverse characters and plots. The metaphor functions to suggest the regular interconnection of characters, the pattern of repetition that constitutes the development of the *roman-fleuve*, "a loosely woven pattern within which parallels, contrasts, repetitions will occasionally occur."[19]

The image of the dancers moving in step also suggests an organization of causality, yet it is a causality that they are perhaps "unable to control"; in this sense the characters are "led a dance," as Tucker has argued, commenting on the irony of the metaphor.[20] This determinism is affirmed as Nick observes, "Nothing in life is planned—or everything is—because in the dance every step is ultimately the corollary of the step before; the consequence of being the kind of person one chances to be" (AW 63). Nick appears to believe that human fate is determined by character, which is basically fixed and unchanging, the same view Trollope expresses in his *Autobiography* and dramatizes in the Pallisers—a view challenged by the erratic evolution within the consciousness of Miriam Henderson in *Pilgrimage*. Nick's interpretation of the dance and the last statement in the initial passage suggest that his creator discerns, however, a tension between determinism and chaos; the unpredictable happenings create contingency, forming a recognizable pattern only in retrospect. Nick comments on the random interconnectedness of life in *A Buyer's Market*, elucidating the statement in the prologue exposition: "Existence fans out indefinitely into new areas of experience, and . . . almost every additional acquaintance offers some supplementary world with its own hazards and enchantments. As time goes on, of course, these supposedly different worlds, in fact, draw closer if not to each other, then to some pattern common to all; so that, at last, diversity between them, if in truth existent, seems to be almost imperceptible except in a few crude and exterior ways" (159). Critics, especially since the publication of the last volume of the *roman-fleuve*, have often perceived a deterministic pattern in *The Music of Time*: "There are many indications in all the subsequent volumes that random lives may be connected in ways that hint at a point, a purpose, some underlying design."[21] Jenkins dallies with the paradox inherent in the idea of contingency: that events depend on contingencies that are unknown but causally motivated—these are the contingencies that initiate the dance to the music of time; contingency holds order and chaos together as conflicting possibilities.

Powell's introduction undermines its agents of narrative desire even as they are introduced, creating another kind of tension. As the focus of the extensive introductory chapter shifts from the street workers, to art and myth, to Widmerpool, and then to Nick's other schoolmates, keeping the narrator always in the background, it is never evident who (if anyone) will emerge as protagonist, an uncertainty that remains unresolved throughout the entire twelve volumes. Widmerpool, who might be regarded as the protagonist (or the antagonist) of the *roman-fleuve*, is a parody of ambitious nineteenth-century protagonists such as Balzac's Rastignac or Stendhal's Julien Sorel, characterized by Brooks as "desiring machines."[22] As an agent of narrative desire, Widmerpool is an equivocal figure. He stimulates curiosity, particularly as he recurs to Nick insistently throughout the twelve volumes as a character who must be understood, part of Nick's personal past to be subjugated in the male masterplot. Yet Widmerpool is an elusive character, neither hero nor villain, politically and personally amorphous, a social chameleon who changes color with each new social era. Nick never grasps Widmerpool's identity, and he is pictured at the end as at the beginning, running a race of social competition, a variant of the work's central dance metaphor. Widmerpool is a character who has often been seen by critics as an embodiment of will. Succeeding General Conyers and succeeded by Scorpio Murtlock, he is one of a series of will figures. Widmerpool epitomizes the will to power in its essential form; he metamorphoses from one social role to another. At one time an admirer of Hitler, at another suspected of Communist allegiance, at another a proponent of occult counterculture values, he is flexible in his ideological affiliation.[23] As the twelve volumes of *The Music of Time* chronicle Widmerpool's various achievements, however, he emerges as an ironic protagonist, ridiculed at each social triumph. The threat Widmerpool poses is insistently suggested, yet the desires that stimulate his social advancement are continually undermined.

Widmerpool's role as agent of desire is also subverted by the depiction of his passive erotic deviance and impotence, traits that undermine the forward movement of the ejaculatory plot and the masculine quest. His tastes run to masochism, the narrator reveals in *A Question of Upbringing*, as he recounts Stringham's anecdote about Widmerpool's masochistic (and implicitly homosexual) pleasure at being pelted with an overripe (and appropriately phallic) banana thrown by the charming Budd, an account that is voyeuristically savored by the self-effacing narrator, Nick Jenkins. In this scene, Nick is increasingly distanced from his own story as he recounts an anecdote that was narrated to him by another: therefore, the introduction presents two passive agents of desire, Widmerpool and Jenkins, both increasingly characterized as voyeurs throughout the novel, displacing desire from protagonist to protagonist, undermining the potency of each—potency being a seeming prerequisite for heroes in masculine plots of adventure or suspense. The oblique multiple exordia stimulate desire sufficiently to move the plot forward, but they function less to introduce conflicts than to establish the pattern of oscillation that typifies the *roman-fleuve* and *écriture féminine*, which begins "on all sides at once."[24]

As narrator, Nick is the center, the supposed hub around which the characters, the dancers, revolve. Yet Jenkins, also a candidate for protagonist, initiates almost no action; he is subordinated to the narrative he relates. Critics are sharply divided on their estimation of Jenkins's role in the action. Thomas Wilcox sees him as "an active participant in the events of the novel," whereas Tucker argues that the narrator does "not influence the course of events," resulting in "a gap, an emptiness . . . at the center of the novel"; Mark Facknitz believes that Jenkins "comes increasingly into being, but at a pace much slower than that of other characters."[25] Although a narrator-protagonist must participate in the action to some extent and cannot totally extricate himself or herself from the tangle of relationships that ensue, Nick is remarkable for the infrequency with which he initiates or influences actions in the novel. The few instances are so rare as to be especially memorable, as, for example, when Nick urges Gwatkin to seduce a barmaid, causing Gwatkin to become so perturbed that he forgets the code word and is subsequently relieved of his company. Generally, Nick's actions are the result of outside circumstances—when he embraces Jean Templer as the car they are riding in passes over a bumpy road or when he makes love to Gypsy Jones in an unpremeditated act motivated by opportunity.

Powell's initial exposition eschews the conventional realism based on plot events for a form that is conceptual and configurational, establishing patterns that suggest recurrence, a synchronic retrospection, rather than the forward movement of diachronic narrative. He is able to accomplish this poetic structure by placing his prologue exposition out of time, eschewing a temporal context that would be concerned with strategies such as beginning *in medias res* and evoking instead a mythical past, commencing outside his primary narrative and establishing a thematic bridge into it. His double exposition reveals both a consciousness of this reality and an effort to fix an appropriate beginning on temporal and historical process. Said defines this problem as one inherent in beginnings: "What sort of action, therefore, transpires at the beginning? How can we, while necessarily submitting to the incessant flux of experience, insert (as we do) our reflections on beginning(s) into that flux?

Is the beginning simply an artifice, a disguise that defies the perpetual trap of forced continuity?"[26] Powell's first exposition is an attempt to "insert," or more precisely to *impose*, a reflection on flux; in this sense it represents what Ricoeur has called the nonchronological, "configurational dimension" of narrative, what I term the static *roman* elements of the text, whereas the second exposition is kinetic, representing the "episodic dimension" of a plot comprised of events,[27] the *fleuve* of narrative itself. Thus, the juxtaposition of the two expositions embodies the tension between the backward pull of the *roman* and the forward drive of the *fleuve* features of the text, even from the first pages of the *roman-fleuve*. Introducing a narrative dynamic that is largely synchronic in effect, it resembles the vertical development of Richardson's *Pilgrimage*, despite its diachronic progression in historical time. The need to impose order on the beginning of the narrative is congruent with Powell's impulse to place himself in what Richardson terms the "male" tradition of realism. He insists upon exordia to shape the organic process of time. However, this impulse thwarts the propensity of the form he has chosen, which privileges the *fleuve* characteristic of *écriture féminine*.

✦ The Contrapuntal Measures of the Dance

The narrative-in-tension that typifies the emplotment of the *roman-fleuve* is most evident in the middle portion of the genre, the series of plot events between exposition and conclusion. This and the related technique of reiterative or synchronic development, a feature of *écriture féminine*, characterize the extensive middle of *A Dance to the Music of Time*; a contrapuntal development is suggested by the central dance metaphor and the characters who recur throughout a sequence of volumes, the "partners [who] disappear only to reappear again." Characters in *The Music of Time* reappear with an intriguing frequency, the number and the persistence of these reappearances suggesting that Powell, as a contemporary writer, is less concerned with traditional realism or character study than with the evocative and linking functions of this device. Some of the linking effect of Powell's reappearing characters is achieved by having them recur in Nick's mind, without a physical appearance, creating a narrative continuity even after characters' deaths. Uncle Giles, for instance, is frequently evoked in Nick's memory after his demise in *The Kindly Ones*. In one unusual case, Scorpio Murtlock claims in *Hearing Secret Harmonies* to be the reincarnation of another character, Dr. Trelawney, providing a mystical pretext for recurrence. Characters recur not only corporally and as reminiscence, a technique made possible by the first-person narrative perspective, but also as resemblance. *The Music of Time* is peppered with hundreds of comparisons as Nick constantly perceives similarities between such characters as Sillery and Le Bas or Sunny Farebrother and Buster Foxe (*QU* 169; 76–77). These recurrences are, of course, the anticipated reappearances of the dancers introduced in the expositional prologue; they illustrate, as Jenkins himself notes when he confuses Barbara Goring and Gypsy Jones, "this latest illustration of the pattern that life forms" (*BM* 258).

In *The Music of Time* the diversity that prevents short-circuit of the plot (a premature finish) is achieved through the constant replenishment of characters. The sheer number of characters—far exceeding Trollope's or Richardson's—sustains the narrative but diverts it from movement toward an end as the corporal presence of characters in the narrative shifts and evolves during the *roman-fleuve*. The exposition seems to establish Nick, Stringham, Templer, and Widmerpool, representatives of varied social strata, as the major characters of the *roman-fleuve*; however, this impression is illusory. Stringham and Templer reappear in Nick's reminiscence even after their deaths, but their centrality fades rapidly after *A Question of Upbringing*. After a brief appearance as a mess waiter in *The Soldier's Art*, Stringham never returns; his capture and death are recounted by Pamela and Widmerpool in *The Military Philosophers*. Templer survives as far as *The Military Philosophers* only to have his death announced in this novel. Obviously, the majority of characters are secondary, yet since the novel never establishes a clear-cut protagonist, they are subordinated to an unstable center, creating a sense of the modernist, decentered narrative.

To revitalize the *roman-fleuve*, Powell is constantly introducing new characters; this technique is most noticeable during the war trilogy and in *Books Do Furnish a Room*, emphasizing the changes brought about by the war, which continues to have an impact on postwar society. In an interview, Powell hints at his technique for introducing new characters while at the same time keeping alive previous ones no longer "active" in the plot: "The greatest technical difficulty, you see, is moving this broad front of characters, which grows with each new book, along. How can you bring them in, keep abreast of everybody's doings, without seeming artificial, that is the greatest problem. But my wife made a point the other day which explains the process somewhat. She said if you leave people out for too long that means something. It's not really necessary to keep some characters on stage to keep in touch with them."[28] Powell's method poses no problem for characters whose demise in the plot corresponds to natural social forces; for example, the death of one's friends is an "expected" outcome of war. Yet the rapid introduction and abrupt disappearance of the "war" characters (such as Gwatkin, Pendry, and Bithel), who are, for the most part, dropped after the war, provide a conflict with the unity of the *roman-fleuve* and the structured novel Powell aims to create. When characters recur, as with Bithel, a member of Murtlock's cult at the end of *Hearing Secret Harmonies*, their appearance outside the context of a wartime society seems incongruous and implausible.

These seemingly extraneous characters may be essential to prevent "short-circuit" of the major plot; in Powell's *roman-fleuve* they provide diverse wartime narratives without draining the force that motivates the major progression of the novel. This is a narrative feature Brooks would describe as furthering the movement toward "discharge," leading to the primary goal of the traditional plot. The use of these characters, clearly subplot material, suggests the possibility of a hierarchy. Yet, at the same time, such conventional features of the narrative are undercut by the way they actually function in the text. The very number of secondary characters undermines hierarchy and teleology. In *The Music of Time*, as in the Pallisers and *Pilgrimage*, digressions, subplots, and detours create the indirect, synchronic progression characteristic of the *roman-fleuve* and *écriture féminine* while working against the effort to link and unify the vast narrative.

Powell's characters function largely as motif, providing his vast and fluid narrative with the referential, backward-moving "bundles" that purportedly organize the plenitude of his text. In an interview, Powell defines his goals for *The Music of Time*: "What I hope to do, among other things, is show the changes in English society, then, from 1914 to the present, but that is only secondary to the investigation of human character."[29] It is ironic, however, that a writer who claims to privilege characterization over plot (as his nineteenth-century predecessor does) uses characters so extensively as a structural device. Characters in *The Music of Time* recur with the astounding frequency that led Evelyn Waugh to criticize Powell's use of an implausible coincidence. At the same time, Waugh himself provided Powell with a list of astounding coincidences connecting their own lives.[30] Others have found this practice only occasionally troublesome. Tucker, for example, shares Waugh's incredulity about Powell's use of coincidence: "Few of us encounter in real life the kind and quantity of coincidences which attend Nicholas throughout the sequence, and which attend other characters."[31] Other critics find these coincidental reappearances "plausible," given the interconnected society Powell is dramatizing.[32]

In his memoirs, Powell associates the technique of recurring characters with "the coherence of a well-constructed novel."[33] Harrington notes the way the reappearances of major characters "bind the moments in the novel together," suggesting Brooks's description of the movement to the climactic plot.[34] However, rather than constantly building toward a highly charged climax, the narrative of Powell's *roman-fleuve* is developed through repetitions, which create a series of unique but inconclusive prototypes. The function of these prototypes, or recurrent examples, is best illustrated by the repeated appearance of Widmerpool, who at various intervals in the text is pelted with a banana, drenched with a castor of sugar, splattered with paint, and pelted with stink bombs. Placed strategically at the beginnings of *A Question of Upbringing*, *A Buyer's Market*, and *Hearing Secret Harmonies* (the first, second, and twelfth volumes), three major incidents correspond to the onset of the principal stages in the lives of Widmerpool and Nick Jenkins— adolescence, adulthood, and advancing age. This sequence of parallel incidents not only chronicles the evolution of Widmerpool, but it also generates an open-ended series, each incident resembling the others without resulting in a clear-cut progression or evident development as examples in the series accumulate. Because such a sequence could be expanded indefinitely, no example can ever be considered final.

This kind of sequence might be contrasted to the completed "microsequence" Barthes describes: "extending one's hand, shaking hands, releasing the handshake."[35] Powell exploits the potential for an incomplete sequence as he creates incidents—and volumes—that are resistant to completion. With each new incident, the reader hopes to understand Widmerpool, his significance in the pattern. But for the reader, as for Nick, the pattern emerges without a full elucidation of its significance. The cumulative effect is that of inconclusiveness; the sequence of prototypes subverts resolution, tantalizing the reader with the ambiguous possibility of either another example or the long-awaited termination of the sequence. The narrative progression of Powell's *roman-fleuve* is characterized by the teasing prospect of a climactic outcome that never arrives.

Although it has been argued that Powell's *roman-fleuve* is not, strictly speaking, an example of spatial form in the sense in which it is defined by Joseph Frank,[36] Powell's use of recurrent characters is one of the devices that give *The Music of Time* the synchronic movement of a spatial novel. As the characters recur in a litany of appearances, they achieve the rhythmic quality of motif and effect the backward referential value of images: "Like flashbacks, recurring images arrest the reader's forward progress, and they also direct his attention to other, earlier sections of the work."[37] This pattern is established not only in Powell's central metaphor of the dancers but throughout the text as well. Jenkins anticipates recurrence when characters such as Farebrother are said to "[pass] out of [his] life for some twenty years" (*QU* 105) or when he quotes a remark that Dicky Umfraville will make in the future (*VB* 47). However, such proleptic snippets are less frequent than their analeptic counterparts, which send the text back to a former appearance. For example, in *The Valley of Bones* Nick meets Jimmy Brent in London, recalling the first appearance of Brent as a passenger in Templer's Vauxhall in *A Question of Upbringing*, and in *The Kindly Ones* Nick discovers that Brent had an affair with Jean Templer during the period covered in *The Acceptance World*. Thus, a single reappearance can generate a ripple of recurrences, moving back simultaneously to several past volumes of the *roman-fleuve*.

Although the recurrent characters do reflect the "unfolding" revelation of "a novel's plot" in their cumulative development, their function as motif, a backward referential function, undermines progression toward climax and resolution. For example, as they recur, many characters take on a symbolic significance that has the static value of artifact. Patrick Swinden has noted the way characters are depicted by reference to visual arts.[38] However, the artifactitious nature of Powell's characters, which resembles Richardson's modernist fetishization of objects, has gone unnoticed. These comparisons with static objects usually refer backward in time. Le Bas, for example, is compared to a historic monument symbolic of the past: "He seemed to represent, like a landscape or building, memories of a vanished time. He had become, if not history, at least part of one's own autobiography" (*AW* 180). Other characters become not monuments but works of art. Widmerpool, as he wears a blue robe in *Hearing Secret Harmonies*, reminds Nick of the painting of robed figures that used to hang in the flat Widmerpool shared with his mother. Norma, a waitress at Casanova's Chinese Restaurant, rendered as a nude by Barnby, hangs on the wall at Stourwater in the manner of Browning's Duchess (*KO* 109–10). These recurrences send the narrative backward in their reference; thus their effect is ultimately synchronic (developing one episode), subverting the diachronic advancement of time (which would continue to the next episode).

One result of Powell's juxtapositions, spread out over such a broad temporal stretch, is Nick's recurrent musing on the changes in his friends and acquaintances over time. A reappearance is frequently met with Nick's observation of the presumed change or lack of change in that character: in *At Lady Molly's* Nick notes that Mona's personality, as she flirts with Erridge, is "much firmer, more ruthless . . . [than when] I had first met her as Templer's wife, when she had seemed a silly, empty headed, rather bad-tempered beauty" (133). By the time of *Books Do Furnish a Room*, the tenth volume, Nick believes that Mona has ceased to change; she is a woman "out of fashion," "a girl not exactly of the present, rather of some years back" (55). Jenkins's tally of various characters' change—or lack of it—over time reveals the difficulty of apprehending character. McLeod observes, "While Powell allows his narrator-as-character to change his views of character, the characters themselves do not change at all—indeed, they remain the stablest element in this sequence dealing with change."[39] Powell's faith in an unchanging core of the self is related to his belief in pattern; time creates outer change, which is reflected in characters, but the "pattern" remains. As Jenkins says of a character in *Temporary Kings*, "Even if Bagshaw's way of life had in certain respects altered, become more solid, a fundamental pattern of unconventionality remained" (182). Moreover, this belief in consistency is extended to all men and women throughout history, as Moreland says of Ben Jonson (in a statement that seems consistent with Jenkins's and Powell's views as well): " 'He's a sympathetic writer, who reminds one that human life always remains the same. . . . How bored one gets with the assumption that people now are organically different from people in the past—the Lost Generation, the New Poets, the Atomic Age' " (*BDFR* 119). The recurrence of characters and events suggests eternal recurrence as the life principle, as implied by the mythical prologue to *The Music of Time*.[40]

While critics have often praised Powell's incremental development of character, a conception of character as motif, artifact, and recurrent history may impede full development of the characters themselves. The characters Powell creates are frequently more symbolic than realistic. Swinden has criticized "the shallowness of [Powell's] insight into what are potentially his most interesting characters—Trapnel, Gwinnett, Pamela Widmerpool."[41] Indeed, it does seem that even his choice of a first-person narrator with limited knowledge of others should not preclude the creation of well-developed characters. The symbolic use of character provides not only structure linking volumes but also incidents within them, creating a high degree of unity and continuity in the *roman-fleuve*, smoothing out what was in Trollope a relatively spastic and discontinuous movement from one well-developed character to another. Powell sacrifices the creation of fully developed and sympathetic characters—the essential appeal of the Pallisers—but in this respect he moves away from nineteenth-century verisimilitude toward a postmodern awareness of the impossibility of comprehending, much less fully representing, a complexly developed human being.

A character such as Pamela Flitton Widmerpool, despite her frequent appearance in the last trilogy of the *roman-fleuve*, has a symbolic significance as a harbinger and instrument of death that far exceeds her development as a human being. Tucker argues that Pamela "receives a degree of character development unequalled among other women,"[42] which is not the same as saying she is a well-developed character. Swinden maintains that so little conclusive evidence is given about her that she "is scarcely a character at all."[43] In point of fact, Powell's female characters are notoriously underdeveloped. Some of his difficulty is elucidated by a statement Nick makes about Jean Templer Duport in *The Acceptance World*: "But descriptions of a woman's outward appearance can hardly do more than echo the terms of a fashion paper. Their nature can be caught only in a refractive beam, as with light passing through the person with whom they are intimately associated. Perhaps, therefore, I alone was responsible for what she seemed to me" (134). This view of women as blanks to be filled in by the male gaze should probably be viewed ironically: as the immature deficiency of the youthful Jenkins. His metaphor also signals the difficulties of perception, a recurrent theme of Jenkins as narrator. In an interview, Powell invokes Pope's famous dictum in justifying his failure to depict credible women characters: "Females are very hard to do. I don't think any male writer has ever done one right. Pope says somewhere that 'Nothing so true as what you once let fall, "Most women have no characters at all.'" I agree. Women are terribly, terribly difficult."[44] Perhaps Powell should be commended for his honest appraisal of his own (or Jenkins's) limitations; his acknowledgment may also explain why his *roman-fleuve* has received more attention from male than female critics. At any rate, a tendency to conceive of character in symbolic and structural terms is exacerbated when the character is female.

Postponing the conventional plot movement toward climax, the synchronic narrative manifests itself in the digressive middle of *A Dance to the Music of Time*. Like *The Eustace Diamonds* in the Pallisers, the war trilogy of *The Music of Time* breaks up the continuity of the primary narrative, providing an inversion of the society depicted, which is nevertheless linked with previous and subsequent volumes through motif, symbol, and repetition. While digressions are a feature of *écriture féminine*, exploited and defended by Richardson, by creating such a prolonged three-volume digression—one that is so extraneous as to be extractable and nearly self-sufficient—Powell reveals his discomfort with this feature of the *roman-fleuve* and reverts to a conception closer to Trollope's: within itself, the micronarrative is highly unified though it presents a major detour from the central narrative of the *roman-fleuve*. Although Nick Jenkins, as narrator-protagonist, cannot be as fully subordinated during any portion of the narrative as Plantagenet Palliser is during *The Eustace Diamonds*, Powell effects a similar shift in perspective by inverting Nick's role in the war trilogy. Instead of an observer set apart from other characters, Nick becomes an active participant and a relatively integral part of the "society" of the army.

Early in *The Valley of Bones* Nick, who has to call on the influence of a family friend in order to gain admittance to the army because of his age, welcomes a chance to be integrated into the war machine: "Now, at last, I was geared to the machine of war, no longer an extraneous organism existing separately in increasingly alien conditions" (39). He is both humanized and in some ways diminished, whereas his social antagonist Widmerpool is grotesquely elevated and almost mythologized. During the war years, Nick is unable to pursue his vocation as a professional writer; instead he turns his talents to transcribing the "undistinguished prose" of the military (*MP* 1). A passive and often almost amorphous observer throughout most of the *roman-fleuve*, Nick suddenly takes on corporeal attributes and becomes more personal and emotional. The reader is almost shocked to witness Nick's physical discomfort or emotional abandon, in contrast to his usual cerebral persona. A chocolate bar, offered by Gwatkin as an apology for dispatching Nick out into the cold without lunch, sends Nick into uncharacteristic sensual raptures that continue sporadically for almost a page (*VB* 86–87). Generally more analytical than emotional, Nick gives in to despair under the influence of discouraging war news and the melancholy associations of Castlemallock (*VB* 171).

In this novel the reader is even admitted to Nick and Isobel's bedroom to overhear a conversation between the two that continues for several pages. Though she is often present at social events in other volumes, Isobel's remarks are seldom reported; as a character she is wholly undeveloped—as one might expect of the wife of a self-effacing narrator—and Nick provides almost no details about their marriage. This passage, however, dramatizes an informal and gossipy chat during Nick's leave, as Isobel fills Nick in on prospective marriage and living-in arrangements of family and friends. The conversation ends with a sparse but cozily suggestive interchange:

> "Anyway, it's nice to meet again, darling."
> "It's been a long time."
> "A bloody long time."
> "It certainly has." (*VB* 148)

The extensive conversation doubles as exposition, of course, bringing the narrative up-to-date on the actions of characters from previous volumes, but it is strikingly intimate compared with Nick's usual reticence about his personal life. Compare the informal tone of the passage above, for example, with Nick's detached, impersonal statement in a postwar volume: "I left London one Saturday afternoon in the autumn to make some arrangement about a son going to school" (*BDFR* 206).

Just as Nick is diminished and humanized by the war in the third movement, Widmerpool is elevated, almost allegorized: the man of will comes into his own during the epoch of Hitler and world war. While Nick can never shake his initial impression of Widmerpool's ineptitude, in the war volumes he finds himself repeatedly dominated by the man he dismissed as a bumbler at school. At the end of the first war novel, *Valley of Bones*, Nick is stunned to realize "I was now in Widmerpool's power" (243). In *The Military Philosophers* Nick's journey to see Widmerpool is described in terms that associate the Cabinet Offices with a mythical underworld and Widmerpool with a figure vaguely suggesting

Pluto, Neptune, or Demogorgon: "I followed the marine down flight after flight of stairs. It was like the lower depths of our own building, though more spacious, less shabby. The marine, who had a streaming cold in his head, showed me into a room in the bowels of the earth, the fittings and decoration of which were also less down-at-heel than the general run of headquarters and government offices" (11). When he arrives at "Kenneth's bower" (14), Nick finds the power has shifted from those early days at school; here he and Templer are expelled from Widmerpool's "brightly lit dungeon," a domain buzzing with "the power principle" (12). In a reversal of the pecking order dramatized in *A Question of Upbringing*, Widmerpool, now a half-colonel, commands, "Do go away, Nicholas. I have some highly secret matters to deal with on the next agenda. I can't begin on them with people like you hanging about the room" (19).

Despite the inversion of civilian roles and social class during the third movement, this digressive portion of the narrative is linked to the rest of the *roman-fleuve* with a function that is more significant than that used in the Pallisers. Whereas the digression of *The Eustace Diamonds* portrays an inversion of the social order that threatens the survival of the aristocratic and upper-middle-class hierarchy, the digression of *The Music of Time* presents an inverted wartime society that threatens civilization itself. The digression is not only historically justifiable, dramatizing the obvious interruptive impact of World War II on British society, it is also carefully prepared for by a plethora of allusions in the prewar volumes that occur with greater frequency as the war approaches.

In spite of its new setting and new cast of characters, the war trilogy is linked to other volumes in the series by recurring characters (who are referred to, if not dramatized) and by the same motific system established in the extended metaphor that comprises the opening of the first novel of the *roman-fleuve*. Echoes of the initial metaphor, which compares the street workers to Poussin's painting of the seasons' dance to the music of time, occur on the first page of *Valley of Bones*:

> Snow from yesterday's fall still lay in patches and the morning air was
> glacial. No one was about the streets at this hour. On either side of me in
> the half-light Kedward and the Company Sergeant-Major stepped out
> briskly as if on parade. Some time in the past—long, long ago in another
> existence, an earlier, less demanding incarnation—I had stayed a night in
> this town, idly come here to cast an eye over a countryside where my own
> family had lived a century or more before. One of them (rather a hard

case by the look of it, from whom Uncle Giles's failings perhaps stemmed) had come west from the Marches to marry the heiress of a small property overlooking a bay on this lost, lonely shore. The cliffs below the site of the house, where all but foundations had been obliterated by the seasons, enclosed untidy banks of piled-up rock against which spent Atlantic waters ceaselessly dissolved, ceaselessly renewed steaming greenish spray: *la mer, la mer, toujours recommençée*, as Moreland was found of quoting, an everyday landscape of heaving billows too consciously dramatic for my own taste. (1)

This passage recalls, both motifically and symbolically, the imagery of the prologue exposition in *A Question of Upbringing*. The images of snow and the winter season establish a climatic and temporal motific link between the openings of these two novels. Both passages describe figures in movement, but whereas Nick observes street workers and mentally evokes the dance of seasons in the first volume, here, characteristic of his changed role in the war years, he participates in the dance and describes himself actually "stepp[ing] out briskly" between his two fellow soldiers. Both passages also depict the recurrence of time: in *Valley of Bones* Nick returns in a new "incarnation" to a place previously visited, a setting with significance for his ancestors—thus a double step backward in time—and as the passage continues Nick compares his situation to that of soldiers in other times, "unnoticed officers of Marines or the East India Company," those serving under Bonaparte, and Celtic warriors (2). The theme of time is also suggested by the refrain "*la mer, toujours recommençée*," evoking the wavelike recurrence characteristic of Powell's narrative technique. The digressive middle of *A Dance to the Music of Time* suggests the synchronous development of *écriture féminine*, but in its extensiveness it resembles the "bagginess" of *The Eustace Diamonds* in Trollope's Pallisers more than the incessant but compressed digressions of Richardson's *Pilgrimage*.

It is not only the digressive war trilogy that suggests the asymmetrical and synchronous narrative of *écriture féminine*: Powell's *roman-fleuve* also uses an analytical self-reflexive development that reiterates narrated material and functions as a digressive supplement to the plot. Creating characters who are writers, Powell adds layers of self-reflexiveness to his work. Not only is Jenkins a writer (who writes about writers such as Burton) writing about his task, but he is writing about the task of his creator as well. Jenkins retraces his own life through memory, at the same time retracing the steps of Powell's life through fictionalized autobiography, just as his character Gwinnett retraces the life of another writer, X. Trapnel. Gwinnett not only writes about Trapnel in a dissertation and in the biography *Death's-Head Swordsman*, but he also relives Trapnel's life by gaining entrance into Trapnel's former circle of acquaintances. As Nick sees it, "Gwinnett's approach, not uncommon among biographers, seemed to be to see himself, at greater or lesser range, as a projection of his subject. He aimed, anyway to some extent, at reconstructing in himself Trapnel's life, getting into Trapnel's skin, becoming Trapnel" (*TK* 190). Through the creation of Gwinnett, Powell accomplishes both a self-reflexive and a reiterative narrative: Gwinnett's efforts to reconstruct Trapnel's life repeat the events, with some variation, already narrated by Jenkins.

Self-reflexiveness is, to state the obvious, referential: one narrative refers to another in that retracing action Brooks argues is inherent in narrative, although Powell's *roman-fleuve* is less experimental and self-reflexive than many postmodern novels. In *The Music of Time* there is a locus for reflexive repetition in the narrator's consciousness, as the mind of Nick Jenkins discovers or unconsciously perceives similarities. One source of repetition is the retrospective nature of the narrative, suggesting that Nick's mind provides the *sjužet*, the *roman* feature of the text—the *fabula* residing, as it always does, outside the text itself as a "mental construction that the reader derives from the *sjužet*."[45] This function of Nick's narrative disrupts the linear chronology of the narrative, the progression of the *fleuve*. Harrington comments that "not only is the forward movement of the narrative an illusion since it circles back upon itself, but the incidents it recounts coexist simultaneously in Nick's memory."[46] Nick's consciousness makes connections that trace the pattern through time and space. For example, in *The Military Philosophers* Nick's observations about a place as his unit passes Great West Road, the location of the billboard depicting the eternally diving woman, link past and present: "I idly wondered what had happened to [Jean], if she were involved in the war; what had happened to Duport, too, whether he had managed to 'sweat it out', the words he had used, in South America" (152). In this sense the whole community exists in Nick's consciousness. As he observes in *Casanova's Chinese Restaurant*, "I was, in one sense, part and parcel of the same community; . . . when people gossiped about matters like Carolo and his girl, one was listening to a morsel, if only an infinitesimal morsel, of one's own life" (25).

Like Richardson, Powell exploits the discursive potential of the genre, albeit through different narrative techniques. Jenkins's meditation on the difficulty of writing a novel about English society—"I began to brood on the complexity of writing a novel about English life, a subject difficult enough to handle with authenticity even of a crudely naturalistic sort, even more to convey the inner truth of the things observed" (*AW* 32)—suggests his awareness of the conflict between the goals of conventional realism and the modernist project of presenting the inner reality. Over several pages, Jenkins moves to compare the difficulties inherent in representing British society with "innumerable Russian stories of the nineteenth century" (*AW* 34). Jenkins's doubts—reminiscent of Bloom's anxiety of influence—express a concern about his place within the realistic tradition.

In contrast to conventional plotting, the recursiveness of this narrative subverts teleology. Nick's reiterations frequently revise former impressions, a process most actively at work in his incessant reevaluations of Widmerpool throughout all twelve volumes of the work. Essentially, Nick's opinion of Widmerpool is formed by that first image of him, jogging through the mist at school, a clumsy and fishy figure, a grotesque image of desire. As Widmerpool's position rises in society, particularly during the war years, Nick realizes there must be something more to Widmerpool than that self revealed to Nick as a younger schoolboy. However, despite Nick's incessant revisions he feels—and we cannot escape his judgment in this—that somehow Widmerpool's self *is* defined by what he was at school. The difficulty of apprehending Widmerpool's essential self is in the mind of the perceiver; Nick cannot segregate an objective view of Widmerpool from the profusion of associations with which he is connected: "One's associations with people are regulated as much by what they stand for, as by what they are, individual characteristics becoming from time to time submerged in more general implications. At that moment, although I had never possessed anything approaching a warm relationship with Widmerpool, his presence brought back with a rush all kinds of things, more or less desirable, from which I had been cut off for an eternity. I wondered how I could ever have considered him in the disobliging light that seemed so innate since we had been at school together" (*VB* 239-40). Nick must continually reevaluate Widmerpool because he cannot reconcile his first impression with Widmerpool's subsequent success. His difficulty is an example of what Brooks terms "significant working through of an unmastered past,"[47] but Powell's *roman-fleuve* never provides a resolution in which such a past is mastered, evading this function of the master-plot.

The reiterative detective function of narrative that Brooks insists upon is most evident in those sections of *The Music of Time* where Nick narrates events he did not witness, as often necessitated by a first-person point of view. Powell compensates for the potential awkwardness of this technique by calling attention to it rather than trying to minimize it. One of the most notable examples of the detective-narrator occurs in *Temporary Kings* as Nick narrates an event witnessed by Bagshaw's father and recounted to Nick by Bagshaw: the discovery of Pamela Widmerpool standing naked in the hallway of his house in the middle of the night. The situation itself is, of course, a reworking of the Billson incident in *The Kindly Ones*. Nick prefaces the narrative with a statement about the essential subjectivity, and concomitant inadequacy, of narrative: "Every story one hears has to be adjusted, in the mind of the listener, to prejudices of the teller; in practice, most listeners increasing, reducing, discarding, much of what they have been told" (190–91).

Powell's adjudicating first-person narrator provides unity in *The Music of Time*, as has frequently been noted. McLeod writes, "Powell has unified his fictional world not through any conventional use of hero or narration but rather through the consistency of tone and viewpoint provided by the narrator's coherent picture of himself and society"; McLeod also details the advantages of the first-person narrator: "Transitions become smoother, events unfold more naturally, and the orchestration of character, incident and dialogue becomes richer and more complex than in short fiction written from an omniscient point of view."[48] The creation of a first-person restricted and retrospective narrator is in no way modern or innovative: it is the technique of the great Victorian bildungsroman, of *Jane Eyre* or *Great Expectations*. The modernity of Powell's narrator is found rather in his self-effacing persona, a technique that contributes to unity by creating a consistent narrative voice while avoiding the disruptive personal intercession of many first-person narrators. The retrospective narrator also mediates the oscillating movement characteristic of the *roman-fleuve* by bringing together diverse plot lines. As McLeod describes it, "The memory of Jenkins-as-narrator shifts backwards and forwards as the project grows, creating an ever widening perspective for the episodes of each successive novel."[49]

In the last volume of the series, Nick's discussion of the "vantage point" of old age applies equally to the advantages of a first-person retrospective narrator: "Two compensations for growing old are worth putting on record as the condition asserts itself. The first is a vantage point gained for acquiring embellishments to narratives that have been unfolding for years beside one's own, trimmings that can even appear to supply the conclusion of a given story, though finality is never certain, a dimension always possible to add. The other mild advantage endorses a keener perception for the authenticities of mythology, not only of the traditional sort, but—when such are any good—the latterday mythologies of poetry and the novel" (HSH 30). The mature narrator provides an organic means to achieve the scope and perspective of a bildungsroman, and because of his age this narrator perceives the archetypal patterns of human experience. Powell's practice unifies the narrative; yet his awareness that "finality is never certain"—there is always another case, the form is ever-expanding—reveals a postmodern skepticism about representation.

Despite the similarities to Trollope's nineteenth-century prototype, the increased unity demonstrated by Powell's *roman-fleuve* situates it as a predominantly modern exemplar. Unlike the Pallisers, *A Dance to the Music of Time* is more obviously one group of novels, resembling in this respect the modernist *romans-fleuves* of Richardson or Proust. Powell's work also has an even more continuous structure than either Trollope's Victorian or Richardson's modernist *roman-fleuve* as a larger number of episodes are linked. It is this linking, rather than the pseudosymmetrical division of *The Music of Time* into titled volumes and four movements, that provides the primary structural principle of the work. By establishing a central metaphor on the first page of the work and prolonging it throughout the twelve volumes of the series, Powell has created an extended metaphor perhaps unrivaled in all literature. Although the volumes and movements provide a framework for emplotting the *fleuve*—it is here that the *roman* features of the genre come into play—the work is not so tightly structured as to violate the primacy of fluidity that is characteristic of *écriture féminine* and the *roman-fleuve*. This fluidity approaches Proust's original conception of *A la recherche du temps perdu* as two huge volumes unmarked by individual titles (titles were later supplied by his publisher, who also insisted he publish the volumes at varying intervals).[50] At the same time, Powell's desire to write about "the whole of one's life,"[51] including a vast social panorama, suggests a conception of the genre that points back to Balzac's vast plan. Similarly, in privileging unity and coherence, Powell allies himself with the nineteenth-century aesthetic of control and structure promoted by Henry James.

❧ The Anticlimax of Extended Narrative

The reiterative pattern of Powell's *roman-fleuve* suggests, as with all narrative, the inadequacy of a single event, an inadequacy that motivates plot itself. Repetition creates a pattern, a plot, and at the same time undermines its own efficacy to push the narrative forward to the end, to complete elucidation, to the fulfillment of desire, to satisfying closure. As repetition is incremental, the effect of the narrative progression is cumulative; the significance of events is postponed as they gradually unfold. Characters who recur are depicted through the progressive accumulation of details. An initial portrait is revised through multiple and often parallel appearances; the complex presentation ends only with the termination of the final volume. The perception of this incremental structure is not only postponed until the end of the work, challenging the reader to suspend comprehension of the whole, but it is also best perceived on a rereading (which the length of the *roman-fleuve* deters), a form of narrative clearly antithetical to the climactic suspense plot. *The Music of Time* has also inspired unusual, nonlinear readings, as I mentioned in my introductory chapter, suggesting its affinity with nonchronological modernist and feminine texts.

It might be expected that the conclusion of each volume of the *roman-fleuve* would embody a miniclimax; at least one critic sees Powell leading up to "dramatic" or climactic moments.[52] The narrative seems always to be working toward the climactic; even the first two "movements" appear to lead up to World War II as a historical climax, a culminating event, in the third. In actuality, however, the most crucial final events of the individual novels in *A Dance to the Music of Time*, as in *Pilgrimage*, are undercut by terminal passages that privilege the insignificant, the anticlimactic. Several volumes end with seemingly sensational announcements of marriages, but in each case Powell minimizes and undermines their climactic potential. For example, Nick's own reaction to his engagement to Isobel Tolland in *At Lady Molly's* undercuts its significance: "A background of other events largely obscured the steps leading up to my engagement to Isobel Tolland. Of this crisis in my life, I remember chiefly a sense of tremendous inevitability, a feeling that fate was settling its own problems" (203). Nick's engagement not only seems inevitable to himself but, as a corollary of his self-effacing quality as a narrator and the lack of information provided about Nick's personal life, it also seems unremarkable to the reader. Far more intriguing in this volume is Widmerpool's engagement to the dashing and controversial Mildred Blaides Haycock. Their engagement is broken in the last chapter, however, apparently because of Widmerpool's failure as a lover, and the volume concludes with Widmerpool's offer to give Nick advice about marriage—ending on an ironic deflationary note. Similarly, the startling announcement of Widmerpool and Pamela's improbable engagement in *The Military Philosophers* is notably underplayed. Although their engagement coincides with the dropping of the atomic bomb in 1945, such events are neither dramatized nor emphasized in the text. Nick hears of the engagement from Archie Gilbert, a minor character who insists on reminding Nick of the time Barbara Goring poured sugar on Widmerpool's head. The text incessantly collapses the climactic into the trivial.

The pattern of teasing desire that characterizes the narrative as a whole is present also in the individual volumes: each purports to offer a conclusion, only to be undermined by the appearance of a new volume. Furthermore, the resolutions of the individual volumes are not only subsequently revealed to lack narrative closure as each new volume begins, but they are also essentially anticlimactic in themselves. For example, *The Acceptance World* ends with Nick meeting Jean for a tryst, the seeming resolution of an infatuation begun in *A Question of Upbringing*. The meeting is revealed to be another serial occurrence, decidedly anticlimactic, however. On the way to meet Jean, Nick contemplates a tacky erotic postcard she has sent him, concluding, "Some of love was like the picture. I had enacted such scenes with Jean: Templer with Mona, now Mona was enacting them with Quiggin: Barnaby and Umfraville with Anne Stepney: Stringham with her sister Peggy: Peggy now in the arms of her cousin: Uncle Giles, very probably, with Mrs. Erdleigh: Mrs. Erdleigh with Jimmy Stripling: Jimmy Stripling, if it came to that, with Jean: and Duport, too" (212-13). The passage becomes a litany of couplings summarizing the erotic adventures of the major characters, launching into the familiar reiterative pattern characteristic of the narrative of *The Music of Time*. Nick's affair is denied its uniqueness, its own climax: it is in no way a high point or a resolution; he and Jean are merely participants in a never-ending procession of lovers. Moreover, the exclusivity of his own attainment of Jean is also undermined as, in a later volume, Nick discovers that Jean was, during the same period of time, also having an affair with the unsavory Jimmy Brent. She is concurrently unfaithful—to her lovers as well as to her husband. Powell's depiction of promiscuity in *The Music of Time*, especially as enacted through the characters of Jean Templer and Pamela Flitton Widmerpool, suggests that sex is a decidedly anticlimactic act.

Powell also diffuses the force of potentially climactic events as his narrator refuses to acknowledge their significance. Near the end of *A Buyer's Market*, Nick loses his virginity with Gypsy Jones, an intriguing event barely discernible in the text, while the emphatically placed final scene of the novel is devoted to Nick's uneventful dinner with Widmerpool and his mother. The penultimate chapter of *Temporary Kings* dramatizes Pamela Widmerpool's vulgar confrontation with Polly Duport, during which she reveals to the group gathered in the driveway of a Regent's Park party the fact that Louis Glober has a "charming little cushion with hair snipped from the pussies of ladies he's had" (258). However, Nick subsequently diffuses the climactic potential of the scene (although he does speculates that Pamela "was working herself up to a climax, possibly a sexual one" [259]) by refusing to validate what happened—the incident was reported to him in conflicting versions by both Odo Stevens and Moreland; he himself was not present. Although the following chapter reveals the extraordinary fact of Pamela's death, Nick mentions it only obliquely, postponing to the next volume an account of how it occurred (an anomalous use of intervolume suspense technique in Powell's *roman-fleuve*). Nick's evasiveness, his lack of participation as a character, and his refusal—or inability—as a narrator to arrive at conclusions about the story he tells contribute to the anticlimactic nature of the narrative. Like the neon diver, he incessantly returns to the springboard.

The narrative of "arrested development," which spirals in a seemingly endless cycle, may be a corollary of a narrator who lacks the insight to push it to a realization, to a resolution. In Poussin's painting the circle is empty at the center; it has no hub, and Nick Jenkins, at the center of *The Music of Time*, may lack the force of personality to center the narrative. Viewed more positively, Nick himself may embody what Richardson would view as a feminine narrative impulse: as a man of imagination, he is essentially contemplative, not active; like Miriam Henderson, he sees no reason to push the narrative toward an end. The volumes with the most climactic endings are those of the digressive war trilogy. In *The Valley of Bones* and *The Soldier's Art*, Powell draws his endings from historical events: the former terminates with the announcement that the German army is reported to occupy Paris, and latter with Germany's invasion of Russia. These endings may suggest that *The Music of Time* is, after all, essentially a historical novel foregrounding society and its fate, a possibility that would explain the lack of a clearly designated individual protagonist. However, although World War II emerges, in retrospect, as the structural apogee of the *roman-fleuve*, the events of the war, even within the third movement, are reduced to anecdotes about the men in Nick's company and to generalizations about historic recurrence.

Jenkins's treatment of the events of war not only subordinates history and war to individual concerns, but also often reduces event to anecdote. The most memorable scenes in the third movement are the slight but comic ones, such as Gwatkin's dance around a stuffed effigy placed in his bed by the men in his company, an event that receives the same mock-epic treatment given to peacetime pranks such as Stripling's attempt to place a chamber pot in Sunny Farebrother's hatbox or Barbara Goring's attack on Widmerpool with the sugar castor. Powell deflates the unprecedented nature of the war by insisting upon its historical recurrence. Most of the military figures are characterized by their similarity to medieval or Celtic warriors, recalling the imagery of the opening passage of *A Question of Upbringing*: Gittins, a member of Nick's company, is described as "another strongly pre-Celtic type" (*VB* 52); Gwatkin resembles "a figure from the later Middle Ages, a captain-of-arms of the Hundred Years War, or the guerrilla campaigning of Owen Glendower" (*VB* 76); and the sight of Belgian troops makes Nick think of "the Middle Ages or the Renaissance, emaciated, Memling-like men-at-arms on the way to supervise the Crucifixion or some lesser martyrdom" (*MP* 88). World War II is thus generalized into a recurrent universal of human history.

The pattern of arrested or unachieved satisfaction in *The Music of Time*, evident in its teasing narrative progression, is reiterated in the erotic response of its characters. The nymphomaniac Pamela Flitton Widmerpool, whose sexuality is described as a "blend of frigidity with insatiable desire," is a figure for the narrative tease. Powell's clustering of what is presented as sexual "deviancy" (nymphomania, impotence, voyeurism, homosexuality) in some of his least attractive characters

(Pamela and Kenneth Widmerpool, Donners, and Murtlock), seems to suggest, especially as it intensifies in the last movement, a fear of social decadence and a certain conservatism and homophobia, despite Jenkins's ostensible liberal tolerance.[53] The exploitative destructive nature of female sexuality, which often motivates the narrative (each conquest of Jean Templer or Pamela Flitton Widmerpool furnishes another episode or incident), contributes concurrently to a denigration of the character. Paradoxically, Powell's female characters are derogated for actions perceived as abnormal, yet their actions stimulate the narrative development.

The personally unconsummated pleasure associated with Pamela also occurs in the portrayal of Widmerpool, as he is characterized by a sexual inadequacy that deviates from the ejaculatory norm. He fails every test of potency: in *A Buyer's Market* he pays for an abortion he did not necessitate; in *At Lady Molly's* he is unable to consummate a premarital liaison with Mildred Haycock; and in *Books Do Furnish a Room* he is said to have given up sexual relations with his wife Pamela as a "bad job" after only two attempts. Pamela also accuses Widmerpool of voyeurism, a passively deviant response that recurs in Sir Magnus Donners, in Gwinnett (at The Devil's Fingers), and in even in Nick himself, who is, it may be argued, passive and voyeuristic as a narrator, though "normal" in his heterosexual response. The stalled and frustrated desires of these characters suggest the teased sensibilities of the reader of the *roman-fleuve*, whose desires are constantly aroused while fulfillment is repeatedly delayed. Readers of *The Music of Time* were simultaneously enticed and thwarted for twenty-five years by the incremental revelation of such mysteries as the nature of Widmerpool's amorous proclivities. The reader, excited by the erotic possibilities of the Widmerpool-Flitton match in *The Military Philosophers* (third movement), is disappointed when they are revealed to be nonexistent in *Books Do Furnish a Room* (fourth movement).

The ideal reader for Powell's *roman-fleuve* is one who appreciates and savors this sophisticated manipulation of expectations, a reader who—perhaps as detached as Jenkins himself—enjoys the play of expectations and deferral. Powell's central metaphor, established in the title and the metaphoric opening of the novel, suggests the oscillating pattern of narrative and the suspension of comprehension characteristic of the *roman-fleuve*: "Partners disappear only to reappear again, once more giving pattern to the spectacle" (*QU* 2). The multitude of repeated details forms a dense network that structures the *roman-fleuve* on a subconscious as well as a conscious level since the length of the work makes comprehension of all of the parallels difficult; as Brooks puts it, "Repetition is a kind of remembering, and thus a way of reorganizing a story whose connective links have been obscured and lost."[54] The revelation of the significance of events is continually postponed, creating an extraordinarily protracted expanse of narrative delight.

Seemingly the most potent agents of desire, female characters, Pamela Widmerpool in particular, instigate the most compelling plots in *The Music of Time*. However, if one looks to Pamela's sudden death to provide a climax in the plot, one must seek it in the margin of the work, since her death is only mentioned, not dramatized in the text. This forceful character is suddenly and surreptitiously disposed of when the narrative desire she stimulates threatens to undermine the primacy of the male protagonists' plots. As an agent, Pamela helps others to achieve their ends, relegating her own story to the subplot. If desire equals a desire to know one's ends, Pamela is an instrument of eschatology for men, just as her actions push these plots to the resolution of closure through death. Her nymphomania is a motivating force in the narrative; she is a Thanatotic narrative catalyst, beckoning her victims— Templer, Trapnel, Ferrand-Sénéschal—to premature deaths, consigning them to one of this multifarious narrative's abortive subplots. Only Gwinnett, an American, escapes death, although Pamela is a vehicle for Gwinnett's knowledge of death, as she apparently commits suicide in order to permit him to fulfill his necromantic fantasies. Powell suggests the potentially annihilatory nature of this brand of eroticism, evident in such scenes as that where, dressed in black, Pamela grabs Gwinnett by the testicles in a church.

However, Pamela represents both knowledge of and dissatisfaction with the end. "Knowing" her sexually permits her victims the knowledge of their deaths, but once dead, they cannot profit from this knowledge. A *belle dame sans merci*, a femme fatale, her nymphomania betokens a desire without satisfaction. The result of Pamela's suicide in the penultimate volume is the precipitous termination of her plot, Brooks's narrative "short-circuit": "the danger of reaching the end too quickly, of achieving the improper death. The improper end indeed lurks throughout narrative, frequently as the wrong choice."[55] The function Brooks attributes to the subplot, "one means of warding off the danger of short-circuit, assuring that the main plot will continue through to the right end,"[56] is evident in Powell's use of the Pamela subplot, which by

its own short-circuit forestalls that eventuality for the male protagonists' plots.

Pamela's death permits Widmerpool, a feebler agent of narrative and
sexual desire but a more representative social force, to accomplish his
ends without the rivalry of her compelling presence. Her subplot, by
premature termination, allows his plot to continue to the finish, giving
the narrative its penultimate inner frame. Pamela provides a stunning—
and ironic—example of what Brooks views as a "female plot": "a resistance and what we might call an 'endurance,' a waiting (and suffering)
until the woman's desire can be permitted a response to the expression
of male desire."[57] The nature of her "response," a suicide that permits
Gwinnett to achieve, vicariously and necrophilically, death without dying, is another suggestive figure for the narrative of *The Music of Time*.
Pamela is an agent for male teleology, whose desire and narratives are
brought to suitable closure through her erotics, yet her own desire is
never satiated—unless its only object is death. *The Music of Time* reflects the feminine dynamics of the *roman-fleuve*, but when the closure
of this *roman-fleuve* is contrasted to that of *Pilgrimage*, it is clear that
Powell does not evade closure to the same extent as Richardson, who
affirms the feminine economy through total refusal of closure. Thus,
while Powell, like Trollope, often employs the feminine features of the
roman-fleuve, his narrative does not *fully* embody an *écriture féminine*.

The depiction of the promiscuous desire Pamela represents continues
after her death and "culminates" in the serial sexual invocation of *Hearing Secret Harmonies*. A variant of the dance metaphor, the cult participants at The Devil's Fingers "should have been all with all, each with
each, within the sacred circle" (167), or so Gwinnett describes their
purpose. The ceremony is anti-erotic, however; consummation signals
not an orgiastic fulfillment of sexual desire ("It wasn't for pleasure,"
Gwinnett tells Nick), but the triumph of the will to power—only Scorpio Murtlock is able to complete a sex act with each participant, achieving mastery over the cult. The desire Murtlock incites is as sinisterly
death-oriented as Pamela's: the objective of the invocation is, after all,
to resurrect Trelawney, and it is Murtlock who drives Widmerpool on
to his final death run. His desire is also rumored to be primarily homosexual, a nonreproductive desire, Powell seems to suggest. There are
surprisingly few children in *The Music of Time*, in a genre that often
exploits its massive scope to present a story of generations, and the

homoerotic is presented as yet one more dangerous component of the cults and one more example of deviant desire in the *roman-fleuve*.

The preeminence of social themes in *The Music of Time* suggests that a resolution to this *roman-fleuve* may be found not in the fates of individuals but in the culmination of society's fate, particularly in the last trilogy. The carefree whirlwind of social events in the first two movements is forever ended by the breakdown of the upper echelon of British society precipitated by World War II, depicted in the third movement. The engagement of Pamela Flitton and Widmerpool at the end of *The Military Philosophers* coincides with the dropping of the atomic bomb, two events representative of the destructive impulse of modern postwar society, auguring the beginning of the end of an era. Characters suffer increasingly from melancholy in the last volumes, a malady that significantly coincides with the male characters' prevalent attraction to Pamela in an erotic death wish. Through Pamela Widmerpool both narrative and male characters reach their ends. Her first appearance, as a bridesmaid who vomits into the font at Stringham's wedding, foreshadows her later emergence as a force that undermines from within the values of the old society, represented by Stringham, and one that literally weds itself to the new society in the parvenu Widmerpool. Reappearing in *The Military Philosophers* as an ATS driver, Pamela is the sexually adventurous new woman (anticipated by Jean Templer), coming into her own after the war years. Her eroticism, that blend of "frigidity and insatiable desire," is a motivating force in the narrative, precipitating the deaths that seem to portend an imminent end to the narrative. However, the urgency of the death wish seems to culminate in the short-circuit of Pamela's own death, between the cracks of narrated action in the last trilogy.

Death as a terminal motif figures frequently in the fourth movement: two major characters, Erridge and Moreland, die. The former is one of the last genuine aristocrats (though hardly a traditional one); the latter is a composer Jenkins compares to Beethoven, a representative of Western culture. Nevertheless, despite the prevalence of death in the last trilogy and the accompanying hints of termination, the last movement continues the narrative pattern of the previous volumes, in particular the pattern of oscillation and cyclical repetition. The techniques of recurrence are even more pronounced in the final volume, *Hearing Secret Harmonies*. The scores of recurring characters suggest both the possibility of final curtain calls for these actors and the continuity of previous appearances. In the first chapter of this novel, forty-three characters from past volumes appear or are mentioned. Some of those summoned are figuratively resurrected from the dead, as in the cases of Ted Jeavons or Jimmy Stripling, but others are evoked only to be followed by exposition that brings their plot lines up to date, suggesting their continued roles in the narrative. Recurrence is also achieved through repeated incidents: Widmerpool is attacked with paint and stink bombs and launches into long-winded speeches reminiscent of his performances at the Old Boy Dinners.

At the same time, continuity is implied by the introduction of a new cast of characters, indicative of a future generation. Unattractive as Scorpio Murtlock, Rusty, Barnabas Henderson, and Fiona Cutts may be, they represent a generation that shows no signs of imminent extinction. Instead, the depiction of these youths suggests recurrence of the past. Not only is Scorpio a fictional reincarnation of Dr. Trelawney, but he also takes his cult to visit "Stone Age" ruins, effecting a link with history and recalling the nomadic tribes of the prologue in the first volume. The members of the caravan are compared to "a medieval lady," a "recreant knight's run-away mistress," and an "unsuccessful troubadour" (6). Both Nick and Gwinnett note a resemblance between the cult movements and previous historical manifestations: Nick compares the hippie rebels to nineteenth-century Romantics (120); they remind Gwinnett of "early seventeenth-century gothicism" (166).

Apropos of endings, Brooks proposes that narrative advances toward a climax of realization: "The ultimate determinants of meaning lie *at the end*, and narrative desire is ultimately, inexorably, desire *for* the end."[58] However, as ending is inherently antithetical to this process-oriented narrative, Powell's lengthy *roman-fleuve* falls short of Brooks's climactic model: its desire terminates in a satisfaction debilitated by the teasing pattern of frustrated desire that motivates its narrative. Like that nymphomaniac dynamo of desire Pamela Widmerpool, compulsively engaging in a frenzy of unfulfilled sexual activity, the narrative of the *roman-fleuve* repeatedly prefigures its end through its teasing pattern of oscillation, evading the climactic resolution it seems to promise.

While after twelve volumes the reader might expect a forceful conclusion to justify the prolonged postponement of the ending, *The Music of Time* terminates with the predictable revelation that the entire narrative has been a flashback in the mind of the narrator. Powell frequently employs similar circular conclusions in the individual volumes of the *roman-fleuve*; for example, as Uncles Giles visits Nick at school in *A Question of Upbringing* and as Nick has lunch with Giles at the end, or as Nick receives postcards from Uncle Giles at the beginning of *The Acceptance World* and from Jean Templer at the end. These circular endings, anticipating the final frame that encloses *The Music of Time*, result from the imposition of parallelism rather than the resolution of events. The ability of the subsequent volume to resume the story reveals the inadequacy of this device for a final termination, though sufficient to close an inner novel of a multivolume work. Although circular endings have been considered "one of the simplest and most effective closural devices,"[59] this technique provides a deliberate yet fragile closure in the *roman-fleuve* because as it circles back, it mimics the oscillating dynamic of its narrative, suggesting not closure but recurrence. The oscillation of the *roman-fleuve*, which works against expectation of closure, is evident in the formal devices that "bind" the narrative, devices that suggest sequence rather than an inherent "termination point." A specific expectancy has been established, and the *roman-fleuve* experiences the same difficulty as the boy-who-cried-wolf: the audience expects a repetition of the usual pattern.

As Kermode points out, we look toward resolution to convey the significance of the whole: "All such plotting presupposes and requires that an end will bestow upon the whole duration and meaning."[60] The prolonged suspension of the *roman-fleuve* may be responsible for creating the expectation of a stupendous resolution (a big bang, so to speak) to compensate for the vast expanse of narrative teasing, a possibility that would account for some critics' disappointment in the last trilogy of *The Music of Time*, particularly in *Hearing Secret Harmonies*. Before the publication of the last trilogy, Brennan anticipated "some grand resolution such as *A la recherche du temps perdu* affords,"[61] a resolution that was not forthcoming. After publication of the last volume, Swinden's disappointment extended, retrospectively, back through the entire series: "But what it offers to our contemplation, especially in much of the later books, is emotionally superficial, intellectually unambitious, and not very funny either."[62] Jones objected to Powell's "refusal to end the sequence with a flourish," and McSweeney was disenchanted with the novel's failure to indulge in "reflexive probing of its own imaginative processes."[63] If the end sheds "retrospective light" on a narrative, as Brooks suggests,[64] the only clear-cut illumination in *The Music of*

Time is that the entire novel has been a flashback, that the end was a time before the beginning.

The genre's resistance to achieving forceful closure, then, is found in its tendency to repeat. Although *The Music of Time* is framed with two conclusions, the ultimate effect is not to reinforce closure but to contest it, reinforcing the predominant oscillating narrative tension of the *roman-fleuve*. Although critics have argued that the long quotation from Burton in the last few paragraphs of *The Music of Time* provides closure for the twelve volumes,[65] the passage actually reiterates the events that emplot the *roman-fleuve*: the events of the war—"daily musters and preparations . . . battles fought, so many men slain"—as well those of peacetime—"[a] vast confusion of vows, wishes, actions . . . whole catalogues of volumes of all sorts, new paradoxes, opinions, schisms, heresies, controversies in philosophy, religion, &c." (271–72). The rhythm of this "torrential" passage evokes both the fluid emplotment of the work itself and the proliferation of incidents generated; its fluidity suggests, at this key moment when the text faces for the last time the possibility of closure, that its dynamic is indeed that of narratives described as feminine. Moreover, the Burton passage ends with statements of reversal that suggest the cyclical movement of recurrence: "Now come tidings of weddings, maskings, mummeries, entertainments, jubilees . . . then again, as in a new shifted scene, treasons, cheating tricks, robberies, enormous villainies in all kinds, funerals, burials, deaths of Princes, new discoveries, expeditions; now comical then tragical matters. Today we hear of new Lords and officers created, to-morrow of some great men deposed, and then again of fresh honours conferred; one is let loose, another imprisoned, one purchaseth, another breaketh; he thrives, his neighbor turns bankrupt; now plenty, then again dearth and famine; one runs, another rides, wrangles, laughs, weeps, &c." (272). By implication, the machinations of a Widmerpool will be followed by a counterforce; the fall of one social agent is followed by the rise of another—a Scorpio Murtlock or possibly a Barnabas Henderson. Depicting society as an endless cycle, the novel spawns a fecund narrative without end.

Any closural force of the Burton passage is subverted not only by its own fluidity and suggestion of recurrence but also by the passage that follows it, supplying the final bracket to the frame tale inaugurated in the prologue, the introduction to the entire multivolume *roman-fleuve*. Even as it enlists a device of traditional closure, the dynamics of Powell's narrative circumvents an end. Although this passage seems at first to offer an even more decisive closure than the quotation from Burton, its imagery and diction actually undermine closure: "The thudding sound from the quarry had declined now to no more than a gentle reverberation, infinitely remote. It ceased altogether at the long drawn wail of a hooter—the distant pounding of centaurs' hoofs dying away, as the last note of their conch trumpeted out over hyperborean seas. Even the formal measure of the Seasons seemed suspended in the wintry silence" (272). The passage circles back to the imagery of the mythical prologue in *A Question of Upbringing*, to winter and the centaurs, to the measures of the season's dance, and to, in the description of the quarry, the excavation of the street workers in the initial passage. The final word, "silence," is appropriately terminal, but the passage leaves ambiguous the reason for the cessation of the music of time. The measures "seemed suspended," the first term undermining any conclusiveness, the second suggesting a temporary interruption or, possibly in reference to the music (as in the measures of Poussin's circular dance), the prolonging of a note into the next chord. The passage, in its circling back to the prologue, is ultimately self-referential: the narrator, for whatever reason— old age, death, fatigue, boredom—has ceased to speak, to record the music. Lacking explanation, the silence seems arbitrarily imposed. The resistance to closure in this passage creates an unstable ending. If, as Brooks suggests, the "desire of the text is ultimately the desire for . . . that recognition which is the moment of the death of the reader in the text,"[66] then that desire must be satisfied with the ambiguous "silence" that ends this *roman-fleuve*, a moderately disconcerting satisfaction.

In affixing double closure, Powell resists the process-orientation of the *roman-fleuve*. The use of two conclusions indicates his anxiety about the sufficiency of a single one, and the contesting relation of the two endings reveals a fundamental inadequacy of closural devices to halt the oscillation of these narratives. If narrative denotes a sequence of events, then closure, the termination of that sequence, must be external to it. The discontinuous nature of closure is especially problematic in the *roman-fleuve*, characterized by the predominance of a hyperbolically extended middle, a genre that ambitiously aims to emulate the unending flow of life itself.

As Powell resists the inherent dynamics of the genre through his closural techniques, he demonstrates a preference for traditional narrative, a need, as Kermode puts it, for a "boundary to make time comprehensible."[67] The repetition characteristic of the extensive middle creates energy, but eventually the system faces the risk of what Smith terms "saturation," which creates an imminent "desire for variation or conclusion."[68] Thus, the form is threatened with overload and premature ending—Brooks's danger of "short-circuit." In the *roman-fleuve* the prolongation of desire runs the risk, to push the coital metaphor to a logical conclusion, of premature finish or exhaustion of desire. However, the enticement of closure may also render narrative tension itself "a source of pleasure," Smith points out,[69] suggesting Irigaray's and Cixous's erotics of an ever-present, multitudinous feminine response.

Powell's ambivalence about the feminine form he has chosen, evident in the various tensions I have identified in *A Dance to the Music of Time*, may be the underlying source of critics' gender-equivocal labeling of his work as "masculine needlework" or "small beer" (see chapter 1). Powell's *roman-fleuve* also refuses many features of the traditional (male) novel, particularly the adventure and quest plots, parodied by Widmerpool's clumsy rise to power. If his female characters are promiscuous and nymphomaniac, their male counterparts are often voyeuristic and impotent. Relations between the sexes form a major issue in this text, yet its interest in gender is subsumed in the larger emphasis on a social decadence, which is ironically shown to be historically recurrent. Powell's narrator exhibits the ironist's skepticism about the possibility of social change, an attitude exhibited by neither Trollope nor Richardson. This irony, skepticism, and ambivalence are reflected in the conflicted gender and genre of *A Dance to the Music of Time*.

Conceiving of the *roman-fleuve* as a traditional novel with a beginning, middle, and end while at the same time choosing a genre with a propensity for *écriture féminine*, which resists these features, Powell mediates between the conflicting *roman* and *fleuve* elements, structure and flow. Ironically, this contradiction embodies a subtle indication of postmodern consciousness in *A Dance to the Music of Time*. The self-effacing Jenkins might be viewed as a postmodern narrator because of his passivity and voyeurism. If, as some critics have suggested, he represents a hollow gap in the text and, more certainly, demonstrates an indifference to the mastery narrators usually exhibit, he may function as a challenge to subjectivity and representation. Like most postmodern texts, *A Dance to the Music of Time* resists closure, and although the ending is duly reinforced, it is, as I have shown, profoundly indeterminate. Most significant, this *roman-fleuve* is protodeconstructive: it is, like

Jenkins himself, deeply skeptical about its own project. These elements, nevertheless, do not seem to override the prevalence of conventional narrative techniques. In the context of genre evolution and literary history, Powell's endeavor is paradoxical: he creates a postmodern example of the genre, but at the same time emulates narratives of the past. Yet the highly developed tension I have traced in this chapter suggests that Powell has carried to an extreme one element inherent in the oscillating *roman-fleuve*—a major narrative innovation and contribution in itself.

The Evolution of the *Roman-Fleuve* and the Canonical Novel

In many ways, the refinements of the *roman-fleuve* during its as yet brief existence mirror the history of the British novel. Trollope, Richardson, and Powell produced novels identifiable, respectively, as Victorian, modern, and contemporary—their *romans-fleuves* each reflect to some degree the prevailing aesthetic of the novel during their lifetimes—yet they also adapt the genre to encompass their individualistic and sometimes innovative conceptions. Despite these writers' achievements, their massive texts have fallen between the cracks of the popular and the canonical novel, revealing the prejudice of both the marketplace and the literary establishment. Any speculation about the future direction of the *roman-fleuve* must account for its past pattern of evolution as well as the cultural and economic factors that have hindered its popular and canonical acceptance.

Anthony Powell began *A Dance to the Music of Time* approximately seventy years after Trollope finished his Palliser novels, a period of time lengthy enough to encompass not only a reaction against the highly plotted realistic nineteenth-century novel but also a transformation of many modernist innovations that had transpired in the interim. Trollope's Palliser *roman-fleuve* has all the characteristics of the baggy Victorian novel; his conception of the genre is that of a Victorian serial exponentially magnified. Yet his dissatisfaction with the artificiality of many of the nineteenth-century novelistic conventions points toward the modernist project. Richardson's *Pilgrimage* is much more one long, continuous novel, unified by the subjective first-person narration of Miriam Henderson. The individual novels are not self-sufficient because of the elliptical presentation of material within each novel and the sizable gaps between them. It might be said that in creating a meganovel, Richardson has pushed the *roman-fleuve* to its most extreme expression—the encyclopedic, interior stream of consciousness novel. Powell also achieves unity by using a first-person narrator as well as recurring characters and circular structure. His *roman-fleuve* is closer to Trollope's than Richardson's, however, in conceiving of each individual volume as a separate novel, yet the whole is far more loosely plotted than any nineteenth-century novel. Accordingly, the evolution of the genre since its origination in the nineteenth century includes the proto–*romans-fleuves* of Balzac and Trollope, the fully realized innovative exemplars of Richardson and Proust, and the completely realized but relatively traditional achievement of Powell.

A Dance to the Music of Time, while it is relatively conventional, defies easy classification into any literary movement: it reflects both the literary conservatism of the 1950s (when its publication began) and the skepticism of the postmodern period. In *The Reaction Against Experiment, 1950–1960*, Rubin Rabinovitz finds a reactionary tendency in twentieth-century literature, particularly in realistic writers such as Powell: "The realistic style of the nineteenth century never really died in England, especially in the fiction of writers like Evelyn Waugh, Anthony Powell, or Graham Greene."[1] The literary movement of the 1950s, according to Rabinovitz, is stylistically indebted to nineteenth-century predecessors and is specifically antiexperimental: "Though the English novelists of this period wrote about contemporary social problems, few of them experimented with the form and style of their novels; nor did they incorporate the techniques of Joyce, Virginia Woolf, or other experimental novelists into their styles. Most of the postwar writers conscientiously rejected experimental techniques in their fiction as well as in their critical writings, and turned instead to older novelists for inspiration."[2] Powell himself supports this assertion as he names writers who influenced him, for instance, his enthusiastic reading of the author of *La Comédie humaine*: "Balzac arrived for me only in middle-age, then wholeheartedly."[3] Rabinovitz's designation of Powell's place in contemporary literature is generally accurate, yet he assumes that narrative technique (especially stream of consciousness) is the primary indicator of experimentation. Powell is not entirely a realistic writer, as my discussion of his characterization in chapter 4 demonstrates; and his subtle innovation in point of view significantly establishes *A Dance to the Music of*

Time as a contemporary rather than a reactionary neo-Victorian novel. Powell deliberately and self-consciously rejects the excesses of postmodernism but is fully aware of its implications for literature, civilization, and history.

While the development of the *roman-fleuve* from Trollope to Richardson to Powell suggests an irregular pattern—neither fully progressive nor reactionary—it is possible to trace other threads by choosing other exemplars. Many characteristics of the *roman-fleuve*, particularly as evident in *Pilgrimage*, surface in the *nouveau roman*; Richardson's *roman-fleuve* also might be considered a prototype for Anaïs Nin's experimental *roman-fleuve*, *Cities of the Interior*. At the same time, most twentieth-century *romans-fleuves* have not been experimental: Lessing's *Children of Violence* is fairly traditional in its narrative until the end of the last novel, *The Four-Gated City*, where the linear narrative breaks down in a way that suggests transcendence through madness.

The pattern of development in the three exemplars I have analyzed suggests that genres do not necessarily evolve toward an ever-greater experimentation, but that the movement may be one of a dialectically swinging pendulum. As Thomas Winner has described this model of genre evolution: "We can think of art as swinging between two poles: from almost complete normativeness, or banality and redundancy . . . to almost total violation of the norm, or of the code. . . . From a diachronic approach, the polar concept defines periods of artistic creation, which appear to oscillate between those which place high value on normativeness at the expense of innovation . . . and those which place high value on innovation at the expense of normativeness."[4] Using this terminology, Trollope and Powell are closer to the "normative" mode, while Richardson violates the norm to emphasize innovation.

Furthermore, as I suggest in the preceding pages, there is a link between particular kinds of adaptations of the form and gendered perception of the genre. James's use of gendered terms to designate literary value not only has personal significance but also has implications for the history of the novel: his efforts to associate certain writers (such as Balzac) and certain novelistic features (such as tight planning) with a more elevated novel than that produced earlier in the nineteenth century comprise an attempt to elevate the profession of writing novels and the genre itself from a popular to a high art form. Gaye Tuchman has documented male writers' proclivity to "edge women out" of the increasingly lucrative and respectable profession of writing novels in the mid-nineteenth century, a move to "invade" the field as "high-culture novelists."[5] The period in which Trollope was writing his Palliser novels (1864–80) fits within what Tuchman defines as the "period of invasion" (1840–79).[6] Trollope's creation of sympathetic women characters and his ambivalent presentation of feminist themes might, therefore, be viewed as an effort to capitalize on the success of women who wrote in a domestic tradition. Moreover, James wrote his criticism of Trollope in 1883, within the second stage of the male takeover, what Tuchman terms the "period of redefinition" (1880–99), during which "men of letters, including critics, actively redefined the nature of a good novel and a great author. They preferred a new form of realism that they associated with 'manly' literature—that is great literature."[7] Surely Henry James, though Tuchman does not mention him specifically, is an agent of this process. His gendered criticism goes beyond mere personal redefinition to situate the genre of the novel in a masculine field of high art.

Therefore, the oscillating evolution of the *roman-fleuve* may also be viewed as a gendered tug-of-war over a literary genre. Trollope moves toward an *écriture féminine* as he undermines an ostensibly antifeminist narrator and appropriates feminine features of the novel. Richardson, reacting against what she perceives as a kind of masculine realism practiced by Balzac, defines the *roman-fleuve* as a fluid and nonlinear feminine narrative. Powell retraces efforts to define the novel—in this case the *roman-fleuve*—as a high-culture form (often perceived as masculine, just as popular forms such as the soap opera are perceived as feminine) by making extensive demands on the reader to comprehend a vast field of characters and an extensive network of allusions to art and literature.[8] His efforts to elevate the novel for a more educated, elite audience parallel the Victorian "reaction against the bourgeois library-subscribers" as well as male writers' appropriation of a previously feminine form in the Victorian period.[9]

The history of the *roman-fleuve* beyond the slice of time from its nineteenth-century inception to the late twentieth century remains to unfold. If Roger Hagedorn is correct in arguing that "serials appear in a medium precisely at that period when the real rival is not so much another serial in the same medium, but another medium,"[10] the successor to the *roman-fleuve* may materialize as a lengthy interactive hypertext novel in the rival medium of the computer. This new mode of publication shares with the *roman-fleuve* a potential for digressions and detours that are significant to the whole ("Nothing is a side issue," Richardson's protagonist insists). Richardson's alternate ordering and reordering of her reading of Proust's *A la recherche du temps perdu* and Powell's readers who purposely took the volumes of *The Music of Time* out of sequence presage reading strategies that demonstrate the hypertext potential of the *roman-fleuve*. Among recent postmodern texts, South American Julio Cortazar's *Hopscotch* offers the reader suggestions for alternate chapter sequences in its preface. Similarly, the "Choose Your Own Adventure" series for children may indicate that personal choice—individual control of the reading experience—is a future direction of the novel. The popularity of the "spin-off" demonstrates the variability of an audience's interest in characters whose primacy may differ, not only from viewer to viewer, but also over time as secondary or minor figures move to center stage.

To support and extend Hagedorn's hypothesis about intermedia competition, it may be observed that the early twentieth century, the period of greatest popularity for the *roman-fleuve*, coincides with the beginning of the cinema's challenge to the book publishing industry, just as the challenge to print media today is posed by computer and laser technology. At the same time, Hagedorn's thesis is based on arguments about the *economic* advantages of serials, that they function to "*promote the medium in which they appear.*"[11] While Dorothy Richardson published a few extracts from *Pilgrimage* in journals, that format of publishing the *roman-fleuve* is rare in the twentieth century, and the contemporary *roman-fleuve* can only promote the book publishing industry. Although the *roman-fleuve* is nearly always published twice—first when it appears in individual volumes, again when a completed or omnibus edition is released—the effects on profits of book publishers have been negligible. The publication of the collected whole is, expectedly, anticlimactic. In spite of a commercial potential rivaling that of the Victorian serial, which could earn profits for author and publisher both as serial installments and as a book, the twentieth-century *roman-fleuve* has not been a boon to publishers. Richardson's experience with her publisher offers the grimmest scenario. When she received her publisher's statement on sales after publication of the twelve-volume edition of *Pilgrimage* it had announced as complete, Richardson wrote, "It is even worse than I had anticipated, revealing the sales, during the vital first three months, to be just 699 <u>volumes</u> not sets. It appears they were right in announcing Pilgrimage as <u>finished</u>."[12] Although the Pallisers and *A Dance to the Music of Time* brought more profits to their publishers, the sales of the *roman-fleuve*, perceived by the mass audience as an esoteric high-art genre, seldom place it at the top of the best-seller lists.

Much of the success of the Victorian novel was the result of a propitious social and economic setting. The rising middle class, the increasingly educated and leisured populace, and the availability of the novel through serial publication and lending libraries all contributed to its popularity among readers and its profitability for publishers. It may be that the next incarnation of the *roman-fleuve* awaits a similarly auspicious era and an even more leisured audience able to appreciate the amplitude of the genre: "Publication formats and literary theory in our century have favored the appearance of the short story over the long novel, just as in the nineteenth century the opposite was the case."[13] Unfortunately, book lovers and academics no longer have the time for leisurely reading they once had. Nevertheless, while the novel's length would seem to be the feature that most hinders its popularity, other long genres—the epic, the sonnet sequence, the dramatic trilogy—have achieved both popular contemporary success and posthumous canonical status, suggesting length is but one factor. My account of reviewers' negative evaluation of the *roman-fleuve* for its feminine features demonstrates the subtle power of gendered denigrations. As critics' gendered exclusion of the *roman-fleuve* reveals, either our valuation of the feminine must increase or the genre must cease to be perceived as feminine if it is to be widely read. The *roman-fleuve* requires not only leisured readers but also an audience receptive to alternatives to the male adventure plot and suspense-driven narratives, as well as a literary establishment free of residual prejudice against women writers and feminine forms.

Aristotle, whose warning against long dramas opened this study, suggests a more optimistic future appreciation of the *roman-fleuve*, "The greater the length, the more beautiful will the piece be by reason of its size, provided the whole be perspicuous" (vii). Granting Aristotle's requirement of perspicuity, the novel without end is the ultimate pleasurable text. Providing an expanse of narrative forepleasure far exceeding the ejaculatory text, the *roman-fleuve* interminably prolongs in its reading a moment of Keatsian arrested passion, privileging desire itself over a climax that is quickly, and inevitably, followed by an anticlimax. The *roman-fleuve* awaits a confluence of cultural transformations that favor its canonical acceptance, particularly an audience receptive to its Rubenesque proportions.

✤ ✤ ✤ *Notes*

Chapter 1 The *Roman-Fleuve*: Flooding the Boundaries of the Novel

1. The nineteenth-century French origins are attested to by Elizabeth Kerr, *Bibliography of the Sequence Novel*, p. 7, and by John McCormick, *Catastrophe and Imagination: An Interpretation of the Recent English and American Novel*, p. 84. According to Kerr, there are no examples of the genre in the eighteenth century; see "The Twentieth Century Sequence Novel," p. 27.

2. Quoted in Robert Selig, *Time and Anthony Powell: A Critical Study*, p. 31.

3. The most extensive discussion of the genre is Kerr's unpublished dissertation, "The Twentieth Century Sequence Novel" (1941). After a summary of the origins of the genre before 1900, she outlines three types of sequence novels classified by content: the individual or biographical sequence (such as Proust's *A la recherche du temps perdu*), the family sequence (Galsworthy's *Forsyte Saga*), and the society sequence (Jules Romains's *Les hommes de bonne volonté*). In this encyclopedic project, Kerr discusses fifty-one twentieth-century novels and touches on many other precursors. While Kerr's work is comprehensive, a veritable key to the sequence novel, it is obviously dated in its critical methodology. In "Some Forms of the Sequence Novel in British Fiction," another unpublished dissertation (1969), Martin Ausmus classifies forms of the sequence novel: he distinguishes between a chronological sequence and a synchronous sequence and outlines four combinations of time and point of view, illustrated by four novels: Galsworthy's *Forsyte Saga* exemplifies the third-person chronological sequence; Bennett's *Clayhanger* trilogy, the third-person synchronous; Sasson's *Memoirs of George Sherston*, the first-person chronological; and Cary's *First Trilogy*, the first-person synchronous. The only published book-length study of the British sequence novel is Robert K. Morris's *Continuance and Change* (1972). Morris's study (which includes a chapter on *A Dance to the Music of Time*) provides a succinct survey of contemporary examples of the

genre, with an emphasis on the themes of time and change as the usual content of the genre.

4. Joyce Reid, comp., *The Concise Oxford Dictionary of French Literature*, p. 549.

5. Frank Kermode, *The Sense of an Ending*, p. 46.

6. Joseph Frank, "Spatial Form: An Answer to Critics," p. 244.

7. Hélène Cixous, "Castration or Decapitation?" p. 52.

8. The following studies have taken varied and often cautious approaches to the gender-genre issue. Linda Kauffman's *Discourses of Desire: Gender, Genre, and Epistolary Fictions* claims *not* to "define women's essence or imagination," p. 25. Nancy Armstrong, in *Desire and Domestic Fiction: A Political History of the Novel*, revises theories about the origins of the novel, arguing that domestic fiction was a major force effecting new cultural conditions contributing to the rise of the middle class. Tania Modleski overturns the "double critical standard" that ignores the romance, the Gothic, and the soap opera, traditionally seen as women's genres, in *Loving with a Vengeance: Mass-Produced Fantasies for Women*, p. 11. For a broad survey of the gender-genre issue, see *Genre Choices, Gender Questions* by Mary Gerhart.

9. Much of this theoretical impasse, a major deadlock in contemporary feminism, results from an unfortunate kind of either-or thinking to which feminists are not immune. However, some of the best recent contributions seek to defuse the overemotional quality of the debate, as Naomi Schor does in "This Essentialism Which Is Not One." Also see Diana Fuss's *Essentially Speaking*, which deconstructs the binary opposition essentialism-constructionism and examines the function of the concept of essentialism for the controversy; Rosi Braidotti's "The Politics of Ontological Difference" questions charges that essentialism is nonpolitical. *Revaluing French Feminism*, edited by Nancy Fraser and Sandra Lee Bartky, contains essays representing both sides of the issue. Among critics of the French feminists, Domna Stanton rejects their use of metaphors she finds to be reductively maternal, while Rita Felski dismisses the whole notion of a feminist aesthetic.

10. Jean-Claude Chevalier et al., eds., *Grammaire Larousse du français contemporain* (Paris: Librairie Larousse, 1964), p. 164.

11. Margaret Whitford, "Rereading Irigaray," p. 121, n. 3.

12. Jane Gallop, "*Quand nos lèvres s'écrivent*: Irigaray's Body Politic," p. 79.

13. Silvia Bovenschen, "Is There a Feminine Aesthetic?" p. 134.

14. Robert Scholes, *Fabulation and Metafiction*, p. 26.

15. Fuss distinguishes between a "real" or Aristotelian essence, which is discovered, as opposed to a Lockean "nominal essence," which is "produced specifically by language" (*Essentially Speaking*, p. 4).

16. Ibid., p. 21.

17. Braidotti, "The Politics of Ontological Difference," in *Between Feminism and Psychoanalysis*, p. 91.

18. Ibid., p. 99. Also see Fuss, who argues that "to give 'woman' an essence is to undo Western phallomorphism and to offer women entry into subjecthood" (*Essentially Speaking*, p. 109).

19. Sir Paul Harvey and J. E. Heseltine, comps. and eds., *The Oxford Companion to French Literature*, s.v. "*roman-fleuve*." Translation mine.

20. J. A. Simpson and E. S. C. Weiner, preparers, *The Oxford English Dictionary*, 2d ed., s.v. "*roman-fleuve*." The second reference to the term listed is from *Bookseller* 1974, in reference to Anthony Powell.

21. Kerr, "Sequence Novel," p. 36.

22. R. H. Super, *The Chronicler of Barsetshire: A Life of Anthony Trollope*, p. 224.

23. Honoré de Balzac, author's introduction to vol. 1 of *La Comédie humaine*, p. lvii.

24. Ibid., p. xlii.

25. Ibid.

26. Selig, *Time and Anthony Powell*, especially pp. 27-69; Philip Thody, "The English Proust," passim.

27. Alastair Fowler, *Kinds of Literature: An Introduction to the Theory of Genres and Modes*. Fowler argues that not all features from a "repertoire" need be present: "When we assign a work to a generic type, we do not suppose that all its characteristic traits need to be shared by every other embodiment of the type. In particular, new works in the genre may contribute additional characteristics. In this way a literary genre changes with time, so that its boundaries cannot be defined by any single set of characteristics such as would determine a class" (p. 38).

28. Wolfgang Iser, "Indeterminacy and the Reader's Response in Fiction," in *Aspects of Narrative*, ed. J. Hillis Miller, p. 17.

29. Peter Brooks, *Reading for the Plot*, p. 108.

30. Ibid., p. 4.

31. Ibid., p. 12.

32. Meir Sternberg, *Expositional Modes and Temporal Ordering in Fiction*, p. 8.

33. Ibid., pp. 8-9.

34. Seymour Chatman, "What Novels Can Do That Films Can't (and Vice Versa)," p. 121.

35. Wolfgang Iser, *The Act of Reading*, p. 148.

36. Kerr, "Sequence Novel," p. 36.

37. Brooks, *Reading for the Plot*, pp. 90, 108.

38. To John Cowper Powys, March 30 [1930], Dorothy Richardson Papers, Beinecke Rare Book and Manuscript Library, Yale University.

39. Paul Ricoeur, "Narrative Time," p. 178.

40. Hayden White, "The Value of Narrativity in the Representation of Reality," p. 14.

41. Scholes and Kellogg, *The Nature of Narrative*, p. 211.

42. To E. B. C. Jones (Mrs. Lucas), May 12, 1921, Richardson Papers, Yale.

43. To Jones, Nov. 1927 [no day], Richardson Papers, Yale.

44. Gérard Genette, *Narrative Discourse: An Essay in Method*, p. 46.

45. See Joseph Boone, *Tradition Counter Tradition: Love and the Form of Fiction*, p. 72. As a (male) feminist, however, Boone does not endorse this association.

46. For useful and succinct definitions of *l'écriture féminine* see Christiane Makward, "To Be or Not to Be . . . A Feminist Speaker," in *The Future of Difference*, Hester Eisenstein and Alice Jardine, eds., pp. 95–105. See also Ann R. Jones, "Inscribing Femininity: French Theories of the Feminine," in *Making a Difference*, ed. Gayle Greene and Coppelia Kahn, pp. 80–112, especially p. 88, and Julia Penelope Stanley and Susan J. Wolfe (Robbins), "Toward a Feminist Aesthetic," pp. 57–71, especially pp. 66–67. Hélène Cixous's "The Laugh of the Medusa" is often considered a manifesto advocating an *écriture féminine*. While there are some variations in the definitions, there is a general consensus that identifies most of the features of an *écriture féminine* that I have outlined.

47. Rachel Blau DuPlessis, *Writing Beyond the Ending*.

48. Susan Winnett, "Coming Unstrung: Women, Men, Narrative, and Principles of Pleasure," p. 506.

49. Linda Hughes and Michael Lund, "Studying Victorian Serials," p. 236.

50. Robert Allen, *Speaking of Soap Opera*, p. 73.

51. J. A. Sutherland, *Victorian Novelists and Publishers*, p. 185.

52. Mary Hamer, *Writing by Numbers: Trollope's Serial Fiction*, p. 13.

53. Sutherland, *Victorian Novelists and Publishers*, p. 109.

54. From John Cowper Powys to Richardson, Oct. 27, 1938, Richardson Papers, Yale. He wrote Richardson: "Shall I or shan't I stop going backwards thro Pilgrimage (now I've got them all) till I've reached the opening words of Pointed Roofs."

55. To Bryher (1925–28), Richardson Papers, Yale.

56. Paul Gaston, " 'This Question of Discipline': An Interview with Anthony Powell," p. 644.

57. Gloria Fromm, *Dorothy Richardson*, pp. 369–70.

58. Hamer, *Writing by Numbers*, appendix 2, "The Initial Publication of Trollope's Novels in England."

59. Ibid., p. 106 and passim.

60. Quoted in Donald Smalley, ed., *Trollope: The Critical Heritage*, pp. 250–52.

61. Ibid.

62. To Richard Church, 1936, Richardson Papers, Yale.

63. Iser, *The Act of Reading*, p. 191.

64. Henry James, "Anthony Trollope," *Partial Portraits*, pp. 98, 100, 101.

65. Leland Person, "Henry James, George Sand, and the Suspense of Masculinity," p. 522.

66. Henry James, "Honoré de Balzac," in *French Poets and Novelists*, p. 68.

67. Ibid., pp. 75-76.

68. Ibid., p. 80.

69. Henry James, "Honoré de Balzac," in *Notes on Novelists: With Some Other Notes*, p. 133.

70. To Peggy Kirkaldy, Dec. 8, 1940, Richardson Papers, Yale.

71. Quoted in Horace Gregory, *Dorothy Richardson: An Adventure in Self-Discovery*, p. 10.

72. Lawrence Hyde, "The Work of Dorothy Richardson," p. 517.

73. Leon Edel, "Dorothy Richardson, 1882-1957," p. 168.

74. To Jones (Mrs. Lucas), Nov. 25, 1938, Richardson Papers, Yale.

75. Anthony West, *Aspects of a Life*, p. 343.

76. Charles Michener, "Powell: The 'Dance' Is Over," p. 80.

77. Robert K. Morris, "Powell's Dance to the Grave," p. 760.

78. Anatole Broyard, "End of the Marathon Dance," p. 33.

Chapter 2. The Pallisers: Trollope's Nineteenth-Century Proto-*Roman-Fleuve*

1. Joseph Boone, "Wedlock as Deadlock and Beyond: Closure and the Victorian Marriage Ideal," p. 79. Also see Marianna Torgovnick's "Closure in the Victorian Novel" and *Closure in the Novel*.

2. Maria Minich Brewer, "A Loosening of Tongues: From Narrative Economy to Women Writing," p. 144.

3. Jane Nardin, *He Knew She Was Right*, and Deborah Denenholz Morse, *Women in Trollope's Palliser Novels*. The recent burgeoning of feminist approaches to literature has brought about a renewed scholarly interest in the vexed issue of Trollope's feminism. In the informal discussion at the end of a 1988 MLA session, scholars dubbed the "Older [Trollope] Critics" in the session title identified the feminist issue as the one they would pursue if they were writing their seminal studies of Trollope today.

4. Rita Felski, *Beyond Feminist Aesthetics*, p. 32.

5. See Lynette Felber, "A Manifesto for Feminine Modernism: Dorothy Richardson's *Pilgrimage*."

6. Alastair Fowler argues, "Whether or not it is meant to be innovative, the assembled form is apprehended as a new genre only from a subsequent perspective. This retrospective critical insight regroups individual works, and sees them

now as belonging to the new genre, now anticipating it, now differing in kind" (*Kinds of Literature*, p. 261). Other recent proponents argue that although genres are mutable and flexible, these characteristics in no way discredit genre criticism. Recognizing that genres are mutable and that classes overlap does not prohibit discussion, definition, and grouping of them. See Ralph Cohen, "History and Genre"; Paul Hernadi, *Beyond Genre: New Directions in Literary Classification*; and the essays by John Reichert, Joseph P. Strelka, and Thomas G. Winner in *Theories of Literary Genre*, ed. Joseph P. Strelka.

7. Northrop Frye, *Anatomy of Criticism: Four Essays*, p. 247; Fowler, *Kinds of Literature*, p. 47.

8. Reichert, "More than Kin and Less than Kind," in *Theories of Literary Genre*, ed. Joseph Strelka, p. 58.

9. See John Halperin, "*The Eustace Diamonds* and Politics" for the history of the classification of the Pallisers, the inclusion and exclusion of various volumes.

10. Steven Wall, Introduction to *Can You Forgive Her?* by Anthony Trollope, p. 22.

11. Janet Husband lists the Pallisers as a sequel in *Sequels: An Annotated Guide to Novels in Series*; Elizabeth Kerr lists it as a sequence novel. Alan Warren Friedman calls it a *roman-fleuve*, p. 126, as does John McCormick, p. xiv.

12. Anthony Trollope, *An Autobiography*, pp. 183–84.

13. Halperin, "*The Eustace Diamonds* and Politics," p. 139.

14. Arthur Mizener, "Anthony Trollope: The Palliser Novels," in *From Jane Austen to Joseph Conrad*, ed. Robert Rathburn and Martin Steinmann Jr., p. 160.

15. Cohen, "History and Genre," p. 216.

16. James Kincaid, *The Novels of Anthony Trollope*, p. 44.

17. Hayden White, "Value of Narrativity in the Representation of Reality," p. 20.

18. Ibid.

19. Scholes and Kellogg, *The Nature of Narrative*, p. 86.

20. Henry Carr, *What Is History?*, p. 10.

21. Paul Ricoeur, vol. 1 of *Time and Narrative*, p. 145.

22. Halperin, "*The Eustace Diamonds* and Politics," also mentions a plethora of connections that this novel supplies with the previous and subsequent volumes (pp. 143–44).

23. McCormick, Introduction to *The Prime Minister*, by Anthony Trollope, p. xvi.

24. Kincaid, *Novels*, pp. 180, 192.

25. Bradford Booth, *Anthony Trollope: Aspects of His Life and Art*, p. 90.

The mere inclusion of a character, however, is not sufficient; otherwise *The Small House at Allington*, in which Palliser is introduced, would also be considered a Parliamentary novel. Although Juliet McMaster includes a chapter on this novel in *Trollope's Palliser Novels*, she describes it as a Barset novel that she has "annexed" to the Palliser series (p. 1).

26. Peter Garrett, *The Victorian Multiplot Novel*, p. 188.

27. Alan Warren Friedman adopts the term "multivalent" to define multi-volume novels with a multiple perspective, those written from a "somewhat different angle or vision and sometimes again and again" ("The Modern Multivalent Novel: Form and Function," in *The Theory of the Novel: New Essays*, ed. John Halperin, p. 122).

28. Susan S. Lanser, "Toward a Feminist Narratology," p. 349.

29. McMaster, *Novels*, discusses the jewel motif at length in chapter 5. Her emphasis is on the diamonds as emblems of lies, and she argues that Trollope's subject in *The Eustace Diamonds* is the same as in Bacon's essay "On Truth."

30. Kerr, "Sequence Novel," pp. 36 and 40.

31. Walter Allen, *The English Novel*, p. 191.

32. Peter Brooks, *Reading for the Plot*, pp. 104-5.

33. Adrian Marino, "Toward a Definition of Literary Genres," in *Theories of Literary Genre*, ed. Joseph Strelka, p. 51.

34. Fowler, *Kinds*, p. 261.

35. Meir Sternberg, *Expositional Modes and Temporal Ordering in Fiction*, p. 194.

36. Lanser, "Toward A Feminist Narratology," p. 357.

37. McMaster, *Novels*, pp. 171-72.

38. Nardin, *He Knew*, p. 28.

39. Sternberg, *Expositional Modes*, p. 17.

40. Ibid., p. 47. Actually, only three characters are presented since, as Sternberg fails to notice, the chapters on Lizzie Greystock and Lady Eustace deal with the maiden and married lives of the same character.

41. Nardin, *He Knew*, pp. 11 and 129.

42. Irving H. Buchen, "The Aesthetics of the Supra-Novel," in *The Theory of the Novel*, ed. Halperin, p. 99.

43. Frank Kermode, *The Sense of an Ending*, p. 45.

44. Jerome Thale, "The Problem of Structure in Trollope," p. 149.

45. Garrett, *Multiplot Novel*, pp. 216-17; Helmut Klinger, "Varieties of Failure"; Jerome Thale, "The Problem of Structure in Trollope"; and Elizabeth Epperly, *Patterns of Repetition in Trollope*, especially. p. 1.

46. Stephen Wall, "Trollope, Balzac, and the Reappearing Character," p. 129ff.

47. Trollope, *Autobiography*, pp. 318-19.

48. Wall, "Trollope," p. 123.

49. Kincaid, *Novels*, pp. 44 and 45.

50. McMaster, *Novels*, p. 109.

51. See John Halperin, *Trollope and Politics*, p. 35ff, and Kincaid, *Novels*, p. 182ff. More recent studies include Morse's *Women* and Nardin's *He Knew*.

52. Kate Flint, Introduction to *Can You Forgive Her?* by Anthony Trollope, p. xv.

53. Ruth apRoberts, "Trollope's Casuistry," p. 25.

54. Aldous Huxley, *Point Counter Point*, p. 408.

55. Trollope, *Autobiography*, pp. 360–61.

56. Halperin, *Trollope and Politics*, p. 87.

57. McMaster, *Novels*, p. 60.

58. Trollope, *Autobiography*, pp. 318 and 320.

59. Mizener, "Anthony Trollope: The Palliser Novels," p. 163.

60. Hermione Lee has discovered that there was actually a horse named The Prime Minister in the 1851 Derby as well as a horse named Plenipotentiary, nicknamed Plinipo (recalling Palliser's nickname, Planty Pall). Too remarkable to be coincidence, these details further thicken Trollope's irony. See Lee, explanatory notes to *The Duke's Children*.

61. See Garrett, *Multiplot Novel*, for a summary of recent discussion of this question, pp. 1–22.

62. Kincaid, *Novels*, p. 30.

63. Garrett, *Multiplot Novel*, pp. 4–9.

64. Julia Penelope Stanley and Susan J. Wolfe (Robbins), "Toward a Feminist Aesthetic," p. 67.

65. Brooks, *Reading for the Plot*, p. 104.

66. Christiane Makward, "To Be or Not to Be . . . A Feminist Speaker," in *The Future of Difference*, ed. Hester Eisenstein and Alice Jardine, p. 96; Hélène Cixous, "Castration or Decapitation?" p. 53.

67. Rachel Blau DuPlessis, *Writing Beyond*, p. 3.

68. Torgovnick, "Closure in the Victorian Novel," p. 5.

69. D.A. Miller, *Narrative and Its Discontents*, p. 273.

70. McMaster, *Novels*, p. 229, n. 2. J.W. Bailey, in *"The Duke's Children:* Rediscovering a Trollope Manuscript," p. 34, speculates that the manuscript was cut by about one-third (22,000 words). However, R.H. Super claims that Trollope cut only twenty percent of the original, "pruning" selectively rather than removing entire chapters (*The Chronicler of Barsetshire*, p. 358).

71. Torgovnick, *Closure in the Novel*, p. 6.

72. Christopher Herbert, "Trollope and the Fixity of Self," p. 230.

73. Barbara Herrnstein Smith, *Poetic Closure*, p. 2.

74. R.C. Terry, *Anthony Trollope: The Artist in Hiding*, p. 120.

75. DuPlessis, *Writing Beyond*, p. 7.

76. According to Kincaid, the theme of acceptance contributes to an open

form: "The series concludes without a conclusion; the form is deliberately suspended" (*Novels*, p. 226).

77. Smith, *Poetic Closure*, p. 210.

78. apRoberts, "Trollope's Casuistry," p. 21.

79. Kincaid, "The Forms of Victorian Fiction," p. 4.

80. John Hagan, "*The Duke's Children:* Trollope's Psychological Masterpiece," p. 20.

81. McMaster, *Novels*, p. 154.

82. Morse, *Women*, p. 139.

83. McMaster, *Novels*, p. 138; Morse, *Women*, p. 122.

84. Patricia A. Vernon, "The Poor Fictionist's Conscience: Point of View in the Palliser Novels," p. 20.

85. Anthony Trollope, *The Warden*, p. 278. For further examples see also the final chapters of *The Small House at Allington, The Last Chronicle of Barset, Phineas Finn*, and *Phineas Redux*.

86. Torgovnick, "Closure," p. 4.

87. Anthony Trollope, *Barchester Towers*, p. 251.

88. D. A. Miller, *Narrative and Its Discontents*, p. 189.

89. DuPlessis, "For the Etruscans," in *The New Feminist Criticism*, ed. Elaine Showalter, p. 276.

90. Ricoeur, vol. 2 of *Time and Narrative*, p. 22.

91. Rebecca West, *The Court and the Castle*, p. 167.

92. Nardin, *He Knew*, pp. xvii–xviii.

93. Cixous and Clément, *The Newly Born Woman*, p. 81.

Chapter 3. *Pilgrimage:* Writing the Consummate Flow

1. Elizabeth Kerr, "Twentieth Century Sequence Novel," p. 74.

2. Rachel Blau DuPlessis, "For the Etruscans," p. 286; Alice Jardine, *Gynesis: Configurations of Women and Modernity*, p. 36.

3. Virginia Woolf, "Romance and the Heart," p. 124. For some of the most productive interpretations of Woolf's statement and/or discussion of Richardson's sentence as a grammatical unit, see DuPlessis, "For the Etruscans," pp. 155–56; Gillian Hanscombe, *The Art of Life*, p. 85; Stephen Heath, "Writing for Silence: Dorothy Richardson and the Novel," p. 138; and Susan Leonardi, "Bare Places and Ancient Blemishes," pp. 150–53.

4. The distinction between the feminine aesthetic proposed by Dorothy Richardson and that of her protagonist Miriam Henderson is so subtle that critics have often found it difficult to distinguish between them. DuPlessis claims that Richardson "re-created herself as the main character of *Pilgrimage*" (*Writing Beyond*, p. 143). Hanscombe suggests that while *Pilgrimage* is not pure autobiography, the relationship between Richardson and Miriam is one of "near-

synonymity" (*The Art of Life*, p. 45); more recently, this critic argues that Richardson purposely "remove[d] the distinction between author and persona by removing the author entirely" ("Dorothy Richardson Versus the Novvle," p. 86). Richardson's principal biographer believes that Richardson "[came] to think of herself and of *Pilgrimage* as one and the same" (Gloria Fromm, *Dorothy Richardson*, p. 371). Throughout his study *Dorothy Richardson*, Horace Gregory blends the two into a composite he calls "Dorothy-Miriam," and he moves back and forth from passages in *Pilgrimage* to Richardson's biography, suggesting they are interchangeable. In contrast, Jean Radford emphasizes the importance of *not* "radically simplif[ying] what *Pilgrimage* has to say" by conflating author and protagonist (*Dorothy Richardson*, p. 68). The problem arises from the autobiographical nature of the work and the first-person perspective of stream of consciousness narrative. Miriam is treated ironically primarily in the first three volumes; in subsequent volumes more insightful opinions contradict, qualify, or illuminate Miriam's previous immature, youthful thought. Throughout this chapter I have tried to distinguish between author and protagonist where it is important to do so. However, Miriam is often a mouthpiece for Richardson's statements about gendered writing, a vehicle to define a feminine aesthetic. The views expressed in her short prose pieces and prefaces are generally consistent with those articulated by Miriam: see Hanscombe, *Art of Life*, pp. 82-83.

5. "Cagey Subconsciousness," review of *Pilgrimage*, by Dorothy Richardson, *Time*, Dec. 5, 1938, p. 70.

6. Luce Irigaray, "This Sex Which Is Not One," pp. 29-30.

7. Because the frequent use of ellipses is characteristic of Richardson's style, I have placed in brackets the ellipses that indicate my omission of irrelevant material from quoted passages [. . .] or my use of a period to end Richardson's ellipses . . . [.].

8. Ellen G. Friedman and Miriam Fuchs, "Contexts and Continuities," in *Breaking the Sequence*, ed. Friedman and Fuchs, p. 8.

9. Maria Minich Brewer, "A Loosening of Tongues: From Narrative Economy to Women Writing," p. 1151.

10. Gustav Freytag, *Technique of the Drama*, pp. 114-15. DuPlessis has also noted the gendered erotics inherent in the narrative Richardson rejects: "She thus sought to revise even the pace of novels, breaking their allegiance to a sexuality perceived only as arousal and climax" (*Writing Beyond*, p. 151).

11. Fromm, *Dorothy Richardson*, p. 287.

12. Ibid.

13. Hanscombe, *The Art of Life*, p. 22. Richardson's position may be inferred from an essay she published in 1917 reviewing four books on feminism. She is aware of the complexities of any solution to the question of an appropriate feminism and the loss implicit in an either-or feminism that grants

women freedom in the public sphere at the expense of domestic satisfactions. In this essay, however, as in *Pilgrimage*, she articulates her belief in women's superior "synthetic consciousness," their ability to "see life whole and harmonious" ("The Reality of Feminism" reprinted in *The Gender of Modernism: A Critical Anthology*, ed. Bonnie Kime Scott, p. 404).

14. *The Future of Difference*, ed. Eisenstein and Jardine, p. xx.

15. Luce Irigaray, "The Power of Discourse and the Subordination of the Feminine," p. 79.

16. Irigaray, "This Sex Which Is Not One," p. 24.

17. Hanscombe, p. 34.

18. Friedman and Fuchs, introduction to *Breaking the Sequence*, p. 3; Ellen Friedman, "'Utterly Other Discourse,'" p. 357.

19. Radford, *Dorothy Richardson*, pp. 111–15.

20. Hélène Cixous, "The Laugh of the Medusa," p. 889.

21. Ibid., p. 877.

22. See Fromm, "Through the Novelist's Looking-Glass," p. 161, and Elaine Showalter, *A Literature of Their Own*, p. 254.

23. Hanscombe, *The Art of Life*, p. 138.

24. Suzette Henke, "Male and Female Consciousness in Dorothy Richardson's *Pilgrimage*," p. 55.

25. Radford believes this word suggests the body of a man to Miriam, with its "phallic 'tails,'" as well as the "'Name of the Father'" (*Dorothy Richardson*, pp. 132–33).

26. Jane Gallop, "Annie Leclerc Writing a Letter with Vermeer," in *The Poetics of Gender*, ed. Nancy Miller, p. 140; Radford, *Dorothy Richardson*, p. 131.

27. Domna Stanton, "Difference on Trial: A Critique of the Maternal Metaphor in Cixous, Irigaray, and Kristeva," p. 170. See also Josette Feral, "Powers of Difference," in *The Future of Difference*, ed. Eisenstein and Jardine, p. 89.

28. Fromm, *Dorothy Richardson*, p. 89.

29. Gregory, *Dorothy Richardson*, p. 31.

30. DuPlessis, *Writing Beyond*, p. 233.

31. Fromm, *Dorothy Richardson*, pp. 95–96.

32. Jane Miller, *Women Writing about Men*, p. 3.

33. Showalter, *Their Own*, p. 250.

34. Irigaray, "Power of Discourse," p. 68.

35. Radford, *Dorothy Richardson*, p. 42.

36. Sydney Janet Kaplan, *Feminine Consciousness in the Modern British Novel*, p. 28; Hanscombe, *The Art of Life*, p. 119.

37. Hanscombe, *The Art of Life*, p. 144.

38. DuPlessis, *Writing Beyond*, pp. 144 and 233, n. 5.

39. See Radford, *Dorothy Richardson*, p. 42.

40. Catherine Stimpson, "Zero Degree Deviancy: The Lesbian Novel in English," pp. 246 and 247.

41. Fromm, *Dorothy Richardson*, p. 73. Dorothy Richardson's papers contain interesting but inconclusive hints about her own sexual preference. When questioned by Horace Gregory, her sister-in-law Rose Odle provided a mixed opinion on this issue. She wrote him on October 1, 1964, that Richardson had been identified as a lesbian by the writer of a book on women's sexual variations and that this might explain the reluctance of Veronica Grad's son David (the son of the fictional Amabel) to let Rose Odle question her about the relationship. Odle concludes that it might "have been a passing phase" with Richardson, but "from the time I knew her–1917 there was no such lesbian tendency." An undated letter from Veronica Grad to Rose Odle written after Richardson's death, however, displays such considerable and forceful ambivalence as to suggest an emotional and lasting relationship. According to Grad, it was described by a mutual friend as "the most astonishing example of enduring & unrequited love." Grad criticizes Richardson for using her closest friends as " 'copy' material not only for books but for stimulation. . . . You know she was rather like a vivisectionist in her attitude to us all." Grad claims that she married her husband, Benjamin Grad (the fictional Michael Shatov), only because Richardson wanted her to. Richardson Papers, Yale. The letter from Veronica Grad to Rose Odle is transcribed in the appendix to Hanscombe's *The Art of Life*, pp. 178–80.

42. Adrienne Rich, "Compulsory Heterosexuality and Lesbian Existence," p. 64

43. Cixous, "Castration or Decapitation?" p. 53.

44. Dorothy Richardson, "Data for Spanish Publisher," p. 19.

45. DuPlessis, *Writing Beyond*, p. 235, n. 18.

46. Hanscombe, *The Art of Life*, p. 28.

47. Arline Thorn, " 'Feminine' Time in Dorothy Richardson's *Pilgrimage*," p. 212.

48. Robert Glynn Kelly, "The Strange Philosophy of Dorothy M. Richardson," p. 80.

49. Margaret Homans, *Bearing the Word*, p. 5.

50. Ibid., p. 9.

51. Ibid., p. 13.

52. Irigaray, "Power of Discourse," p. 80.

53. Radford, *Dorothy Richardson*, p. 108.

54. For a more detailed discussion of Richardson's evaluation of James, see Shirley Rose's "Dorothy Richardson's Theory of Literature: The Writer as Pilgrim," pp. 22–24.

55. Fromm, *Dorothy Richardson*, p. 260.

56. DuPlessis, *Writing Beyond*, p. 143.

57. Hanscombe, *The Art of Life*, p. 34.

58. DuPlessis, *Writing Beyond*, p. 151.

59. Fromm, *Dorothy Richardson*, pp. 297 and 310.

60. Ibid., p. 308.

61. Ibid., p. 312.

62. Ibid., pp. 369–70.

63. Friedman and Fuchs, "Contexts and Continuities" in *Breaking the Sequence*, ed. Friedman and Fuchs, p. 12.

64. Radford, *Dorothy Richardson*, p. 125.

65. Cixous, "Castration or Decapitation?" p. 53.

66. Thomas F. Staley, *Dorothy Richardson*, pp. 120 and 124.

67. Gregory, *Dorothy Richardson*, pp. xi, 82.

68. Fromm, *Dorothy Richardson*, p. 397.

69. Friedman, "Utterly Other Discourse," p. 357; DuPlessis, *Writing Beyond*, chapter 9; Showalter, *Their Own*, p. 261.

70. DuPlessis, *Writing Beyond*, p. 144.

71. Or, as Radford interprets it, "the myriad 'I ams' of the woman 'Mir-i-am'" (*Dorothy Richardson*, p. 61).

72. Hanscombe, *The Art of Life*, 33.

73. Ibid., p. 159.

74. DuPlessis, *Writing Beyond*, p. 144.

75. Ibid., p. 3.

76. Susan Gubar, "The Blank Page and the Issues of Female Creativity," p. 299.

77. Showalter, *Their Own*, p. 261.

78. Cixous, "The Laugh of the Medusa," p. 878.

Chapter 4. *A Dance to the Music of Time*: A Text of Arrested Desire

1. Peter Brooks, *Reading for the Plot*, pp. 101–2.

2. Alastair Fowler, *Kinds of Literature*, p. 42.

3. Robert Selig, *Time and Anthony Powell*, argues that Powell employs many of the same narrative techniques as Proust: the iterative, pseudo-iterative, etc. (pp. 41 and 46). Yet these time-deforming techniques are used much less frequently by Powell than by Proust.

4. Anthony Powell, *Faces in My Time*, p. 212.

5. Neil Brennan, *Anthony Powell*, p. 127.

6. See Lynette Felber, "The Fictional Narrator as Historian: Ironic Detachment and the Project of History in Anthony Powell's *A Dance to the Music of Time*."

7. Henry Harrington, "Anthony Powell, Nicholas Poussin and the Structure of Time," p. 441.

8. Roland Barthes, *The Pleasure of the Text*, p. 8.

9. Powell, *Faces in My Time*, p. 47.

10. Allan James Tucker, *The Novels of Anthony Powell*, p. 179. The example Tucker chooses—the Modigliani—is a detail that is *not* lost from the narrative, but his point is that not all readers may have read every volume, and even those who have done so may not recall every detail.

11. Paul Gaston, " 'This Question of Discipline': An Interview with Anthony Powell," p. 645.

12. Richard Jones, "Anthony Powell's *Music*: Swansong of the Metropolitan Romance," p. 354.

13. Linda Hughes and Michael Lund, *The Victorian Serial*, p. 245.

14. Meir Sternberg, *Expositional Modes*, p. 238.

15. Harrington, "Anthony Powell, Nicholas Poussin and the Structure of Time," p. 441.

16. Selig, *Time and Anthony Powell*, argues that the flashback ending perceived by critics is invalidated by "textual details" (p. 27ff). He challenges the assumptions that the same voice is narrating from beginning to end and that the street repairs that seem to frame the novel are a single instance.

17. Edward Said, *Beginnings: Intention and Method*, p. 50.

18. Brennan, *Anthony Powell*, p. 133; Tucker, *Novels*, p. 177.

19. Arthur Mizener, "*A Dance to the Music of Time*: The Novels of Anthony Powell," p. 85.

20. Tucker, *Novels*, p. 77.

21. Patrick Swinden, *The English Novel of History and Society*, p. 97.

22. Brooks, *Reading for the Plot*, p. 39.

23. The contrast between figures of will and of imagination has become a standard of criticism on *The Music of Time*. Perhaps the theme is analyzed most fully by Robert K. Morris, *The Novels of Anthony Powell*, p. 9. See also Donald Gutierrez, "The Discrimination of Elegance: Anthony Powell's *A Dance to the Music of Time*."

24. Hélène Cixous, "Castration or Decapitation?" p. 33.

25. Tucker, *Novels*, pp. 103 and 105; Thomas Wilcox, "Anthony Powell and the Illusion of Possibility," p. 227; Mark A. R. Facknitz, "Self-Effacement as Revelation: Narration and Art in Anthony Powell's *A Dance to the Music of Time*," p. 522 and passim.

26. Said, *Beginnings*, p. 43.

27. Paul Ricoeur, "Narrative Time," p. 178.

28. Douglas Davis, "An Interview with Anthony Powell, Frome England," p. 535.

29. Ibid., p. 533.

30. Gaston, "'This Question of Discipline': An Interview with Anthony Powell," p. 641.

31. Tucker, *Novels*, p. 161.

32. Dan McLeod, "Anthony Powell: Some Notes on the Art of the Sequence Novel," p. 51.

33. Anthony Powell, *The Strangers All Are Gone*, p. 88.

34. Harrington, "Anthony Powell, Nicholas Poussin and the Structure of Time," p. 436.

35. Roland Barthes, "An Introduction to the Structural Analysis of Narrative," p. 254.

36. John Russell, *Anthony Powell: A Quintet, Sextet, and War*, pp. 86, 90.

37. David Mickelsen, "Types of Spatial Structure in Narrative," in *Spatial Form in Narrative*, ed. Smitten and Daghistany, p. 68.

38. Swinden, *English Novel*, p. 121.

39. McLeod, "Anthony Powell: Some Notes on the Art of the Sequence Novel," p. 53.

40. On Powell's use of Nietzsche's eternal recurrence, see Selig, *Time and Anthony Powell*, p. 51.

41. Swinden, *English Novel*, p. 128.

42. Tucker, *Novels*, p. 124.

43. Swinden, *English Novel*, p. 108.

44. Davis, "An Interview with Anthony Powell, Frome England," p. 536.

45. Brooks, *Reading for the Plot*, p. 13.

46. Harrington, "Anthony Powell, Nicholas Poussin and the Structure of Time," p. 434.

47. Brooks, *Reading for the Plot*, p. 123.

48. McLeod, "Anthony Powell: Some Notes on the Art of the Sequence Novel," p. 52.

49. Ibid., p. 52.

50. Kerr, "Sequence Novel," p. 89.

51. Powell, "Taken from Life," p. 53.

52. Selig, *Time and Anthony Powell*, p. 137 and passim.

53. Selig and others have often praised Powell for the "tolerant amusement" with which his narrator regards homosexuals (p. 115). Yet homosexual characters are relegated to marginal roles and "tolerant amusement" might seem oxymoronic to some.

54. Brooks, *Reading for the Plot*, p. 139.

55. Ibid., p. 104.

56. Ibid.

57. Ibid., p. 330, n. 3.

58. Ibid., p. 52
59. Barbara Herrnstein Smith, *Poetic Closure*, p. 256.
60. Kermode, *The Sense of an Ending*, p. 46.
61. Brennan, *Anthony Powell*, p. 132.
62. Patrick Swinden, "Powell's *Hearing Secret Harmonies*," p. 59.
63. Jones, "Anthony Powell's *Music*: Swansong of the Metropolitan Romance," p. 369; Kerry McSweeney, "The End of *A Dance to the Music of Time*: The Novels of Anthony Powell," p. 56.
64. Brooks, *Reading for the Plot*, p. 92.
65. McSweeney, "The End of *A Dance to the Music of Time*: The Novels of Anthony Powell," p. 48; Swinden, *English Novel*, p. 94.
66. Brooks, *Reading for the Plot*, p. 101.
67. Kermode, *The Sense of an Ending*, p. 162.
68. Smith, *Poetic Closure*, p. 42.
69. Ibid., p. 3.

Epilogue. The Evolution of the *Roman-Fleuve* and the Canonical Novel

1. Rubin Rabinovitz, *The Reaction Against Experiment*, 1950–1960, p. 5.
2. Ibid., p. 2.
3. Anthony Powell, *Messengers of Day*, p. 116.
4. Thomas Winner, "Structural and Semiotic Genre Theory," in *Theories of Literary Genre*, ed. Joseph Strelka, p. 256.
5. Gaye Tuchman, *Edging Women Out: Victorian Novelists, Publishers, and Social Change*, p. 14.
6. Ibid., p. 7.
7. Ibid., p. 8.
8. Mark A.R. Facknitz discusses the importance of aesthetic appreciation as a standard of value in *A Dance to the Music of Time* and the narrator's significant role in this process ("Self-Effacement as Revelation: Narration and Art in Anthony Powell's *A Dance to the Music of Time*," p. 529 and passim).
9. Tuchman, *Edging Women Out*, p. 47.
10. Roger Hagedorn, "Technology and Economic Exploitation: The Serial as a Form of Narrative Presentation," p. 12.
11. Ibid., p. 5; italics in original.
12. To E.B.C. Jones, April 3, 1939. Richardson Papers, Yale.
13. Linda Hughes and Michael Lund, *The Victorian Serial*, p. 236.

❧ ❧ ❧ Works Cited

Abel, Elizabeth, ed. *Writing and Sexual Difference*. Chicago: University of Chicago Press, 1982.

Allen, Robert C. *Speaking of Soap Opera*. Chapel Hill: University of North Carolina Press, 1985.

Allen, Walter. *The English Novel: A Short Critical History*. London: Phoenix, 1954.

Aristotle. *Aristotle's Theory of Poetry and Fine Art with a Critical Text and Translation of the Poetics*. Translated by S. H. Butcher. N.p.: Dover Publications, 1951.

Armstrong, Nancy. *Desire and Domestic Fiction: A Political History of the Novel*. New York: Oxford University Press, 1987.

apRoberts, Ruth. *The Moral Trollope*. Athens: Ohio University Press, 1971.

————. "Trollope's Casuistry." *Novel* 3, no. 1 (Fall 1969): 17–27.

Ausmus, Martin Russey. "Some Forms of the Sequence Novel in British Fiction." Ph.D. diss., University of Oklahoma, 1969.

Bailey. J. W. "*The Duke's Children*: Rediscovering a Trollope Manuscript." *Yale University Library Gazette* 57, no. 1–2 (October 1982): 34–38.

Baker, Robert S. "Anthony Powell." Review of *The Novels of Anthony Powell*, by James Tucker, and *Infants of the Spring* and *Messengers of Day*, by Anthony Powell. *Contemporary Literature* 20, no. 2 (Spring 1979): 251–59.

Balzac, Honoré. Author's Introduction to vol. 2 of *La Comédie humaine*. New York: Century, 1911.

Barthes, Roland. "An Introduction to the Structural Analysis of Narrative." *New Literary History* 6, no. 2 (Winter 1975): 237–72.

————. *The Pleasure of the Text*. Translated by Richard Miller. New York: Hill, 1975.

Bergonzi, Bernard. *The Situation of the Novel*. London: Macmillan, 1970.

Birns, Margaret Boe. "Anthony Powell's Secret Harmonies: Music in a Jungian Key." *Literary Review* 25, no. 1 (Fall 1981): 80–92.

Blake, Caesar R. *Dorothy M. Richardson*. Ann Arbor: University of Michigan Press, 1960.

Boone, Joseph. "Modernist Maneuverings in the Marriage Plot: Breaking Ideologies of Gender and Genre in James's *The Golden Bowl*." *PMLA* 101, no. 3 (May 1986): 374-88.

―――. *Tradition Counter Tradition: Love and the Form of Fiction*. Chicago: University of Chicago Press, 1987.

―――. "Wedlock as Deadlock and Beyond: Closure and the Victorian Marriage Ideal." *Mosaic* 17, no. 1 (Winter 1984): 65-81.

Booth, Bradford: *Anthony Trollope: Aspects of His Life and Art*. Bloomington: Indiana University Press, 1958.

Bovenschen, Silvia. "Is There a Feminine Aesthetic?" *New German Critique* no. 10 (Winter 1977): 111-37.

Braidotti, Rosi. "The Politics of Ontological Difference." In Brennan, ed. (q.v.), 89-105.

Brennan, Neil. *Anthony Powell*. New York: Twayne, 1974.

Brennan, Teresa, ed. *Between Feminism and Psychoanalysis*. London: Routledge, 1989.

Brewer, Maria Minich. "A Loosening of Tongues: From Narrative Economy to Women Writing." *MLN* 99, no. 5 (December 1984): 1141-61.

Brooks, Peter. *Reading for the Plot: Design and Intention in Narrative*. New York: Alfred A. Knopf, 1984.

Broyard, Anatole. "End of the Marathon Dance." *New York Times*, March 25, 1976, 33.

Buchen, Irving H. "The Aesthetics of the Supra-Novel." In *Theory of the Novel*, Halperin, ed. (q.v.), 91-108.

Burton, Robert. *The Anatomy of Melancholy*. Vol. 1. London: J.M. Dent, 1932.

"Cagey Subconscious." Review of *Pilgrimage*, by Dorothy Richardson. *Time*, December 5, 1938, 70.

Carr, E.H. *What Is History?* London: Macmillan Publishing, 1961.

Chatman, Seymour. "What Novels Can Do that Films Can't (and Vice Versa)." *Critical Inquiry* 7, no. 1 (Autumn 1980): 121-39.

Cixous, Hélène. "Castration or Decapitation?" Translated by Annette Kuhn. *Signs: Journal of Women in Culture and Society* 7, no. 1 (Autumn 1981): 41-55.

―――. "The Laugh of the Medusa." Translated by Keith Cohen and Paula Cohen. *Signs: Journal of Women in Culture and Society* 1, no. 4 (Summer 1976): 875-93.

Cixous, Hélène, and Catherine Clément. *The Newly Born Woman*. Translated by Betsy Wing. Vol. 2 of *Theory and History of Literature*. Minneapolis: University of Minnesota Press, 1975.

Cohen, Ralph. "History and Genre." *New Literary History* 17, no. 2 (Winter 1986): 203-18.

Davis, Douglas M. "An Interview with Anthony Powell, Frome England." *College English* 24, no. 7 (April 1963): 533-36.

DuPlessis, Rachel Blau. "For the Etruscans." In Showalter, ed. (q.v.), 271-91.

_____. *Writing Beyond the Ending: Narrative Strategies of Twentieth-Century Women Writers*. Bloomington: Indiana University Press, 1985.

Edel, Leon. "Dorothy Richardson, 1882-1957." *Modern Fiction Studies* 4, no. 2 (Summer 1958): 165-68.

Eisenstein, Hester, and Alice Jardine, eds. *The Future of Difference*. New Brunswick, N.J.: Rutgers University Press, 1985.

Ellmann, Mary. *Thinking about Women*. New York: Harcourt Brace Jovanovich, 1968.

Epperly, Elizabeth. *Patterns of Repetition in Trollope*. Washington, D.C.: Catholic University of America Press, 1989.

Facknitz, Mark A. R. "Self-Effacement as Revelation: Narration and Art in Anthony Powell's *A Dance to the Music of Time*." *Journal of Modern Literature* 15, no. 4 (Spring 1989): 519-29.

Felber, Lynette. "The Fictional Narrator as Historian: Ironic Detachment and the Project of History in Anthony Powell's *A Dance to the Music of Time*." *CLIO: A Journal of Literature, History, and the Philosophy of History* 22, no. 1 (Fall 1992): 21-35.

_____. "A Manifesto for Feminine Modernism: Dorothy Richardson's *Pilgrimage*." In *Rereading Modernism: New Directions in Feminist Criticism*, edited by Lisa Rado, 23-39. Wellesley Studies in Critical Theory, Literary History, and Culture, William E. Cain, gen. ed. New York: Garland, 1994.

Felski, Rita. *Beyond Feminist Aesthetics: Feminist Literature and Social Change*. Cambridge: Harvard University Press, 1989.

Feral, Josette. "The Powers of Difference." In Eisenstein and Jardine, eds. (q.v.), 88-94.

Flint, Kate. Introduction to *Can You Forgive Her?* by Anthony Trollope. Oxford: Oxford University Press, 1982.

Fowler, Alastair. *Kinds of Literature: An Introduction to the Theory of Genres and Modes*. Cambridge: Harvard University Press, 1982.

Frank, Joseph. "Spatial Form: An Answer to Critics." *Critical Inquiry* 4, no. 2 (Winter 1977): 231-52.

_____. "Spatial Form in the Modern Novel." In *Critiques and Essays on Modern Fiction*, edited by John W. Aldridge, 43-66. New York: Ronald, 1952.

Fraser, Nancy, and Sandra Lee Bartky, eds. *Revaluing French Feminism: Critical Essays on Difference, Agency, and Culture*. Bloomington: Indiana University Press, 1992.

Freytag, Gustav. *Technique of the Drama: An Exposition of Dramatic Composition and Art.* 6th ed. Translated by Elias J. MacEwan. Chicago: Scott, Foresman, 1894.

Friedman, Alan Warren. "The Modern Multivalent Novel: Form and Function." In *Theory of the Novel*, Halperin, ed. (q.v.).

Friedman, Ellen G. " 'Utterly Other Discourse': The Anticanon of Experimental Women Writers from Dorothy Richardson to Christine Brooke-Rose." *Modern Fiction Studies* 34, no. 3 (Autumn 1988): 353-70.

Friedman, Ellen G., and Miriam Fuchs. "Contexts and Continuities: An Introduction to Women's Experimental Fiction in English." Introduction to *Breaking the Sequence*, Friedman and Fuchs, eds. (q.v.), 3-51.

————, eds. *Breaking the Sequence: Women's Experimental Fiction.* Princeton: Princeton University Press, 1989.

Friedman, Norman. "Point of View in Fiction." In *Approaches to the Novel: Materials for a Poetics*, edited by Robert Scholes. San Francisco: Chandler, 1961.

Fromm, Gloria Glikin. *Dorothy Richardson: A Biography.* Urbana: University of Illinois Press, 1977.

————. "Through the Novelist's Looking-Glass." In *H. G. Wells: A Collection of Critical Essays*, edited by Bernard Bergonzi, 157-77. Englewood Cliffs, N.J.: Prentice-Hall, 1976.

Frye, Northrop. *Anatomy of Criticism: Four Essays.* Princeton: Princeton University Press, 1971.

Fuss, Diana. *Essentially Speaking: Feminism, Nature, and Difference.* New York: Routledge, 1989.

Gallie, W.B. *Philosophy and the Historical Understanding.* 2d ed. New York: Schocken, 1964.

Gallop, Jane. "Annie Leclerc Writing a Letter with Vermeer." In Nancy Miller, ed. (q.v.), 137-56.

————. "*Quand nos lèvres s'écrivent:* Irigaray's Body Politic." *Romanic Review* 74, no. 1 (January 1983): 77-83.

Garrett, Peter K. *The Victorian Multiplot Novel: Studies in Dialogical Form.* New Haven: Yale University Press, 1980.

Gaston, Paul L. " 'This Question of Discipline': An Interview with Anthony Powell." *Virginia Quarterly Review* 61, no. 4 (Autumn 1985): 638-54.

Genette, Gérard. *Narrative Discourse: An Essay in Method.* Ithaca: Cornell University Press, 1980.

Gerhart, Mary. *Genre Choices, Gender Questions.* Norman: University of Oklahoma Press, 1992.

Greene, Gayle, and Coppelia Kahn, eds. *Making a Difference.* New York: Routledge, Chapman, and Hall, 1985.

Gregory, Horace. *Dorothy Richardson: An Adventure in Self-Discovery*. New York: Holt, 1967.

Gubar, Susan. "The Blank Page and the Issues of Female Creativity." In Showalter, ed. (q.v.), 292–313.

Gutierrez, Donald. "The Discrimination of Elegance: Anthony Powell's *A Dance to the Music of Time.*" *Malahat Review*, no. 34 (April 1975): 126–41.

——. "Power in *A Dance to the Music of Time.*" *Connecticut Review* 6, no. 2 (April 1973): 50–59.

Hagan, John H. "*The Duke's Children:* Trollope's Psychological Masterpiece." *Nineteenth Century Fiction* 13, no. 1 (June 1958): 1–21.

Hagedorn, Roger. "Technology and Economic Exploitation: The Serial as a Form of Narrative Presentation." *Wide Angle* 10, no. 4 (1988): 4–12.

Halperin, John. "*The Eustace Diamonds* and Politics." In *Anthony Trollope*, edited by Tony Bareham. London: Vision, 1980.

——. *Trollope and Politics: A Study of the Pallisers and Others*. London: Macmillan, 1977.

——, ed. *The Theory of the Novel: New Essays*. New York: Oxford University Press, 1974.

——. *Trollope Centenary Essays*. London: Macmillan, 1982.

Hamer, Mary. *Writing by Numbers: Trollope's Serial Fiction*. Cambridge: Cambridge University Press, 1987.

Hanscombe, Gillian. *The Art of Life: Dorothy Richardson and the Development of Feminist Consciousness*. London: Peter Owen, 1982.

——. "Dorothy Richardson Versus the Novvle." In Friedman and Fuchs, eds. (q.v.), 85–98.

Harrington, Henry R. "Anthony Powell, Nicholas Poussin and the Structure of Time." *Contemporary Literature* 24, no. 4 (Winter 1983): 431–48.

Harvey, Sir Paul, and J. E. Heseltine, comps. and eds., *The Oxford Companion to French Literature*. Oxford: Clarendon Press, 1959.

Heath, Stephen. "Writing for Silence: Dorothy Richardson and the Novel." In *Teaching the Text*, edited by Susanne Kappeler and Norman Bryson, 126–47. London: Routledge, 1983.

Henke, Suzette A. "Male and Female Consciousness in Dorothy Richardson's *Pilgrimage.*" *Journal of Women's Studies in Literature* 1, no. 1 (Winter 1979): 51–60.

Herbert, Christopher. "Trollope and the Fixity of Self." *PMLA* 93, no. 2 (March 1978): 228–39.

Hernadi, Paul. *Beyond Genre: New Directions in Literary Classification*. Ithaca: Cornell University Press, 1959.

Homans, Margaret. *Bearing the Word: Language and Female Experience in*

Nineteenth-Century Women's Writing. Chicago: University of Chicago Press, 1986.

Hughes, Linda K., and Michael Lund. "Studying Victorian Serials." *Literary Research* 11, no. 4 (Fall 1986): 235-52.

―――. *The Victorian Serial.* Victorian Literature and Culture Series, gen. eds. Karen Chase, Jerome McGann, and Herbert Tucker. Charlottesville: University Press of Virginia, 1991.

Husband, Janet. *Sequels: An Annotated Guide to Novels in Series.* Chicago: American Library Association, 1982.

Huxley, Aldous. *Point Counter Point.* London: Chatto and Windus, 1935.

Hyde, Lawrence. "The Work of Dorothy Richardson." *Adelphi* 2 (November 1924): 508-17.

Irigaray, Luce. "The Power of Discourse and the Subordination of the Feminine." In *This Sex Which Is Not One,* by Luce Irigaray, 68-85. Translated by Catherine Porter with Carolyn Burke. Ithaca: Cornell University Press, 1985.

―――. "This Sex Which Is Not One." In *This Sex Which Is Not One,* by Luce Irigaray, 23-33. Translated by Catherine Porter with Carolyn Burke. Ithaca: Cornell University Press, 1985.

Iser, Wolfgang. *The Act of Reading: A Theory of Aesthetic Response.* Baltimore: Johns Hopkins University Press, 1978.

―――. "Indeterminacy and the Reader's Response in Prose Fiction." In *Aspects of Narrative,* edited by J. Hillis Miller, 1-45. New York: Columbia University Press, 1971.

James, Henry. "Anthony Trollope." In *Partial Portraits,* by Henry James. 1888. Reprint, Westport, Conn.: Greenwood Press, 1970.

―――. "Honoré de Balzac." In *Notes on Novelists: With Some Other Notes,* by Henry James. New York: Biblo and Tannen, 1969.

―――. "Preface to 'The Tragic Muse.'" In *The Art of the Novel: Critical Prefaces by Henry James.* Boston: Northeastern University Press, 1984.

Jardine, Alice. *Gynesis: Configurations of Woman and Modernity.* Ithaca: Cornell University Press, 1985.

Jones, Ann R. "Inscribing Femininity: French Theories of the Feminine." In Greene and Kahn, eds. (q.v.), 80-112.

Jones, Richard. "Anthony Powell's *Music:* Swansong of the Metropolitan Romance." *Virginia Quarterly Review* 52, no. 3 (Summer 1976): 353-69.

Kaplan, Sydney Janet. *Feminine Consciousness in the Modern British Novel.* Urbana: University of Illinois Press, 1975.

Kauffman, Linda. *Discourses of Desire: Gender, Genre, and Epistolary Fictions.* Ithaca: Cornell University Press, 1986.

Kelly, Robert Glynn. "The Strange Philosophy of Dorothy M. Richardson." *Pacific Spectator* 8, no. 1 (Winter 1954): 76-82.

Kermode, Frank. *The Sense of an Ending*. New York: Oxford University Press, 1967.

Kerr, Elizabeth. *Bibliography of the Sequence Novel*. Minneapolis: University of Minnesota Press, 1950.

———. "The Twentieth Century Sequence Novel." Ph.D. diss., University of Minnesota, 1941.

Kincaid, James R. "The Forms of Victorian Fiction." *Victorian Newsletter* 47 (1975): 1–4.

———. *The Novels of Anthony Trollope*. Oxford: Oxford University Press, 1977.

Klinger, Helmut. "Varieties of Failure: The Significance of Trollope's *The Prime Minister*." *English Miscellany* 23 (1972): 168–83.

Lanser, Susan S. "Toward a Feminist Narratology." *Style* 20, no. 3 (Fall 1986): 341–63.

Lee, Hermione. Explanatory notes to *The Duke's Children*, by Anthony Trollope. Oxford: Oxford University Press, 1983

Leonardi, Susan J. "Bare Places and Ancient Blemishes: Virginia Woolf's Search for New Language in *Night and Day*." *Novel* 19, no. 2 (Winter 1986): 150–53.

Lund, Michael. *America's Continuing Story: An Introduction to Serial Fiction*. Detroit: Wayne State University Press, 1993.

McCormick, John. *Catastrophe and Imagination: An Interpretation of the Recent English and American Novel*. London: Longmans, 1957.

———. Introduction to *The Prime Minister*, by Anthony Trollope. Oxford: Oxford University Press, 1983.

McLeod, Dan. "Anthony Powell: Some Notes on the Art of the Sequence Novel." *Studies in the Novel* 3, no. 1 (Spring 1971): 43–63.

McMaster, Juliet. *Trollope's Palliser Novels: Theme and Pattern*. New York: Oxford University Press, 1978.

McSweeney, Kerry. "The End of *A Dance to the Music of Time*: The Novels of Anthony Powell." *South Atlantic Quarterly* 76, no. 1 (Winter 1977): 44–57.

Makward, Christiane. "To Be or Not to Be . . . A Feminist Speaker." Translated by Marlene Barousm, Alice Jardine, and Hester Eisenstein. In Eisenstein and Jardine, eds. (q.v.), 95–105.

Marino, Adrian. "Toward a Definition of Literary Genres." In Strelka, ed. (q.v.), 41–56.

Michener, Charles. "Powell: The 'Dance' Is Over." *Newsweek*, April 5, 1976, 79–81.

Mickelsen, David. "Types of Spatial Structure in Narrative." In *Spatial Form in Narrative*, edited by Jeffrey R. Smitten and Ann Daghistany, 63–78. Ithaca: Cornell University Press, 1981.

Miller, D. A. *Narrative and Its Discontents: Problems of Closure in the Traditional Novel.* Princeton: Princeton University Press, 1981.

Miller, J. Hillis. *The Form of Victorian Fiction.* Notre Dame, Ind.: University of Notre Dame Press, 1968.

———. "Narrative and History." *ELH* 41, no. 3 (Fall 1974): 455–73.

———. "The Problematic of Ending in Narrative." *Nineteenth-Century Fiction* 33, no. 1 (June 1978): 3–7.

Miller, Jane. *Women Writing about Men.* London: Virago, 1986.

Miller, Nancy, ed. *The Poetics of Gender.* New York: Columbia University Press, 1986.

Mizener, Arthur. "Anthony Trollope: The Palliser Novels." In *From Jane Austen to Joseph Conrad: Essays Collected in Memory of James T. Hillhouse,* edited by Robert C. Rathburn and Martin Steinmann Jr., 160–76. Minneapolis: University of Minnesota Press, 1958.

———. "*A Dance to the Music of Time:* The Novels of Anthony Powell." *Kenyon Review* 22, no. 1 (Winter 1960): 79–92.

Modleski, Tania. *Loving with a Vengeance: Mass-Produced Fantasies for Women.* Hamden, Conn.: Archon Books, 1982.

Morris, Robert K. *Continuance and Change: The Contemporary British Novel Sequence.* Carbondale: Southern Illinois University Press, 1972.

———. *The Novels of Anthony Powell.* Pittsburgh: University of Pittsburgh Press, 1968.

———. "Powell's Dance to the Grave." Review of *Hearing Secret Harmonies. Nation,* June 19, 1976, 758–60.

Morse, Deborah Denenholz. *Women in Trollope's Palliser Novels.* Ann Arbor: University of Michigan Research Press, 1987.

Nardin, Jane. *He Knew She Was Right: The Independent Woman in the Novels of Anthony Trollope.* Carbondale: Southern Illinois University, 1989.

Pei, Lowry. "*The Duke's Children:* Reflection and Reconciliation." *Modern Language Quarterly* 39, no. 3 (Sept. 1978): 284–303.

Person, Leland S., Jr. "Henry James, George Sand, and the Suspense of Masculinity." *PMLA* 106, no. 3 (May 1991): 515–28.

Powell, Anthony. *Faces in My Time.* Vol. 3 of *To Keep the Ball Rolling: The Memoirs of Anthony Powell.* New York: Holt, 1978.

———. *Messengers of Day.* Vol. 2 of *To Keep the Ball Rolling.* New York: Holt, 1978.

———. *The Strangers All Are Gone.* Vol. 4 of *To Keep the Ball Rolling.* London: Heineman, 1982.

———. Interview, "Taken from Life," by W. J. Weatherly. *Twentieth Century* 170, no. 1010 (1961): 50–53.

Rabinovitz, Rubin. *The Reaction Against Experiment in the English Novel, 1950–1960.* New York: Columbia University Press, 1967.

Radford, Jean. *Dorothy Richardson*. Key Women Writers Series, edited by Sue Roe. Bloomington: Indiana University Press, 1991.

Ray, Gordon N. "Trollope at Full Length." *Huntington Library Quarterly* 31, no. 4 (August 1968): 313–40.

Reichert, John. "More than Kin and Less than Kind: The Limits of Genre Theory." In Strelka, ed. (q.v.), 57–79.

Reid, Joyce, comp. *The Concise Oxford Dictionary of French Literature*. Oxford: Clarendon Press, 1976

Rich, Adrienne. "Compulsory Heterosexuality and Lesbian Existence." *Signs* 5, no. 4 (Summer 1980): 631–60.

Richardson, Dorothy. "Data for Spanish Publisher." *London Magazine*, June 1959: 14–19.

―――. Papers. Beinecke Rare Book and Manuscript Library. Yale University, New Haven.

―――. " The Reality of Feminism." In *The Gender of Modernism: A Critical Anthology*, edited by Bonnie Kime Scott, 401–7. Contributing editor for Richardson, Diane F. Gillespie. Bloomington: Indiana University Press, 1990.

Ricoeur, Paul. "Narrative Time." *Critical Inquiry* 7, no. 1 (Autumn 1980): 169–90.

―――. *Time and Narrative*. Translated by Kathleen McLaughlin and David Pellauer. 2 vols. Chicago: University of Chicago Press, 1985.

Rose, Shirley. "Dorothy Richardson's Theory of Literature: The Writer as Pilgrim." *Criticism* 12, no. 1 (Winter 1970): 20–37.

Rosenberg, John. *Dorothy Richardson*. New York: Alfred A. Knopf, 1973.

Russell, John. *Anthony Powell: A Quintet, Sextet, and War*. Bloomington: Indiana University Press, 1970.

―――. "The War Trilogies of Anthony Powell and Evelyn Waugh." *Modern Age* 16, no. 3 (Summer 1972): 289–300.

Said, Edward W. *Beginnings: Intention and Method*. New York: Columbia University Press, 1985.

Scholes, Robert. "Afterthoughts on Narrative II: Language, Narrative, and Anti-Narrative." *Critical Inquiry* 7, no. 1 (Autumn 1980): 204–13.

―――. *Fabulation and Metafiction*. Urbana: University of Illinois Press, 1980.

Scholes, Robert, and Robert Kellogg. *The Nature of Narrative*. London: Oxford University Press, 1966.

Schor, Naomi. "This Essentialism Which Is Not One." *Differences* 1, no. 2 (Summer 1989): 39–58.

Scott, Bonnie Kime, ed. *The Gender of Modernism: A Critical Anthology*. Bloomington: Indiana University Press, 1990.

Selig, Robert L. *Time and Anthony Powell*. London: Associated University Presses, 1991.

Showalter, Elaine. *A Literature of Their Own: British Women Novelists from Brontë to Lessing.* Princeton: Princeton University Press, 1977.

————, ed. *The New Feminist Criticism.* New York: Pantheon, 1985.

Simpson, J. A. and E. S. C. Weiner, preps. *The Oxford English Dictionary.* 2d ed. Oxford: Clarendon Press, 1989.

Smalley, Donald. *Trollope: The Critical Heritage.* London: Routledge and Kegan Paul; New York: Barnes and Noble Books, 1969.

Smith, Barbara Herrnstein. "Afterthoughts on Narrative III: Narrative Versions, Narrative Theories." *Critical Inquiry* 7, no. 1 (Autumn 1980): 213–36.

————. *Poetic Closure: A Study of How Poems End.* Chicago: University of Chicago Press, 1968.

Staley, Thomas F. *Dorothy Richardson.* Boston: Twayne, 1976.

Stanley, Julia Penelope, and Susan J. Wolfe (Robbins). "Toward a Feminist Aesthetic." *Chrysalis,* no. 6 (1978): 57–71.

Stanton, Domna C. "Difference on Trial: A Critique of the Maternal Metaphor in Cixous, Irigaray, and Kristeva." In *The Poetics of Gender,* edited by Nancy Miller, 157–82. New York: Columbia University Press, 1986.

————. "Language and Revolution: The Franco-American Disconnection." In Eisenstein and Jardine, eds. (q.v.), 73–87.

Sternberg, Meir. *Expositional Modes and Temporal Ordering in Fiction.* Baltimore: Johns Hopkins University Press, 1978.

Stimpson, Catherine R. "Zero Degree Deviancy: The Lesbian Novel in English." In Abel, ed. (q.v.), 243–59.

Strelka, Joseph P., ed. *Theories of Literary Genre.* Vol. 8 of *Yearbook of Comparative Criticism.* University Park: Pennsylvania State University Press, 1978.

Super, R. H. *The Chronicler of Barsetshire: A Life of Anthony Trollope.* Ann Arbor: University of Michigan Press, 1988.

Sutherland, J. A. *Victorian Novelists and Publishers.* Chicago: University of Chicago Press, 1976.

Swinden, Patrick. *The English Novel of History and Society, 1940–80.* New York: St. Martin's Press, 1984.

————. "Powell's *Hearing Secret Harmonies.*" *Critical Quarterly* 18, no. 4 (Winter 1976): 55–60.

Terry, R. C. *Anthony Trollope: The Artist in Hiding.* Totowa, N.J.: Rowman & Littlefield, 1977.

Thale, Jerome. "The Problem of Structure in Trollope." *Nineteenth-Century Fiction* 15, no. 2 (Sept. 1960): 147–57.

Thody, Philip. "The English Proust." In *Studies in French Fiction in Honour of Vivienne Mylne,* edited by Robert Gibson, 323–37. Valencia, Spain: Grant and Butler, 1988.

Thorn, Arline R. " 'Feminine' Time in Dorothy Richardson's *Pilgrimage.*" *In-*

ternational Journal of Women's Studies 1, no. 2 (March–April 1978): 211–19.

Torgovnick, Marianna. *Closure in the Novel.* Princeton: Princeton University Press, 1981.

———. "Closure in the Victorian Novel." *Victorian Newsletter* 71 (Spring 1987): 4–6.

Trollope, Anthony. *An Autobiography.* London: Oxford University Press, 1950.

———. *Barchester Towers.* Oxford: Oxford University Press, 1985.

———. *Is He Popenjoy?* Vol. 1. New York: Dodd, Mead, 1913.

———. *The Small House at Allington.* Oxford: Oxford University Press, 1980.

———. *The Warden.* Oxford: Oxford University Press, 1985.

Tuchman, Gaye, with Nina Fortin. *Edging Women Out: Victorian Novelists, Publishers, and Social Change.* New Haven: Yale University Press, 1989.

Tucker, Allan James. *The Novels of Anthony Powell.* London: Macmillan Publishing, 1976.

Vernon, Patricia A. "The Poor Fictionist's Conscience: Point of View in the Palliser Novels." *Victorian Newsletter* 71 (Spring 1987): 16–20.

Wall, Stephen. Introduction to *Can You Forgive Her?* by Anthony Trollope, 7–26. Middlesex: Penguin, 1972.

———. "Trollope, Balzac, and the Reappearing Character." *Essays in Criticism* 25, no. 1 (January 1975): 123–44.

Warhol, Robyn. *Gendered Interventions: Narrative Discourse in the Victorian Novel.* New Brunswick, N.J.: Rutgers, 1989.

West, Anthony. *H. G. Wells: Aspects of a Life.* London: Hutchinson, 1984.

West, Rebecca. *The Court and the Castle.* New Haven: Yale University Press, 1957.

White, Hayden. "The Fictions of Factual Representation." In *Tropics of Discourse: Essays in Cultural Criticism*, 121–34. Baltimore: Johns Hopkins University Press, 1978.

———. *Metahistory: The Historical Imagination in Nineteenth-Century Europe.* Baltimore: Johns Hopkins University Press, 1973.

———. "The Value of Narrativity in the Representation of Reality." *Critical Inquiry* 7, no. 1 (Autumn 1980): 5–27.

Whitford, Margaret. "Rereading Irigaray." In Brennan, ed. (q.v.), 106–26.

Wilcox, Thomas W. "Anthony Powell and the Illusion of Possibility." *Contemporary Literature* 17, no. 2 (Spring 1976): 233–39.

Wilson, Keith. "Pattern and Process: The Narrative Strategies of Anthony Powell's *A Dance to the Music of Time.*" *English Studies in Canada* 11, no. 2 (June 1985): 214–22.

Winner, Thomas G. "Structural and Semiotic Genre Theory." In Strelka, ed. (q.v.), 254–68.

Winnett, Susan. "Coming Unstrung: Women, Men, Narrative, and Principles of Pleasure." *PMLA* 105, no. 3: 505–18.

Woolf, Virginia. "Romance and the Heart." Review of *The Grand Tour* by Romer Wilson and *Revolving Lights* by Dorothy Richardson. In *Contemporary Writers*, 123–25. London: Hogarth Press, 1965.

Wright, Andrew. "Trollope Revises Trollope." In *Centenary Essays*, Halperin, ed. (q.v.), 109–33.

About the Author

Lynette Felber is associate professor of
English at Indiana University–Purdue
University in Fort Wayne. She is general
editor of CLIO: *A Journal of Literature,
History, and Philosophy of History* and the
author of many book chapters and articles
published in journals such as *Mosaic,
Genre, Frontiers, The Victorian Newsletter,*
and *Tulsa Studies in Women's Literature.*